All To Bring
Victoria Home

AMBASSADOR

BELFAST, NORTHERN IRELAND
GREENVILLE, USA

Dedicated to
our persecuted brothers and sisters
in Christ

Our thanks to
all those who helped us
and prayed for us over the years.

All To Bring Victoria Home

Delwyn Jones-Schmidt

AMBASSADOR

BELFAST, NORTHERN IRELAND
GREENVILLE, USA

All To Bring Victoria Home
© Copyright 2002 Delwyn Jones-Schmidt

Names of most of the people
mentioned in this book have been
changed to protect their privacy.

ISBN 1 84030 33 3

Ambassador Publications
a division of
Ambassador Productions Ltd.
Providence House
Ardenlee Street,
Belfast,
BT6 8QJ
Northern Ireland
www.ambassador-productions.com

Emerald House
427 Wade Hampton Blvd.
Greenville
SC 29609, USA
www.emeraldhouse.com

Contents

1

The raid - Delwyn
February 10 1993

The dawn raid

5:30 a.m. Axel had just left to catch the train to work. I liked to be up to see him off, but for the moment I wanted to get a little more sleep. It seemed I had only just lain down on the sofa a minute when the doorbell rang. 6:00 a.m. It could only be him. What could he have forgotten ?

Strangely, through the peep-hole there seemed to be movement in the corridor beside him. I must be seeing things, I thought.

I opened up anyway.

"Police!" Three plain-clothes police officers barged their way in – you'd have thought they were on a drugs haul. What did they think they would find here, I wondered. Just what was the meaning of all this? In reply to our questions they would only say that it was a case "*contre X*" – accusations against an unknown person. But we "weren't to worry", we were only being called on as "witnesses".

Witnesses of what – what accusations ? And I knew nothing about procedural rules in France – weren't they supposed to have a search warrant ? We had little choice anyway. I started feeling sick and a little light-headed. These French police officers were so arrogant: you're the enemy, just do as you're told.

The one who seemed to be in charge was sticking to Axel. He was youngish, not very tall, and his aggressive attitude gave him the look of someone who was out to make a name for himself – probably needed to get himself promoted, I thought. The woman was very businesslike, a little older, more approachable, probably more experienced. The third was definitely the youngest – he looked like a trainee, with a darker complexion than the others, smooth-talking, and he had a Spanish-sounding name.

They were going through everything in the living room, systematically. I had to ask them to be quiet, to let the children sleep as long as possible.

Victoria, our 3-year-old daughter, was still fast asleep in her little dark wooden bed with a white net cover over the head of it. Asleep with her white comfort blanket up against her face, and her favourite toy rabbit, Jacquot, tucked into the corner above her pillow. When she woke she would sing out "*Bonjour, Maman*" with the same little tune every morning, and I would sing it back to her "*Bonjour, mon bébé*". My heart tightened at the thought. I mustn't let this morning be any different. I would make sure Victoria was shielded from their…intrusions.

They insisted on waking the children at 7:30. I went into the bedroom where Victoria was asleep. The policewoman said she would try not to make too much noise, but she was going through the chest of drawers – very thoroughly. Apparently they were determined not to leave any stone unturned. It of course woke Victoria. I sat between her and the police officer so she wouldn't be too alarmed, but there was no fooling her. So I told her that there was a "nice lady" there, that she didn't need to worry…The two boys in the next room were awake by now as well and looked confused and uneasy. I couldn't tell them anything that would help, since I had no idea what was going on. They had stayed overnight in order to go to the physiotherapist's – they had an appointment that morning. The family, who were good friends of ours, had recently moved out of the area, so Paul and David stayed with us sometimes and I took them to the physio round the corner. The police made it difficult for me to talk to them, listening to every word and hurrying us all the time.

After they had been through the whole house – even the fridge and freezer – they told us we would have to go to the police station for questioning. We would be back by lunchtime, they said. I was feeling uneasy, though. It was something in their attitude towards Victoria and I. I didn't feel free to leave her for a minute. I didn't usually trust in these kinds of feelings too much – they could be right, and they could be very wrong. Maybe this unease was totally unwarranted. One thing I knew for sure : the God we trusted was in control of it all, whatever feelings I may have had.

It was a cold winter morning and the children had to be bundled up in their warm coats and hats. When everyone was ready Axel prayed briefly with the children and I in the lounge. On the way to the police car the policewoman took Victoria's hand as I was locking the appartment door. I hurried to take the other hand, torn between wanting to keep everything as normal as possible, and a dreadful, growing apprehension of what could possibly be behind it all.

They put Axel and Paul in another car in front. From the beginning they had separated us from each other and we had been unable to talk about anything. We stopped on the way and the policewoman went to get the children something to eat from the baker's – with my money, of course. We finally drew up in front of a big grim-looking building in a gloomy down-town part of St-Germain-en-Laye that I had never been in before. We were marched through the front door, where I was told to go upstairs for questioning, so I went to leave Victoria with Axel downstairs. The look on his face shook me, there was something terribly forboding about it… but I smiled at him.

"It won't be too long, will it ?"

He didn't answer.

All the police officers invariably made the same sort of remark when they saw Victoria: *"Qu'est-ce qu'elle est mignonne!"* ("What a little darling!"), often accompanied by a chuck on the chin. She just observed them quietly with her big brown eyes, weighing them up in her mature little 3-year-old mind. She was such a special little girl to us both …

The romance

Axel and I had met in 1984. We were both students at the time and I for one was not thinking about settling down and getting married. I was fully enjoying my studies in a two-year "*cours préparatoire*" which was preparation for an entrance exam into the *Ecole Normale Supérieure*, the highest teacher-training school in France, and that also counted as the first two years of university. Axel though, was nearing the end of his studies in law, and was definitely interested in getting married fairly soon.

I knew Axel as someone who was enthusiastic in the church, often one of the first to pray or share a text in the meetings. He came across to me as a very earnest, sincere kind of person. He had an old brown two-tone *2-Chevaux* and sometimes if he met my friend Michèle and I on the way home from classes, he would offer us a ride. However, he never really spoke to me personally very much, so I had no idea of what was brewing, and I had so much else going on in my life to keep me busy.

Guys and gals were usually pretty discrete groups within the church, so the first thing I noticed was that little things seemed to throw us together. Then we started talking, and found we wanted the same sorts of things in life… In May 1985, I had just spent two very special days fasting and praying, asking God for direction in my life, when Axel told me, on the evening of the second day, that he wanted to talk to me. I had a fair idea of what was coming, but I still had the butterflies. He sat me down very seriously – in fact, he seemed a little nervous himself. What surprised me was that when Axel asked me to marry him, he warned me we might not have an easy life together – in the sense that we could have outside opposition to face. Little was I to know how true that would be.

I told him I would think about it, and with the cruelty of youth I left him to stew for a couple of hours, even though I was almost certain of my answer already. Since we had come to know each other better I had found Axel to be a gentle, sensitive and serious person, someone I knew I could depend on, and there was something very clear-cut and straightforward in his character that made him special to me. I felt I had stumbled on a gem – and he wanted to marry me – what could I say ? Besides, he was tall, dark and hand-some and reminded me of my Dad... When I went to give him my answer he looked relieved. We prayed together, and that night, at the very outset of our togetherness in life, I knew in my heart that Axel was right for me.

My parents were a little skeptical at first. They somehow didn't seem to have much faith in my judgement of 'men' (I was only 19, etc.), but a photo of Axel reassured them and my Mum and my sister Sheryl visited in October of that year (the original date for the wedding, but we had moved it back to December) and Mother was much struck with her future son-in-law.

"You do make a lovely couple, darling girl," was her first reaction, as she met us at the airport. Unfortunately my parents weren't able to come for the wedding in December because of my Dad's work.

Axel's parents were more than a little skeptical – they were down-right discouraging. It made no sense to them for Axel to get married when he was still a student and not sure he would be able to provide for his family. It was doomed to be a "catastrophe", according to them. When Axel took me to meet them, however, they seemed to have come round a little, and we spent an enjoyable evening with them.

An acquaintance of my mother's told her at the time that it was an impossible match: laid-back New Zealanders just do not get on with nervy, wound-up Continentals such as the French were generally perceived to be... Now it was true that we came from very different backgrounds – I was the humble shepherdess from the distant hills of a faraway island, and he was the son of a well-to-do French banker then civil servant in Algeria, followed by Columbia – a good *bourgeois* family with links to the de Gaulles. So apparently we didn't have much going for us genetically – two very different bloodstreams. But we, of course, were completely oblivious to such speculation.

After the "civil" wedding in the town hall, the "religious" ceremony, as they say in France, took place in the church where by then we had both been members for a while. The ceremony was simple, but I thought it beautiful. We had one of the girls in the church play a violin solo as I entered, and a special moment just before we exchanged the traditional vows when we both spoke to express in a more personal way our commitment to each other. "Ever faithful" were my words and they were to be proven. I glimpsed my elderly French teacher at the back of the room with tears in his eyes.

It was also a special time with Axel's family, especially his Mum and Dad. In fact, there were so many of Axel's relations there that I couldn't remember even half of their names. All Roman Catholics, of course, the family was traditionally Catholic though Axel and his brother had both become Bible-believers after attending our church. They all fully enjoyed themselves, anyway.

It was only some time after the wedding that Axel's parents started putting the church down. Axel and I, who were very close to our friends in the church, felt quite wounded and puzzled – there was no reason for them to suddenly start being insulting about our friends, criticizing the church, and looking down on us all the time. It gradually got worse until finally it was impossible to have any dialogue with them at all. We learned later that several former members of the church had gone to them with personal criticism of those who had remained in the church and that was what had brought about this contemptuous, judgmental attitude in Axel's parents.

They had also been contacted by an unscrupulous lobby group called UNADFI, which ran under the guise of National Union of Associations for the Defence of the Family and the Individual. In reality, their self-appointed job, somewhat like a modern-day Inquisition, was to attack any group whom they labelled a 'cult', of which the 'biggies' were Hare Krishna, Moon, the Church of Scientology, etc. Unfortunately, or perhaps to suit their purposes, UNADFI had never been able to decide on the exact definition of what a 'cult' was, and therefore mixed truly dangerous groupings with Christian churches. Nevertheless, it was proving to be a profitable business, and they were always on the lookout for other groups whom they considered 'suspicious'.

So we had had to keep Axel's parents at a distance over the past few years. Unfortunately, things had not got any better…

Back in the police station, the questioning started. After a while, Axel came upstairs and gave Victoria into my arms. They were taking him elsewhere. This time my confident smile died at the devastated look on his face. I tried to ask him what was happening, but he couldn't speak – he just kissed us sadly goodbye.

In spite of this, I wasn't extremely worried about Axel himself. He had a legal mind and a legal background and could keep a cool, clear head in the midst of all this turbulence. He was of the quiet thinker type, and anyone would have had a hard job pulling the wool over his eyes, especially where the French Judiciary were concerned!

No, I wasn't worried about Axel. What was worrying me was that he was clearly worried about us. Was he maybe just looking on the dark side ? What did he think was going on ? I would have dearly loved to be able to have just a few words with him. Surely Victoria and I couldn't be touched, we were both New Zealand citizens – they wouldn't dare. In any case, whatever happened, wherever they took us, we would stay together. They had absolutely no reason to separate us. They only had to look at Victoria to see she was perfectly well cared for, and they had said it themselves, she was a little darling. I loved my little girl. Victoria had always been like a gift to me. Like many mums, I felt I just had to put everything I had into the care I gave my child – probably the result of the kind of attentiveness I had seen in the families in the church, perhaps a throwback from my own childhood too.

Rotorua, New Zealand – to Tahiti – to France

It was true that I came from a close family, and a large one too: seven girls – but no boys – and I was right bang in the middle. Every day my Mum and Dad read to us from the Bible and said the Lord's Prayer, and every Sunday they took us all to the local Baptist church and Sunday school. We lived on a big sheep-farm overlooking Lake Rotorua in the Bay of Plenty, North Island, New Zealand. My Dad managed the farm for a wealthy landowner, all the 1200 rolling acres of it along with its 33 000 sheep and a few hundred cattle for beef. We had our own cow, warm milk every morning (if we liked it that way), and real cream, and once we were older, the farm motorbikes to ride practically whenever and wherever we liked.

My Dad was quite a handyman and built us a little swimming pool that you could heat, the most enormous swing that I have ever seen on the side of a hill, and almost anything else you could ever think we would need, from rabbit hutches to a trampoline to a wind turbine, which he imagined could well produce electricity for the house one day. Although he had chosen farming, he had a grammar school education and I clearly remember him helping me with my homework. Above all he gave us an example. Intelligent, hard-working, God-fearing, he was a loving father who could be firm when he had to, and after all, with seven girls, he had to. He was well respected as far as I cared to know, at the tender age of 17 when I left home for a job as an *au pair* in Tahiti.

My Mum was a homely person, but full of spark too. We knew she was always there for us. She was worried when I left for Tahiti, but I had a determination to travel which stemmed from a deep dissatisfaction with life up to then. I had no idea where I was going in life. I knew I needed God in my life and had taken "decisions" to be a Christian, but I felt a failure. To me it was a "be-good" religion, and time after time I found I didn't measure up. I had been baptized, but once again it didn't have a great deal of meaning for me – it was something everyone did, something I was expected to do, sooner or later. Although I believed certain people in the church in Rotorua had a real faith, including my parents, I had no idea how to obtain it for myself. Perhaps I hadn't listened enough – I was quite frivolous and avoided 'serious' discussions. Underneath, though, I was longing for a meaningful knowledge of God (and a meaningful romance somewhere along the line too). As far as church-going went, though, I was gradually turning rebellious about it all.

School was easy for me, I had lots of friends, I got my University Entrance examination (approximate equivalent of A-levels) accredited. I was in Form 7, preparing for university like all my friends were, but without really knowing what I wanted to do. I wasn't a model pupil. If I had found school more difficult I might have been better. As it was, exams weren't usually too much of a stress and many were the times when we were almost caught by the deputy headmaster playing cards in the Form 7 common room or the library instead of studying. I suppose I had life too easy. I had done well in French at school, and France held a sort of fascination for me which must have been inspired by my teachers, or perhaps one of my older sisters. So when the school received a letter asking for *au pair* girls in Tahiti, it seemed like the perfect opportunity.

Tahiti, though, was difficult. Behind the beautiful scenery it was hot, dirty and often smelly. The worst were the cockroaches – I even found one in my hair during the night once, because my bed was a good size, but it was less then six inches off the ground. The roaches just scuttled into the ground-level house, which was open practically day and night because of the heat. I had been supposed to help a mother of four who was a secondary school teacher and had had to cope on her own when a hurricane had hit Tahiti a short time before – especially as her husband had left her there with the children and returned to France to work. However, the very first night I spent there I was woken in the dead of night by someone opening the door of my room – a strange man ! I must have kind of gulped and sat straight up in bed, in that weird lost-in-between world you sometimes find yourself in when you're somewhere strange and still half asleep, but then he simply said, *"Oh, pardon!"* and shut the door. That was her husband back from France. Anybody else would probably have headed back to New Zealand there and then, but I was too stubborn to run for home so soon.

Tahiti was lonely, above all. The family I was with despaired of me, for I was forever writing or phoning friends or family, even when they had a handsome brother to stay. They really did their best to give me a social life, and I did enjoy it, but didn't really make any close friends – my heart was not in Tahiti. It was especially a time of personal soul-searching. That was when I seriously started reading the Bible regularly, searching it. It meant something, but I couldn't get at it. I believed it, but I felt helpless when it came to actually putting it into practice. And I was getting overweight, which made everything ten times worse, in my eyes.

The family were to return to France at the end of the school year, and when they offered to try to find me another *au pair* family in France, I gladly accepted. And so I came to live in a tiny *chambre de bonne* on the sixth floor of an apartment block on a busy Parisian boulevard. I enjoyed it; and I got to experience life in Paris. I opened the tiny window to the morning sun and all the sounds of a busy city, I did a bit of housework, went to fetch the baby from the *crèche,* attended a few courses at the Alliance Française (especially useful for meeting other English people), and travelled with my new 'family' to the centre of France for their holidays. I also started to attend a small evangelical church on the outskirts of Paris …

The questioning

"And how did you come to be a member of this church?" The police officer's question demanded a precise answer. Why did he want to know that, I wondered. What were they trying to get at? I had to explain that a friend of my family in New Zealand had given me the address and that when I came, I was interested to find in the church a real, practical faith that I had never been able to share in before.

"The true Christian life," took up the police officer with an ironic smile.

And when speaking of fasting:

"The point is to lift your soul into a higher realm," he mocked, making the gesture of spinning something skywards. What was a police officer using clichés like that for, I wondered.

The questioning went on and on, endless questions about my Christian friends, our church, our beliefs - nothing about Victoria.

The novelty of the place and the people was fast wearing out for Victoria. The room we were in was just a small office, with room enough for a desk, another little table, another door, a small window and that was it. At least through the window you could see some trees and what looked like a little path through them, if I remember well.

She was getting very restless. They had brought her a colouring-in book and felt pens when I asked for them, but no food, though I had asked several times. The only thing she had eaten all morning was the croissant we had bought on the way. Of course, she started wandering around the room, trying the doors. I was ready to make allowances, but one of the policemen told her off when she took out a key, so I had to explain that she mustn't touch that...She discovered that by asking to go to the toilet we could go downstairs together. Not long afterwards she was asking to go again ! Poor baby, it was becoming ridiculous. Just how long was this going to last ?

At two o'clock I asked when we would be able to go. The officer said he would have to see. So we waited. The policeman said once that I might have to go into police custody. I said that Victoria would have to come with me then. He said that it was cold there, not really a place for kids. I said OK, I'll go with her then, wherever she goes. Nothing could be simpler.

Victoria was tired and started lying down on the floor, so I made her a kind of bed with two chairs, my coat and her jacket, but it was impossible for her to rest. Besides, she didn't have her comfort blanket, or Jacquot her little rabbit. It was hard for her. I read her a story and she told me *Papa* had read her one too. I asked again for something for her to eat. Not once had she cried, but she was having to make an effort now to hold out against hunger and tiredness. She was only 3 years old... Of course, she thought everything depended on me, and kept asking me for something to eat, something to drink, to go outside. I couldn't understand what was so difficult about bringing her a sandwich. She was getting to the stage of not wanting to do anything else except get out of there. I managed to hug her so hard that she laughed.

The policeman went out for a minute. I opened the window and, looking through it with Victoria, promising her we would go for a walk afterwards. We said a little prayer together. The policeman returned. No news.

The critical moment

I was just asking for food for Victoria for the hundredth time, politely – though it made you want to shake them – when the policewoman who had been at our home that morning put her head in the door and said casually, holding out her hand to Victoria: "Do you want to come with me for lunch ?"

I started up from my chair but Victoria had already taken the hand of the "nice lady" trustingly, dying to get out of that shut-up room and eat something.

"You'll bring her straight back, won't you?" I asked. What else could I say ?

"Mummy's waiting for you," I said to Victoria, a little uncertainly. "See you after lunch."

The policeman shut the door behind them. It was ten to four. Usually a meal didn't take Victoria more than twenty minutes, maybe half an hour, let's allow 15 minutes while she washed her hands, and if she has to wait a bit... maybe she would go outside a little ... but it surely couldn't go on later than five o'clock.

So I waited again. 4:15. The policeman handed me the police custody register, saying, oh, he'd forgotten to ask me to sign. I hardly noticed. But some change in his attitude made me feel edgy. I couldn't hear anything at all.

I opened the door and said I was going down to see Victoria, but he wouldn't let me.

"You are to stay in here, Madam. Why are you so nervous ? You weren't like that this morning."

He was getting sarcastic. I did not like this. I still had Victoria's hat and jacket. Surely they couldn't ... He had been downstairs once, but there had been others outside the door, watching. I asked him what Victoria was eating.

"Oh, I'm not sure, noodles or rice or something."

No green vegetables, I thought, automatically.

Once I thought I heard Victoria's voice repeating something about "Maman". My heart leapt, I held my breath, waiting to hear footsteps on the stairs, but there was only silence. 4:45. The policeman was going to sleep with his feet on the desk. I opened the door and started downstairs.

"I'm just going to see…"

"Madam, you are supposed to be under surveillance. You must stay here."

"It's taking a very long time," I said pointedly.

"OK, I'll go and see."

When he came back I kept asking questions, so he phoned down to the kitchen, very briefly.

"It's almost finished," he said.

Ten minutes later two others came into the room.

"Your child has been placed in State care," they announced.

I exploded. What ! The police had lied to me, mocked me, cheated me out of my daughter. **Why?** What an abuse of confidence, authority, everything – there was no reason for this – they had no right... Coming from New Zealand I suppose my naïve image of the police was more that of the friendly, helpful British 'bobby'. No longer.

"People are going to know about this," I vowed to them.

It wasn't their fault, they said. It was the prosecutor who decided. A prosecutor who had never set eyes on my daughter or myself – or even my husband.

Oh, it was "normal" for me to react in this way, they said. Normal – and I suppose it was normal for the police to rip a family apart behind their backs, in such a civilised, "human rights" banner-carrying country like France.

Then they wanted Victoria's hat and coat. I refused, though of course they could make me if they wanted. Why hadn't they asked before taking her away ? I was furious. In spite of that terrible apprehensiveness I had felt all along, I was still extremely shocked. This just could not be happening to me. Not with Victoria.

Fight or break

Now that Victoria wasn't there their politeness dropped. I was told I was going to be put into "*garde à vue*" (police custody). I was taken away in a police car to a station in a neighbouring town where I was body-searched. Tearfully I told the police on duty there that the other officers had taken me in for questioning and then kidnapped my daughter. They looked uneasy, but they still locked me up in a cell for three hours. That was when Victoria's hat and coat finally disappeared.

The time in the cell was also – probably deliberately – a test. Pacing around the small cell, it suddenly seemed as though I was about to fall – not into a faint, it wasn't physical – but into a sort of mental black hole. They were just waiting for me to give in. The only thing that kept me was the name of the Lord Jesus. That was all I could cry, inwardly. And then that Bible blessing came to me with startling clarity:

"Blessed are ye, when men shall revile you, and persecute you, and shall say all manner of evil against you falsely, for my sake."

Yes. That was so exactly it. All the suggestive questions, the hinted accusations, the aggressiveness – I understood; and grasping this gave me the strength I needed.

When one of the policemen on duty asked me if I wanted something to eat, I actually hissed at him that it was scandalous for me to be in there. Not long after that, towards 8:00 p.m., I was returned to the original 'Children's Brigade' where we had been that morning, for more questioning, they said. On the way back the police officers joked and made lewd remarks about me, saying I was too skinny for their liking, etc. Once there though, instead of questioning me, they told me I was free to go home.

I refused to leave without my daughter. They had absolutely no reason to separate us. I refused to sign out. I had to protest. If I was free, why wasn't Victoria ? If she wasn't free, why should I be ? It was totally illogical, impossible, unbearable

In the end the police officers carried me out by force and left me alone in the dark in an unknown part of the town, bereft of my daughter, and not knowing what had happened to my husband except that he was "still in custody". Shakily, I had to ask passers-by how to get to the train station, and when I got home, the silence of the apartment was overwhelming.

Life had been turned upside down, just when we had been happily settled. I remembered going out to get the bread one morning just a few days earlier, and feeling a special kind of 'contentedness' that's hard to describe. As though, yes, your life is on the right track… Strangely enough, as I came home that morning a police car had passed me and it struck me that they were looking at me in an observant sort of way that quite chilled me – and now look where I was. I needed to keep my head clear and talk to someone, make some sense out of this day, do something about all this after being made to feel so helpless. I grabbed the phone...

For days afterwards it was impossible to eat. I just managed to drink a minimum. Now I really was just skin and bones. The nights were endless, tossing and turning, my empty, knotted stomach would not let me sleep. Then there were the sudden tears, the anguish of being helpless to help my child. One doctor, a former French resistant, was horrified to hear what had happened. He called it "Nazism" – and he had the same advice as our GP: "You have to fight for your child. And you have to be strong to fight for your child." It had to be done. Sarah-Jane, one of our American friends, took several of us into a fast-food bar that day and persuaded me to have some coke. Then a bit of burger ... Oh, yes, we would be strong and we would fight – for Victoria.

But for the moment, what had happened to Axel ? With the terrible ache of Victoria's absence in my heart, I longed for his release.

2

The raid - Axel

February 10-11, 1993

Police custody

The cell was filthy and the bare concrete bench stone-cold. It had been a long day so far, and Axel was forced to just sit and wait, not knowing if or when they would be taking him out for questioning or whether he would have to go before a judge to be formally indicted, and maybe sent to prison. They were capable of it, he knew that. It didn't matter if the accusations were based only on hearsay, without the slightest shred of evidence. The French Judiciary could detain him in prison pending a hearing for as long as they liked. It was an eerie feeling. He would just have to take it as it came. He was putting his trust in God - that would make all the difference.

The police officer on duty appeared with a sandwich, but Axel refused to eat. Even when the police officer insisted, apparently thinking Axel couldn't really mean it, he refused again. Pure gut reaction, a blunt refusal of everything they were doing, and a way of crying to God for justice. The police officer was quite taken aback and left it there on the floor. He had probably never seen anybody in *garde à vue* refuse to eat, for it was usually the only welcome break of normality in the abnormal monotony of the cell.

Axel's thoughts went back over the events of the day.

When he had walked out of the apartment at 5:30 a.m. on that Wednesday, February 10, 1993, he had been in a hurry to get a train to Paris in order to catch the first long-distance train from Paris to Lille, in the north of France. There, several bank employees would have been waiting for him to give them a day's training on various aspects of fiscal and commercial law.

It was a cold, quiet, early winter morning, with nobody about except for one car with a couple of passengers in the middle of the carpark. Probably others leaving early for work. With a quick gesture to the driver, Axel indicated that he needed to get his car out from behind theirs, got into it, and heaved his well-packed satchel onto the seat beside him.

Suddenly the door was wrenched open – "Police!" A young man in plain clothes was holding out his police identification card. Axel was under arrest. That vehicle had been an unmarked police car. The police had had to wait to get into the house, for under French law police officers can only enter and search private homes after 6:00 a.m. They left Axel very much to himself as they waited around outside the apartment block entrance.

His first thought was that they could well be messing up all the hard work he had put into getting his own business going – and it had been going well. Surprisingly well, considering he had been a child who hadn't even gone to school normally before the age of 10!

The ups and downs of life

Axel was born in Algiers, Algeria, while his father was a civil servant there, and he spent his early childhood there and then in Columbia, where he picked up Spanish. It was only back in France that he got to school, and then he hated it, and didn't do well. He was a sensitive child. To make up, in a way, he got very much into sport – football and then cycling especially. As a teenager he had also been very involved in the Catholic church where his parents attended, as an *animateur* for the young people, but had ended up feeling exploited. Disillusioned, he threw it all in and went off to seek for 'truth and enlightenment' in monasteries. But he never seemed to find what he was really looking for. He had struggled through his *baccalauréat* (the French equivalent of A-levels).

Just before going to university he had spent the month of August away on a solitary cycling holiday, leaving from Menton, right down on the south coast where the family went for their holidays, and heading back up to Paris. Something had given him the idea that solitude would bring him closer to God. And he had actually taken a Bible with him and read through Proverbs, though without understanding a thing. Depression was setting in. What was the sense of living, anyway ? As it got worse, it was as though he could feel his mind slipping away - crazy. He couldn't face anything anymore, he seemed to be sinking - titanically fast. He liked reading Albert Camus, (*"L'Etranger"*, *"La Peste"*) because of this same sense of the absurdness of life. Yet he still had a deep conviction that if anyone could rescue him from this headlong, downward slide, it would only be God Himself.

Because of the cloud of depression that had descended upon him, it was extremely difficult for him to concentrate on his studies. After a year, he was fairly sure that his exam results would be proof enough that this was not the way for him. He had walked out of one exam without even handing in his paper, and without a decent mark for that exam he couldn't possibly pass. When in June of that year he dropped in to see the results board, he couldn't believe his eyes. For that very exam he had been awarded 14/20 (70%) ! He still doesn't know how - he assumed that when they couldn't find the paper, they had given him the same mark as he had got for his class work - but that mark got him through to his second year. At that stage in his life, he certainly wasn't going to contest it. He took it as meaning that he should continue to study law. He took it, maybe a little superstitiously, as being from God.

It was amazing that he got through that first year at University.

Still, a second year at university was a daunting prospect. He decided to take a one-year break to Scotland on a social work holiday. Perhaps this way he could find some sense of purpose and usefulness for his life. His work a couple of years beforehand with the group of young people in the Catholic Church where he had grown up – before he became disenchanted with the whole set-up, and stopped attending – had given him the idea that he could maybe work with children or adolescents. The work in Scotland with disturbed children was difficult – he was only 20 – but he stuck it for the year and even got himself the nickname of 'the man with a big heart' – for he really wanted to help those kids, and if that meant taking them on outings, organising activities, talking things through with them, he was ready to do it all. But the end result was not what he had hoped for. He came out of it discouraged, and determined never to go into social work. In an environment like that, at any rate, he didn't feel he could really do anything to help those children. After all, he himself hadn't found any answers to life – what could he do for anyone else?

So he had come back to struggle through his second year in law at university. By Easter he decided he needed out for a while and went for a week to a Jesuit retreat centre just outside of Paris. A life of silence - even during meals - solitude, nature walks and jogging, spending his spare time reading up on the life of a Catholic priest who worked with the down-and-outs of Paris... His *directeur de conscience* (director of conscience), who was of Irish descent, had known Axel since the time he had been involved in the Catholic church in his home town a few years before. He told him that when in difficulty he should cry to God, and recommended that Axel read the Psalms, Psalm 139 in particular. Verse 2 of that psalm stayed with him :

"Thou knowest my downsitting and mine uprising, thou understandest my thought afar off ..."

In spite of this, Axel still had that sense of culpability – it was fine to cry to God but He seemed such an awful way off, it was like crying into a void. During one of the many conversations they had, "Father" O'Reilly even told him that he was cut out for "exceptional situations", but it left Axel indifferent. He still hadn't found any answers.

Discovering Christ

Around the same time Axel had noticed an interesting, and

apparently genuine change in his brother René, who along with his wife and little son were now attending a small evangelical church in the outskirts of Paris. Until then they had been scraping along on a very modest income and living in a run-down area of outer Paris. Mireille, his wife, was working too, and they had a young son, Luc, who always seemed grizzly and discontented. Now, though, their visits showed a happier, more confident and united family.

One day while they were visiting with the family, they invited Axel's parents to come along with them to church. When his parents refused, they turned to Axel. Well – yes, all right. He was curious to see what had wrought this change in his brother's life.

And there it was – the answer. Why had nobody ever told Axel so clearly that all he needed was Christ ? It was more than a turning point in his life, it was an about-face. His former indecision, lack of conviction, of direction, was gone. Sometimes he would still get discouraged, sometimes he still got so down he felt sure he could never get up again. But that was where he found a secret that has never left him since: you have to rely on God and no other, He alone will get you through.

It was an old church building, small and simple. The service was divided into three parts: first there was a Bible reading by the presiding elder, who preached on the text and then threw open the meeting for the rest of the congregation to share a text, give a testimony or suggest choruses; secondly came the communion service; and thirdly there was the message preached by a different elder. During the first part of the meeting, one of the elders who stood up, Richard was his name, spoke of how a Christian should stand for God, even if that meant losing some of your hair (his was becoming rather sparse!). The remark was to leave a deep and lasting impression on Axel. He had always thought that God was worth taking a stand for, but had never heard anyone say as much - someone whose actions obviously testified to his convictions. The presiding elder asked René to introduce Axel to the small congregation, and left Axel the opportunity to say a few words too. Axel felt that these people were honest – so he would be honest. He spok e slowly.

"I would like to take this opportunity to say that everything I have heard so far today has deeply touched my heart. Thank you."

And he sat down.

At the end of the service he was left with the savour of having tasted the goodness of God, and the thought of returning to his usual everyday life loomed before him like a prison sentence. It held nothing for him. As he was about to leave, his brother came over with one of the elders.

"Axel," said the elder, "Do you want to start your life with Christ now ?"

Axel's answer was an unhesitating yes. And when asked if he wanted to be baptized straight away or later, Axel unhesitatingly replied "now".

"Are you quite sure about this ?" they asked. Yes. He was sure all right.

So a meeting was convened at an elder's house. There, the way of salvation was explained to Axel, and he came to Christ in repentance and thanksgiving and commitment. After which he was baptized and left the house amidst the rejoicing brethren, a liberated man.

He was late home and his Mum and Dad were still up waiting for him.

"*Papa, Maman*," he said, "I found Christ tonight." The announcement was greeted with silence, and his parents looked uneasy and anxious. He tried to explain that for him Christ was the answer he had been looking for, that it was great news. Unfortunately, his parents didn't see things quite like that. They have never been able to. But they couldn't deny the change in Axel himself, for he had returned to his studies with a completely different attitude.

When Axel was called in for his *service militaire* (obligatory military training) the following year (1982-1983) he went at it with that same attitude. It shaped his life too, not only the discipline but the fact that he was a fairly new Christian being plunged into an army environment. He came through with flying colours: a medal on his shirt and the hard-earned trust of his superior officers to his honour. On his return he settled into more organised and purposeful studies, and his hard work brought him good results. And so, year after year, as he grew spiritually, he had been able to start work as a training consultant in law and taught as an assistant lecturer at the University where he had once studied – and he would never forget that it was all thanks to the grace of God in his life.

Now it looked as if all that was about to be ruined – how could he possibly explain to his clients why he had failed to turn up for a day's training that had long been arranged ?

The attack

Axel continued to pace around outside the entrance to the apartment block, wondering where it was all leading to and how it would all finish. It was almost as though the police were deliberately giving him lots of space and the chance to make a run for it - but there was no way he would try anything so daft. They were armed, of course. The last few months had been extremely tense, and now he understood the terrible pressure he had suddenly felt bearing down on him the previous evening. This was a fresh attack, and a heavy one at that – but why?

At six o'clock a locksmith joined them. They certainly weren't messing around. Axel had to agree to let them in, obviously. He knew they wouldn't have hesitated for a second in breaking down the door. He had no choice but to follow orders – stand in front of the door and ring the bell. All three immediately slammed themselves against the wall on either side, and when I confidently opened the door, they barged through.

The officer in charge, who had obviously been assigned to shadow Axel, was soon carefully searching his desk, examining photos and even inspecting scraps of torn-up paper in the waste-paper basket. What exactly were they looking for behind the cushions on the sofa ? Incriminating evidence ?

"For certain offences there sometimes is no evidence," said the officer. What was that supposed to mean ? That they would be trying to get evidence some other way ? That was typical – accusations first, then they back it up with whatever they can find.

Well, they would find nothing anyway. There was nothing to find, and Axel told them as much.

The phone shrilled – "Don't answer!" Axel was ordered. It was only 6:15 a.m. Who could be ringing at this hour except a friend – maybe a friend in trouble ?

The officer sat beside him and ordered him to lift his right hand and swear to say "the truth, the whole truth and nothing but the truth". Axel almost laughed outright in spite of the circumstances, it was so ludicrous. But he simply replied that he only swore on oath before a judge, in court. The officer busied himself elsewhere.

The phone rang again, ominously. Nobody was allowed to answer. So… there must be others going through something similar. This must have been a long time in the planning, something coordinated, something…ruthless.

Victoria was asking for him, so he went through to comfort her. She had been so hyper the day before – as though she could feel this coming. She had felt stress in the past too, even as a little child. Once she had cried all day when there had been legal proceedings going on that she couldn't possibly have known about. Now she wanted reassurance from her Daddy. After all, waking up to find strangers in her bedroom, strangers searching all over the house, strangers ordering her parents around – it was enough to upset any child. Yet she wasn't crying.

Now the officer was asking Axel for Victoria's date and place of birth, which he gave him. He also decided to show him her health book, in which the paediatrician had written, less than two months before: "superb child". It would do no harm for them to know just how well Victoria was cared for with her Mum and Dad. Actually, it would do no harm to warn them exactly what they were getting themselves into.

"This is a case of religious persecution, you know. People who were with us left our church and now they've turned to lying against us."

The police officer told him he was a Protestant.

"If you are a Protestant," answered Axel, "you ought to know that these things can happen."

Separations and accusations

Then there was the scene at the police station later, when he took Victoria up to me. When the police had told him that he was being put into *garde à vue* (police custody), they had wanted to "look after her" themselves, and had even tried to tempt her away from him with colouring-in pens, etc. Victoria had been far too comfortable on her Daddy's knees though, and wasn't even interested. Without really knowing why, he sensed it was dangerous to leave Victoria with them... He carried her upstairs and put her firmly on her Mummy's lap as he kissed her goodbye, and she gave him a smacker back. Axel was reasoning to himself that since they were putting him into *garde à vue*, they were perhaps intending to release me. Walking back downstairs he shouted out to me: "When everything is over, go back home with the children!" But the police officer had already closed the door...

Now here he was. Through the dull transparent surveillance pane beside the cell door he suddenly recognized a friend who had just come in – Richard. They must have been into central Paris as well then, where he lived, and brought him all the way out here. If he had been arrested, what about their other friends? Just how big was this?

Towards the end of the afternoon, not long after Victoria had disappeared and I had been taken elsewhere to be locked up, Axel was taken back to the Children's Brigade for questioning. In the car on the way there he asked the police officer if they were going to make the headlines with this escapade. To his surprise, the officer assured him, in a rather irritated voice, that they would not. Axel was surprised. That was a change of tactics, for the media usually loved this sort of thing. Was the whole operation perhaps not going quite as they had planned ?

The accusations were becoming more specific now. They had questioned Paul and David and were now using their so-called 'statements' against Axel. He was perfectly aware of how police statements were drawn up in France; a joke by British standards. Nothing was ever taped and the interrogating officer usually never typed the questions he asked, but was free to rephrase the answers – to fit in with the accusations, if that was what they were after - and it was especially easy if they were interviewing a child. Even an innocent adult had to be extremely careful. Axel didn't trust them an inch.

The police officer started by asking him if he had 'beaten' David, which he flatly denied. David was the youngest son of Philippe, the very church elder who had preached at the first meeting Axel had attended in the church. Axel hadn't really had much to do with David except for once during the summer holidays of 1987, but I had looked after him and his brother Paul quite a lot.

In 1987, while a few of us had been on holiday together during the summer, Axel had promised to keep an eye on David for his parents, Philippe and Rebecca, when they had to return to work in Paris. Looking back, it was perhaps unwise, but at the time it seemed perfectly natural to help friends out. The little fellow was only 4 years old then and he enjoyed the attention of an adult, especially as Axel played sports with him and let him help with little jobs around the house, which needed a bit of fixing up. He even started David reading and writing a little. Sometimes David used to make a fuss about eating his meals, so Axel had sternly told him where things were at. Occasionally he had had to send him to the corner for time out or give him a tap on the bottom to make him understand that this was serious. And sure enough, he had got back into good eating habits once again and had never had any problems since. His Mum and Dad came back at the weekend and after about two weeks he returned home with them, and life went on as usual.

But why was this being brought up now ? It dated back more than five years !

Since then, Rebecca had sometimes arranged with me to look after the boys during the day along with Victoria, since I wasn't working and we lived in the same town. Then Philippe and Rebecca had moved to central Paris around the end of 1992, so Paul and David had been back a few times, usually in order to go to the physiotherapist's (their GP had recommended preventive exercises for their backs), sometimes staying overnight if it suited Rebecca. Axel rarely saw them because he was often late back in the evening and left early in the morning. The boys got on well with Victoria, and I didn't mind having them...

The police officer still maintained that the children themselves had 'confessed' that Axel had beaten David. It was a nasty accusation, but with his conscience clear, Axel denied it even more strongly. The officer grew angry and stormed out of the office. A few minutes later he stormed back in with papers in his hands – the so-called 'statements' by Paul and David, typed out by his colleagues. He read them out aloud, obviously convinced that he had vital evidence against Axel in hand. They were full of vulgarities and the words couldn't possibly have been the boys' at all. They had both been well brought-up and taught to use decent language. Axel was actually relieved, for he knew that the boys themselves had nothing to say against him, and here was proof of it. The police could manipulate them all they liked, as they obviously had done, but these were not the boys' words. He immediately contested the authenticity of the statements.

"You think that's the result of police manipulation ?" shouted the officer, rather red in the face.

Axel had absolutely no doubt about it.

He confirmed once again that he had not beaten any child, nor done a child harm in any way. When the police officer started to argue, Axel reminded him that his job was to type what he, Axel, had to say. And the officer lowered his head and started to type!

The policewoman who had been present at the six o'clock raid that morning came in to tell the officer in charge that she had finished and was going home. Only later would Axel learn about the dirty job she had done that day.

"Thanks very much for your help," was all the officer had to say.

Axel asked him what had happened with Victoria and I, and was told that his wife was in *garde à vue* and his daughter was being 'looked after'.

"How did things go with Victoria?"

The officer brushed the question off. "Oh, it wasn't easy, but then it's never easy in such circumstances – anyway, everything turned out all right in the end." Axel was obviously not going to get a straight answer.

Axel was silent. What had they done? What had they done to his little girl? And me, in *garde à vue* ? What on earth for ? If Victoria was in care, she had better be back with us quick...

Immediate reactions

After a while he asked who was in charge of the investigation. The officer gave him the name of an investigating judge, Mlle Roussel.

"My instructions are that my wife and daughter should be immediately released, and I want these instructions conveyed to the judge!"

What else could he do? He refused to sign the statement typed out by the officer. He had to show his opposition somehow.

He was returned to his cell in the police station in Saint-Germain. It was late already. Sharing the small, dim cell with two other men meant that Axel had to sleep on the floor, unable to stretch out full-length, with only his coat to cover him. The other two obviously knew each other, but Axel didn't feel like talking. As he thought things over he realized that although the police had initially called him as a witness, they were actually wanting to indict him in order to justify whatever they were doing with Victoria... In spite of the noise of the place – policemen talking, doors banging, keys jangling – he managed to get a little sleep somehow.

The following morning the other two men were pestering to get out, fed up with being cooped up in such a small space without knowing when it would end.

Later in the morning he was taken out, at the same time as Richard, and both were handcuffed – treated like dangerous criminals... It was probably part of the strategy – the psychological demoralising process. In spite of the grimness of the situation, Richard had an encouraging smile for him. They were taken by car to the Children's Brigade for more questioning. Richard had managed to keep his Bible with him and they shared a few verses on the way, but apart from that they didn't feel like talking much. The police officers seemed tenser, if anything, than they had been the day before. A senior police officer had also been brought in, to question Richard. Maybe that meant they were getting desperate – good news.

Axel was taken upstairs to the room where he had left Victoria and I the day before. The police officer (the same one as the day before) was trying to make him feel at ease, but Axel suspected it was probably only an attempt to get a confession out of him about the alleged mistreatment of Paul and David. That was the way the French police worked – confession was always the 'queen' piece of evidence.

"You intend to keep me a little longer, then indict me and send me to jail, is that it?"

The officer brushed it off as if the thought had never crossed his mind.

Since he was trying to be pleasant in order to get his prisoner talking, Axel took advantage of it to ask him how old he was – "26" – and how long he had been in the police – "five years". The officer even went on to explain why he had chosen to work in the Children's Brigade... Axel was amazed that a case involving several arrests and the removal of at least one minor-aged child had been assigned to such a young, relatively inexperienced fellow.

He wanted to know now exactly what had happened to Victoria and I and was told this time that Victoria had been placed in State care at the request of the Public Prosecutor and that there was nothing anybody could do about it. Concerning me – I had been released, they said. Axel simply didn't believe it. After all, the police had lied from the outset, telling him he was going in for questioning and then putting him into *garde à vue*, to start with; and telling me that I would be back home in a couple of hours; and then, if I was released, why was Victoria not with me ? No, he didn't believe it, and so demanded that I be released immediately. Then Victoria could be returned to me.

The officer seemed to be at the end of his tether with the whole business, and raised his voice.

"She *has* been released, I tell you ! You have my word as a police officer !"

Axel fell silent once again. So his wife was free but Victoria wasn't. So it was Victoria they were after, in their crazy, illogical, heinous way of reasoning. Make an innocent child suffer, and you should have her parents eating out of your hand. France was his mother country, his "*patrie*"; but how ashamed he was of it now.

Prison – or not ?

Not long after Axel's return to the now familiar cell (his two other cell-mates had disappeared), Richard was released. That was definitely good news. At least *he* wasn't going to prison ! Axel had been worried about him, because he had been through so much already. After three years of investigations into every aspect of his life, which had ended with a non-suit order two years before, they couldn't have had anything left to accuse him of ! He left Axel his Bible and in spite of the pressure and worry, he was able to read in peace - and await his fate. And since Richard had been released and not him, it was beginning to look like it might be prison.

In the middle of the afternoon it was time for yet another session of questioning – the third time round. Could they still be hoping for a confession ? But now, because he understood that they had targeted Victoria, Axel wanted more than ever to be able to fight for her. And of course, he had to be free to fight for her.

Until then he had always dictated his statements, but this time when the police officer asked him politely for answers to his questions, he consented. True, it would give them an opportunity to add to or modify or twist the meaning of what he said to suit their purposes, but at the same time he didn't want to be too hard-headed. Anyway, the officer was now dealing with minor issues, such as previous addresses, and questions about friends. He typed up the report and asked Axel to sign it; and this time he agreed to.

They sent him handcuffed to the *Tribunal de Grande Instance* in Versailles to be presented to the examining judge, stopping *en route* only to allow the police to collect other statements, of which there seemed to be a great number, apparently faxed in from several different places. What a nasty job these French police officers had done in just thirty-six hours, he thought. They marched him handcuffed down the street to the Tribunal, in full public view, just to humiliate him, of course. Usually prisoners entered through the basement.

Upstairs he waited in a small room walled with compartments just big enough for one person to sit down in - custom-made for people in *garde à vue*. A little while later Paul and David's mother Rebecca was brought in, escorted by police officers, and sat down in the compartment beside him. She was a gentle, sweet lady and looked extremely out of place in those surroundings. She appeared to be in brave spirits though, and even gave him a smile, with her typical serenity. She spoke in a quiet voice.

"It's terrible, what the children have said against you. We denied everything."

He told her tranquilly not to worry about it. They both seemed to have a strangely peaceful sense of *que sera, sera*. They certainly couldn't do anything about it now. Their fate was about to be decided by a young woman judge who could send them to prison right away if she wished.

Rebecca was taken in first, and a short while later was escorted back through the corridor between two police officers. Someone shouted the word "*dépôt!*". That meant she was going to prison ! Shock hit him. He couldn't even begin to imagine what she could possibly have been indicted for.

It was now Axel's turn. He entered the judge's office and sat down in the chair provided, in front of the examining judge. Beside him was the police officer who had been there the morning before, the one who had questioned him three times. He was quiet, and any confidence he had had over the last two days seemed to have completely evaporated.

The judge asked Axel to confirm his personal details.

"You are a consultant in law ?" she asked with a slight smile. Her face was very vaguely familiar. He replied in the affirmative. From her position behind the court clerk, the judge was checking everything that was being typed. She then returned to her chair.

"I indict you for mistreating the child David Legrand in Carquebut."

She asked him if he wished to speak then, or later in the presence of a lawyer. He chose the latter. Curiously, the more Axel looked at the judge, the more he felt convinced that he had seen her somewhere before. She continued.

"I am going to release you on bail, with one condition. You are forbidden to have any contact with David or his brother or sisters."

Axel nodded.

Then he asked her where Victoria was. She replied that that was not her job - a judge for children was in charge of the case.

Axel nodded again and left her office – free.

The poor police officer was still sitting on his chair, clutching his pile of statements and looking rather bewildered. After all his hard work, there was Axel, walking free !

Free to fight

Downstairs in the tribunal, it was great to be free. He felt relief for himself, but grief for Rebecca. How must Philippe be feeling ? What could he, Axel, possibly do to help ? After downing a cup of black coffee from the slot machine, Axel thought he may as well return upstairs on the chance that he might be able to speak to the examining judge again. The building was now empty, for it was late afternoon already. He found the judge's office, where she was on her own, about to leave. He told her that the accusations were false, that there was absolutely nothing true in it.

"You will explain it all when you have your lawyer with you," she replied, smiling, with a dismissive gesture. There was nothing more to be done.

Heading for the telephone box to phone me, he suddenly remembered where he had seen the judge before. She used to attend Nanterre University when he was also a student there. He had stood today before his judge – practically a university classmate!

For now though, he wanted to speak to me and find out how Richard was, and who else had been through this – and how they had come through these traumatic two days.

3

The aftermath
February 1993

Reeling from the blow

The numbers said it all. Out of our small group of friends, four families had been targeted on February 10, and out of 16 people, seven minor-aged children had disappeared without warning into state care, two mothers had been jailed, and a third was in hospital after unsuccessfully resisting police attempts to forcefully remove her two-year-old son from her.

"Now I know what it must have felt like to wear the yellow star," that little boy's mother, Isabelle, told me later. I knew what she meant. Whatever we said or however we protested, the judgement had already been pronounced, however arbitrarily - our children were to be taken from us. The way they took her little son by force proved to Axel and I that whatever we had done, they would have taken Victoria anyway, by whatever means necessary. It was tyranny. From four whole families we were down to just 6 adults – and that was including Richard and Anutza's daughter Lydia who was just over eighteen, so they couldn't force her into care. Only friends who were single or who had grown-up children had escaped the blitz. Innocent children and loving mothers were being made to suffer the most. Once more, it was the *total separation* that was so incomprehensible. How could the French Judiciary do this to us ?

According to the judge for children in her February 12 judgment, when some of the older children were questioned by the *gendarmes* (rural police) they "monotonously reeled off stereotyped phrases specifying that they [were] persecuted because of their religious beliefs; that they [were] happy and content, and want to live their faith freely; that they do not belong to a cult but are part of a group of friends with a practical faith …". The children had obviously done all they could to be returned home.

Little by little during the second day people started resurfacing. When Axel actually phoned I could scarcely believe my ears. After he had left us the day before, I had guessed from some of the questions they had been asking that they were trying to frame him, but here he was free!

It was only by the grace of God that Axel and I were together again, because we both knew the Judiciary could have jailed him without proof – accusations were enough. The strategy of splitting each couple up meant that it was very difficult to try and regain custody of our vanished children. I don't know how I would have managed by myself.

Worst of all was the fact that the Judiciary had cut Victoria off from us so completely – we were forbidden all contact, forbidden to know even where she was in State care. Faced with Victoria's sudden absence, I found myself putting my feelings on freeze. After all, we still had to go about our everyday lives - go to work, do the shopping, get some sleep, carry on with our lives successfully in order to be able to fight for Victoria. The only way forward was to hope and trust in God and channel our strength into the battle to regain custody of Victoria. I unconsciously buried my feelings down as low as I could in the depths of my soul.

Sometimes when I dared to think of what had happened, the feelings escaped in spite of myself. It was worse at night, when the torture of not being able to comfort my little girl or do anything to help her just got too much, and the tears would come welling up again uncontrollably. Sometimes circumstances were too much and the feelings I tried to keep under would rattle against the bars of their confinement. When I was at home alone, for example, and a noise would make me think I should check on Victoria - but then she wasn't there; or the time one of my English students told me he and his wife wanted to name their new-born daughter after me (they had wanted an English name) and they wanted to check the spelling - but *I* wasn't allowed to have my own little daughter at home with me.

I got into the habit of shying away from anything that touched my feelings. I could laugh and joke and make small talk, talk about serious subjects as long as they were impersonal, or even talk about Victoria's case in an objective sort of way. All of this was alright if it took my mind off *that*. It was an instinctive reaction, and in some ways the habit partly remains with me today. At the time, it was simply the only way I could cope.

Back at our flat, word had got around that our daughter had been removed and placed with Social Services – and Victoria's absence was evident enough. The neighbours hardly looked at us. It was true that we hadn't been living there long. Only the caretaker, a single Mum with two daughters of her own, whom we had talked to on several occasions, was touched enough to actually write a statement about seeing Victoria going in and out regularly with us, a happy, smiling little girl. After all the disturbing events of February 12 we were grateful for this token of goodwill.

It was impossible to talk to anybody official about Victoria's case. The Public Prosecutor said there was a Judge for Children in charge of it, but the Judge for Children said she hadn't received the file from the Public Prosecutor yet. At any rate, there was no news of Victoria and no way of knowing where she was being held.

The New Zealand connection

On February 11 I was distraught about Victoria and waiting to hear what had happened to Axel, but one of the first things I did was to ring the New Zealand Embassy in Paris. Back in April 1992, when Victoria was only 2 years old, we had made sure that she was registered as a New Zealand citizen, and we had obtained a New Zealand passport for her – if the worst came to the worst, well, there *was* an escape route. Because of this and my own New Zealand citizenship, we thought that surely the Embassy would be able to put pressure on the French authorities for Victoria to be returned to me. After all, a somewhat similar situation in France where Dutch people had been involved had been resolved in just that way.

The Embassy in Paris told me that they would be looking into the matter. I could only keep phoning to ask for news and to remind them that this was urgent – our little girl of only 3 years of age had been completely cut off from her loving parents and placed in the strange and bewildering environment of a State institution ! Many were the desperate prayers we sent up to God as we struggled to keep our heads clear and fight back intelligently. Surely our loving Father would not allow such a situation to last for long.

Then I had to break the news to my Mum in New Zealand. Surprisingly, she had already been informed of my arrest through diplomatic channels. But she just could not believe they had gone so far as to take Victoria from us. She had been to stay with us a few months before, and only days before February 10, I had been on the phone telling her about Victoria saying English words I had been teaching her. There was such a strange gulf between the reality we all knew and this vicious attack on our family and our friends' families. It was outrageous, and my Mum was soon talking about going to the New Zealand press about Victoria. After talking it over with Axel, we gave her the go-ahead. Surely it couldn't do any harm?

A few days later we learnt that the local Rotorua paper, the "Daily Post" had given my Mum front page coverage, and it continued to give positive coverage regularly for some time thanks to the compassion of one of their reporters.

What we naïvely *hadn't* expected was to be flooded with calls ourselves from the different New Zealand media. Newspaper, radio and finally television reporters interviewed us, and in particular me, of course, being 'the' New Zealander in question. This was some-times difficult to face, especially as I was still feeling raw. From my point of view, I couldn't imagine that these people would be trying to do anything but help me and my little daughter. Unfortunately the world of the press is not so good-natured ! And they are scarcely interested in the <u>proof</u> of the truth of a matter – they prefer sensational headlines and tasty rumours, whatever will go down best with the general public or whatever suits their own position.

So I had my work cut out for me, trying to explain how Victoria's withdrawal had come about without falling into the traps which reporters set for unsuspecting members of the public. I suppose from the outside it looked extremely damning for us. You had to really go into the whole story to be able to understand the monstrosity of it all, and the French Judiciary knew this full well. They had deliberately made the whole case look even more complicated than it really was, for it made it extremely difficult for us to explain. How could anyone explain such subtle persecution ?

Fighting for our lives

We were hardly home at all over the next couple of weeks, spending a great deal of our spare time getting together with our fellow 'survivors' to work out how best to proceed. Far from splitting our group of friends up and turning us against each other, as the French Judiciary had undoubtedly hoped would happen on or after February 10, the children's removal rallied everybody to the fight. And for us it was the natural thing to do. We had all known the reality of life in the church, and we had all come under the same senseless, devastating attack on our families.

So we left our ground-floor residential area apartment, with the pedestrian paths winding between high-rise apartment blocks, the playgrounds and the greenery, to meet in one home then in another, in a leafy Paris suburb or in somebody else's apartment. The situation was talked inside out and upside down and prayed over, and every possible course of action was discussed. The phone never seemed to stop and there was always someone busy writing a letter, or preparing for a meeting. We appealed to anybody we could think of to help.

Lydia, Richard's daughter, went straight to the top to ask for her mother's immediate release from prison and her twin brothers' return home. She went personally to the halls of power in Paris, the great white-pillared building of the *Assemblée Nationale* (the French

Parliament), to give letters personally to numerous Government Ministers and MPs.

American friends from the church contacted Christians in America for help and prayer. I was on the phone to New Zealand, and my Mum and several of my sisters wrote to the French authorities demanding that Victoria be returned home. Some of our friends' business contacts were also informed – and were outraged. People from different countries who had visited the church over the years were shocked at the news – including my own family's Baptist minister from New Zealand who had visited us twice with his wife for a while, back in 1987 and 1988. How many happy photos we had of their time with us!

There was also the tedious business of bringing out the proof that the accusations brought against our loved ones were false. It shouldn't have had to be done of course, since a person should be presumed innocent until proven guilty, but in practice that simply is not the way the French legal system works. For the two mothers in prison especially, this work was vital. After a week in prison, their lawyers were allowed to ask for their release on bail. So each accusation had to be carefully refuted, with a full file of evidence. This not only meant getting a lot of detailed reasoning clearly onto paper, which was mainly what Axel was busy at, with his legal background, but also more practical work like typing or carefully searching through family photos, which then had to be laser-copied and displayed with captions. The work would often continue late into the night and we usually ended up putting together an evening meal for everyone, as the work went on.

The whole story was told over again to American, African, Romanian, Japanese and British Christians, amongst others, and many wrote to the French authorities to voice their indignation, but we couldn't see that their protests were having any effect on the ground – the two mothers remained in prison, as bail was refused by the examining judge. By the harrowed lines on their husbands' faces when they returned from visiting them in prison, we all knew that the situation was very grim. Anutza in particular was suffering badly in prison. Because of a heart condition she was supposed to be following a cholesterol-free diet, but the prison would not allow her to be treated any differently from everyone else – so she practically wasn't eating. In spite of her generally frail health and the trauma of being separated from her family and especially her twin sons, they seemed to be singling her out for harsh treatment.

Family doctors also had to be visited, the situation explained and health certificates obtained. On hearing what had happened, many friends wrote personal testimonies or letters asking for the imprisoned mothers to be released and the children returned home. And each family had to get their own lawyer, arrange meetings, present their evidence, etc.

Axel met with a lawyer with whom he had been following other cases – one of the most famous lawyers of the French bar. He had agreed to take on Victoria's case and immediately dictated a letter to the Versailles Judge for Children, demanding Victoria's release. Looking at Axel he remarked: "You've lost weight !" Observant people, lawyers… The strain of the past few days was obviously taking its toll.

The fact that we were able to pray and work together to defend our children and release the two mothers kept us busy, and I think it also kept us sane. In such a situation there is nothing so encouraging, though unfortunate, as knowing that those around you are going through the same inner turmoil and anguish. By God's grace we were able to pull together at that absolutely crucial time for us all.

Tell us who you are

One question that came up a lot in those days, for example when talking to the New Zealand press, was "Well, what kind of church were you ?" We may have had a very definite idea of who we were and what we believed, but it was difficult to put a label on it, except to say that we were a small, independent, evangelical church. We didn't belong to any particular denomination or federation, but we were very definitely Bible-based, Lutheran and Calvinistic in principle, as was evidenced by our 'declaration of faith' by which the church had been constituted. Several members had also been Pentecostals. We weren't aware of it at the time, but it was our very independence as a church that was going to cost us dearly: because we weren't affiliated to a "mother" church under whose wing we could find refuge, we were in fact sitting ducks for predators such as UNADFI, the anti-'cult' lobby group which was out to target any religious minority in France whom they branded as a "cult".

"Could you say you're basically Baptist ?" was the question my family's minister in New Zealand asked me. I could only say yes – I couldn't see any doctrinal differences between the Baptist church I had grown up in in New Zealand and our church in France, though for me personally it was much more meaningful. The only thing I hadn't known in New Zealand was fasting – but that may have been simply because of my age. My family's minister from New Zealand had been to see the church in France for himself anyway, and as a former President of the Baptist Union in New Zealand, he started circulating petitions destined for the French authorities around the various Baptist churches there.

One day not long after the story came out in the New Zealand press, we received a phone call from a Christian in New Zealand who wanted to find out whether the children's removal really was based on our Christian faith. The editor of the "New Zealand Beacon", a Christian magazine, was not the sort of person who would interrogate you cold-bloodedly and turn the knife in the wound as you lay on the bed of torture. Derek Pearce wasn't interested in our nametag – it was the down-to-earth, everyday reality he wanted to grasp. He spoke to me initially, but also to Axel and other friends, and was confirmed in his perception that this was real persecution – attacks based simply on our faith – and that there was nothing to justify such barbaric actions being taken against us.

Derek and his wife Liliane became very dear friends over the next few years and we were much strengthened simply by knowing that their whole family and Christian friends were actively praying for us during those very trying times. Not only that, Derek Pearce acted. Thanks to his organising skills, a protest was staged in front of the French Embassy in Wellington, with placards reading "Victoria needs her mother!" and "Stop Vel d'Hiv rafle[1] !"

[1] *Vélodrome d'Hiver* – Winter Cycle-Racing Track where the Jewish families arrested were held as the first stage of a fateful journey which led eventually to the Nazi extermination camp of Auschwitz and the ethnic cleansing of France. The Jews could not imagine that the French Police would set upon women and children, and even the Germans themselves (who had not planned on deporting children) were obliged to ask Berlin for the go-ahead in order to take advantage of such ready cooperation offered by the French Vichy Government.

He later remarked to Axel that the efficacy of that last slogan was quite astounding, although he had been a little dubious about carrying a placard written mostly in French. Apparently the French Ambassador's jaw literally dropped when he saw it!

This contact with concerned and active Christians was the greatest encouragement we could have had. Derek introduced us to Dr Peter Trumper in Wales, himself a great and faithful encouragement to us in spite of his own trials and battles. These dear people were a ray of light for us in the midst of darkness. Here were like-minded Christians, whom you felt you had known for years straight off. Here were praying Christians with a deep compassion for the trials of others and a loyal, upright heart. These were Christians who believed in the power of God – they had experienced it in their own lives, and knew God never makes mistakes. They were all to show an understanding and a compassion for our situation which only comes from tested spiritual maturity. They had all been tried themselves. Derek and Lilian's favourite verse of encouragement was Romans 8:28: "And we know that all things work together for good to them that love God, to them who are the called according to His purpose." How we thank God for them and others like them still today !

A glimpse of church life

My first impressions of the church and my main memories of the seven years I spent as a member, are probably the best glimpse I can give of "who we were" as a church.

When I started attending in June 1984, I soon realised that this was no Sunday religion, it was a way of life. There was a serious-ness about these Christians' faith which I had rarely seen in New Zealand or anywhere else, and a deep concern for others. Although as a family we would have had other Christian families out to dinner on a Sunday in New Zealand, it was really much more of a social "entertainment" visit, as I saw it, whereas this was a sort of 'caring-for-other-people' atmosphere. Anutza in particular was a hard worker, often providing a meal for single girls like me after the Sunday service, when she always found time to come and chat with us in spite of having three children of her own to look after, including the twin boys who were then very lively 5-year-olds.

That day the church had met in Richard and Anutza's home, where folding chairs had been set out in the lounge / living room. There must have been around 60 people present, and their enthusiasm was almost palpable. There was a spirit of praise and intercession that seemed to bring you right up close before God. The service was like a spring of water for someone dying of thirst. People I spoke to afterward had a warm welcome and seemed genuinely concerned for me. Although I still had hang-ups about my weight, etc., all that seemed completely irrelevant here. There was so much more to life.

I was still working as an *au pair* in inner Paris at that time, but was able to arrange to go on holiday with others from the church who were going to Corsica, as they had already been doing over the past couple of years.

The mid-summer train journey from St Etienne in the centre of France, near where I was staying with my *au pair* family, down to Marseilles, was quite an experience, in the old-type French train with compartments and a side corridor. There weren't too many people, so I put my feet up on the bench and plugged my walkman in – that was my New Zealand lack-of-inhibition side coming through. So the train ride was fairly enjoyable, but the heat that met me when I got out at Marseilles was overwhelming – it seemed almost as hot as Tahiti. Then I got mixed up between the new port and the old, and had to struggle my way round to the old one, tugging my suitcase, while the sophisticated French sat under shady umbrellas in their cafés, sipping cool drinks and watching me toil by with some amusement.

Finally, on arriving at what I hoped was the right boat, I couldn't find the people from the church whom I was supposed to meet there – until about five minutes before we were due to leave. Being the happy-go-lucky, enjoy-what-you've-got type, I wasn't really worried, but looking back I have a feeling the others were. They at least had a sense of responsibility. I'm afraid I was far too used to enjoying God's protection – my Mum and Dad were undoubtedly faithfully praying for me back home. As a teenager travelling alone, first to Tahiti for nine months, then on to California for two weeks, England and Scotland for two weeks, then *beau* Paris for two months and finally on to Corsica, I never realised until much later just how much I was unknowingly protected.

The view as we sailed out of Marseilles was like a dream – all I remember is a vision of blue sea and blue evening sky and rocky coasts, with a warm sea breeze in my hair. Somehow I made it to my upper berth and fell asleep.

Corsica was beautiful. Us girls were lodging in a semi-detached bungalow all to ourselves, with Anutza and her family in the semi-detached next door. The bungalow was rented out in the summer by the owner of an orchard, which was round the back of the house. It was as though I'd found another bunch of sisters – the usual morning rush for the shower etc. – and being used to a big family of girls made it even more family-like for me. The other families rented different houses around the area – some of them really nice, like the one where Jacques and Mireille stayed with their three children – a charming little villa, cool and clean and very well-kept. Some were further up in the mountains where the air was cooler and the view fantastic. Richard and Anutza's little semi-detached was very simple and small in comparison, but they didn't seem to mind. The beach was only 5 minutes away by car, and almost every afternoon was spent down there, then in the evening we would all meet up in the big outside area next to our bungalow where there was a swing sofa and parasol and room for everyone.

The holiday atmosphere was relaxing and gave me time for thought. It was interesting to see how the other girls – and the other families, when we saw them – lived their Christianity. The seriousness with which they all applied themselves to it was in sharp contrast with my light-hearted approach to everything, but it reflected the seriousness I found in the Bible. This was surely the place, if any, where I was going to learn to reach the meaning in all those verses which had always eluded me. At last I felt I was getting somewhere.

I was struck by the richness of church life. Until then I had only been to the Sunday service, but now I was introduced to the women's Bible study and prayer meeting – a study time and then we knelt down to really pray and praise God together – as well as the young people's meeting on the Friday evening and the family meeting on the Saturday: always lively and enthusiastic.

Sometimes, usually on a Sunday, there was a day of prayer and fasting, and the adults who wished to participate were welcome. Personally, I was sincerely seeking to know the Lord better and stumbling on the secret of fasting and praying[2] was a real find – not in an outward exercise, but in focussing on the important things – straightening my life out, getting my priorities right before God. And to be able to fast with others was encouraging. It was a uniting force.

The children were encouraged to do a little holiday schoolwork in the mornings, and because many of the girls I was with were students, and were studying a little too, I decided to take up my German again. Anutza and some of the others spoke it, and I enjoyed getting back into some wracking of the brain cells. I also got talking with Anutza about where I was going in my life, and found her input to be lucid and very relevant. I also much appreciated her work of organisation and coordination with the other women. Many of them seemed to go to her for advice but she never seemed to mind, she just gave ungrudgingly of her time and efforts without counting. The whole holiday actually demanded a lot of commitment on her behalf. They were all obviously used to helping each other out in practical ways – an arrangement which made a lot of sense.

For me, it was a thoroughly enjoyable, invigorating holiday time. My *au pair* family, seeing the change in me when I returned from holiday, were not surprised when I told them I wished to start study-ing and move out closer to the church.

After that I was able to enjoy church life *and* study. 1984-85 was the best year of my single life. Church life as I had come to know it in Corsica simply continued on back in Paris, except that by now I was in my first year of studies, and I loved it. I owe much to Michèle, who was doing the same studies as I was and who patiently explained to me all the errors in my French essays.

---

[2] Fasting as we practised it meant going without food and drink until around 6:00 p.m., when a full evening meal was taken.

One of the families from the church had very kindly offered to board me and the church was readily accessible, too. I was also enjoying viola lessons (after a year they became violin lessons, on my teacher's recommendation), which I had taken up after hearing Anutza and Richard's children play. I seemed to have everything going for me.

The only blots on those times were when people from the church left. Not understanding why, I was left puzzled at these disappearances, which inevitably created a slight undercurrent of tension. But they weren't made an issue of and such discouraging business was left to the elders of the church... And by then my life had taken on another dimension : by May 1985 I was engaged to be married to Axel.

A wedding in the church

The wedding made for much excitement in the church naturally – and much hard work too, as everybody lent a hand to prepare the new church meeting room for the 'big occasion'. A couple in the church had moved home and made the whole bottom floor of their house available for the church to meet in. Once all the work was finished it was a beautiful spacious room with three pairs of French windows opening onto their quarter-acre garden. With wood-panel walls and soft mid-blue curtains, it looked gorgeous for the wedding, and of course it would serve afterwards for the church too.

Axel was a great help to me in my Christian walk. We had agreed that we would always pray together briefly when we got up in the morning and again at night. Our lives, our marriage, our family, friends and future were always placed firmly in the hands of God. Axel's natural seriousness helped me consider things more deeply – and usually admit he was right, of course! Perhaps most of all, Axel was patient with me in the difficulties that every young married couple faces as they adapt to life together. We had a strong basis for our marriage in the Bible, but it was the patience and love Axel showed me in those first few years that I was never to forget.

As a couple in the church we found ourselves spiritually much stronger, though materially speaking we hadn't 'two pence to rub together', as they say. Although still students at the beginning, we had a 'granny' flat downstairs in another family's house, which we took Axel's Mum and Dad to see after the wedding. Somehow I don't think they were very impressed, but we were happy – so what did it matter ?

Being married also brought me closer to the other married women in the church. Two in particular, Rebecca and Anutza, were great examples for me in their commitment to others and to their children. I remember looking at the two of them and thinking "Lord, if only I could be a little like them !"

As we gradually made our way into the working world and started our own family, we were glad to be able to contribute more to the 'mutual help' that we had benefited from so much ourselves.

Unfortunately, not all those in the church were to prove as exemplary as Philippe and Rebecca or Anutza and Richard, and the change we saw take place in most of those who left the church was staggering.

4

How it came about
1980s-1993

Questions, questions

As we worked on in the aftermath of February 10 1993, people were asking us questions, but we were also asking ourselves – how did we get into such a mess ? What had possessed our accusers to make them go so far ? Couldn't we have avoided the dragnet, or shouldn't we at least have seen it coming ? Just what was the aim of the French Judiciary in it all ?

There was a nagging worry that we must have done something wrong to bring this upon us. But what ? The accusations against the church were sometimes downright stupid but sometimes so vile too, and our accusers so virulent, yet we had done them no harm. God knew our hearts. Why had He allowed all this to happen ?

We turned to the Bible and found that

"Yea, and all that will live godly in Christ Jesus shall suffer persecution." (2 Timothy 3:12.)

It's just 'the way things are'.

"Beloved, think it not strange concerning the fiery trial which is to try you, as though some strange thing happened unto you : But rejoice ..." (1 Peter 4:12)

And we had work to do :

"Resist the devil and he will flee from you." (James 4:7.)

So the work went on.

Axel and I were spending much more time together and I quite often accompanied him to Paris. We were forever talking it all over – in the car, in cafés, before meetings, after meetings. He had restaurant tickets from work he hadn't used, and we were eating out more – there was a pizzeria on the Champs-Elysées that did great thin stone-cooked pizzas, so big that one was enough for the two of us. Gradually the whole picture became clearer to me. I had only joined the church in 1984, so Axel filled me in on events before then. Little by little I was piecing together how it had all come about.

Departures from the church

Axel told me about the few members of the church whom he had known personally and who had left in the early eighties – people who for personal or religious reasons had no longer wanted to continue attending the church. Well, they had been free to come and they were free to go, it was their choice. It can happen in any church.

These were the kind of people who seemed to 'drift', never staying long in the same fellowship. They appeared very enthusiastic to start with, but then perhaps their conscience was pricked about some aspect of their life they knew should change but felt they couldn't or simply wouldn't, or perhaps they disagreed on some triviality which they blew up out of all proportion – and after that they just started looking for an excuse to leave. When people around you are sincere, you can't pretend forever, a mere façade will not do the job – especially when trials come along.

The rest of the church remained enthusiastic. There was of course a certain order in the church – the Lord is a God of order. But above all there was an agreement between the preached Word of God and the lives of the church members. This struck both Axel and I. This church was alive. That was what stayed with me after the first service I attended there - yes, Jesus Christ truly is alive ! As a Christian visitor remarked to Axel one day : "There's life in your church !"

This 'life' stemmed of course largely from the church's enthusiasm for Bible teaching and prayer meetings – getting earnestly down to the essentials. As well as the service on Sunday there were often two Bible study and prayer meetings during the week, and others were sometimes arranged spontaneously, especially meetings for the group of elders (those responsible for church leadership). We were also faithfully taught to take the witness of our life in Christ wherever we went.

There would often be business acquaintances, friends or family of one or other of the church members visiting the church. Michèle and I invited our French teacher to dinner in 1985 and my 2nd-year French teacher attended our wedding. My Mum and my sister Sheryl came to see us in 1985, and then our family minister from New Zealand was over in 1987-88, as well as a cousin of mine and her husband in 1989. In fact, people from quite a range of different nationalities, Christian and non-Christian, visited the church at different times – Japanese, Romanian, African, American, German, British, as well as French people from many different backgrounds. Axel's Mum and Dad had been to the church several times before I appeared on the scene, and I had seen his Mum at a few of the ladies' prayer meetings. In fact, life was so full that I had to be careful not to neglect my studies.

The church falls prey to UNADFI

However, this vibrant church life which I found so enriching came under violent attack. One man who had left the church went to see a certain Madame Beauchamp who, incidentally, had with some difficulty allegedly 'rescued' her own husband from a so-called 'cult'[1] where he had been a member. She was at that time the Vice-President (later to become President) of UNADFI, the anti-'cult'

[1] The translation of an official document issued by the French Parliament about 'sects' or 'cults' deliberately uses the word 'cult'. The translator notes: "the actual French word is 'secte'. I have been using cult' because that's the sense in which it's used in the report... To my knowledge, there is no separate word for 'cult'." This is why I use the word 'cult' in this book – we were not simply being accused of not belonging to main-stream Protestantism, as the word 'sect' can imply.

lobby group. Certain sections of French society seemed rather prone to being swayed by influences like UNADFI – swift to jump on the bandwagon and point the finger.

This man's visit must have seemed like a windfall. Mme Beauchamp actually lived near where our church met – this was going to be a 'cult' story right on her doorstep. She took the bait hook, line and sinker, without even thinking of – or perhaps she deliberately avoided – investigating the matter for herself, i.e. coming to see what the church was really about. This was fresh meat for her table, and therefore more publicity, hopefully more funds, and UNADFI obviously wanted it as tasty as possible.

So a pattern was set: as soon as somebody left the church, they were contacted by Mme Beauchamp who invited them to join her in what she called 'exposing the church for what it was' – which she in fact knew absolutely nothing about. Rumours were soon circulating and people were starting to look at us sideways in the street. Many of those attending the church resisted for a good while before giving in – but they finally judged the cost to be too much. Others left when their particular friends left, creating a snowball effect. Things were looking good for Mme Beauchamp.

UNADFI contacted Axel's parents in 1986. Our Christian Bible Church was a legally constituted 'religious association' in accordance with the French law passed in 1905 (with internal regulations accessible to the public) and had fully as much right to exist as UNADFI itself. Nevertheless, UNADFI told Axel's parents that the church was a dangerous 'cult', that their two sons and their families were in dire danger because they belonged to it, and that they themselves really should be doing everything they could to 'free' their poor, misled offspring. All this without anybody from UNADFI ever having been to a service at the church or attempting to make any sort of unbiased inquiries.

Little by little, Madame Beauchamp was gathering together all the former church members she could muster, encouraging them all to 'speak out' and providing them with contacts in the media where they could air their 'complaints', which only grew wilder as time went on. And so the campaign against the church was stepped up.

Then in December of 1986, after intense pressure was applied from family and former church members, there came the withdrawal of Axel's brother René from the church. He was the very person who had introduced Axel to the church and had been one of the most enthusiastic members of the church. He had also been helped by other church members in his work, his family, and even financially: he had qualified as a doctor since he joined the church, spontaneously dedicating his thesis to his friends in the church, and he had – with considerable help – been able to move his family to a new home where they were very content. Now that he had everything going for him, he was backing away.

"I'll never do you any harm," he said as he left. They were treacherous last words.

The build-up of accusations

In June 1987, Madame Beauchamp hit out first of all in a slanderous article against the church published in the local council magazine. And it hurt. It took my breath away when I read it. Some of the church members, fearing that they could come under persecution, opted out. It all depended on how deep your convictions were.

Today we know that most of those who turned against the church never thought their complaints would go as far as they actually did. UNADFI proved to be a deadly catalyst and once exposed to it, slight or even imagined personal grievances became criminal accusations. Not once was an accusation made against our church without having been concocted in the UNADFI melting-pot.

By deforming and amplifying the slightest grievance or suspicion, the most *banal*, everyday incidents or habits took on a hidden, sinister connotation. Those of us at university, who like most students tended to study until late at night and eat when we could, were said to be forced to do this – not allowed to sleep or eat properly. If two brothers in the church had come to a friendly financial arrangement, it was now said to be extorsion and financial fraud. If two mothers left their children doing their homework together one day with a third Mum while they went out shopping or doing other errands, why, this was separating those poor children from their parents, they were being 'enlisted' into the 'cult', like little soldiers in an army.

Everything was perverted, blackened and exaggerated until our church was the spectre of a foul, monstrous imagination. The church services were said to be too long – they were now termed 'brain-washing sessions'. Any meal taken together – and we have many photos showing the abundance of food – were now called 'frugal'. Fasting, which was something for each member to decide on personally, was now supposed to be 'imposed' (how, I wonder ?). The list was potentially endless. As loving parents, our friends in the church would also discipline their children, but not unreasonably. This was transformed into "mistreatment". Paradoxically, it was the couple who had helped us the most in the church who was especially targeted at that stage, and that was Richard and Anutza.

Richard had come to France at the beginning of the seventies on a grant from the French Government and had just been joined there by Anutza for a short holiday when Christian literature was discovered in their home in their native, then-communist, Romania, and they had had to take the difficult decision to stay in France, leaving their little daughter trapped in Romania. But that is their story… Most importantly, the guidance and spiritual support which they provided us with ungrudgingly, as well as the practical help they gave us, in our studies for example, were of incalculable value.

Personally speaking, I wouldn't even have been able to attend university in France if it hadn't been for Richard, who visited the head of the school personally to request with much perseverance that my late application be received favourably – and to make matters worse my New Zealand University Entrance certificate was not strictly at the same level as the *baccalauréat* (the French equivalent of 'A-levels'). Not to mention the many times they helped me financially. The same went for Axel if not more, and they had shown the same generosity and concern towards his brother René and many of the other church members who had since departed. That was just the way they were, and the way they wanted to be. They gave of themselves, of their time and of their worldly goods, without counting the cost. It seemed extremely cruel and grossly unfair that now they were the ones who had to bear the brunt of UNADFI attacks which were constantly referring to their national origin in order to discredit them in the eyes of the French public and the authorities.

It was not common in France for people to be as spontaneously compassionate and generous as Richard and Anutza without expecting to receive something in return. What this couple had grown up with in their native Romania, where Christians shared everything though they had little, was something foreign to the mind of many people in France. Add to this a good pinch of racism, and it will be clear why Richard and Anutza were a perfect target for an organisation like UNADFI, which was expert at inciting public hatred.

This general mindset also explains how the accusation that we were living as a 'community' – in spite of the fact that we all had our own homes – immediately evoked, in the mind of the average French citizen, the idea of promiscuity; how a photo of the 'sisters' of the congregation made the word 'harem' spring to the mind of the general French public; how, although it was never actually an accusation, our children were labelled as the 'children of the community' not as belonging to a particular family. This was another subtle way of blackening and cheapening our church – all the *sous-entendus* which the French public understood perfectly well, and which even the authorities never failed to pass on orally whenever they needed to discourage anybody from coming to our assistance.

The UNADFI strategy

The situation we were now up against was becoming deadly serious. The press were homing in on the 'cult story' mounted by UNADFI and the church's detractors, and the judicial machine, which eventually was to split our family with a devastating blow in 1993, was being set in motion.

In all fairness, it must be said that on 23 March 1988, the one and only positive article to be published in the French press appeared in '*Libération*', a left-wing daily newspaper. The paper had published one slanderous article against us, but after our vigorous protests they had agreed to arrange a meeting. Credit is due to '*Libération*' for the interview they gave us and the ensuing article, for it was the only time French reporters ever attempted to find out the truth of the matter. It was a small consolation in the flood of delirious, unsubstantiated accusations which appeared in all the other main French newspapers.

The horror articles which appeared in the local, then regional and national newspapers in 1987-1988 were only the beginning. UNADFI also had contacts in several French Government Departments, and this soon resulted in the launch of multiple inquiries. There was an inquiry into financial fraud in the church; an inquiry into tax fraud in Richard's business; Axel's brother René attacked Richard for taking money off him (of all things – when Richard had helped him out financially countless times); the mother of my friend Michèle, who I went to university with, lodged a complaint for lack of care of her daughter. Michèle's case even hit the international press in January 1988.

Inquiries meant house searches, and house searches meant being invaded by the police, usually early in the morning, without knowing how long it would last or how it would end.

In October 1987, for example, four police cars screamed to a halt early in the morning outside a friend's house; police poured out of them, jumped onto and then over the six-foot paling, military-style; and then tore up to the front door, demanding entry. At other times, children were woken by the shouts of the police and subjected to the stress of a prolonged police presence in the house. Police intrusion left the children very distressed, tearful and fearful for the future.

The police were so conditioned by the accusations spread by UNADFI and the slander published in the newspapers that they arrived on the scene absolutely convinced that they would be the heroes of the day, come to rescue tortured children and put an end to what they had been told was a cruel, immoral exploitation of human beings. When they found people living normally, it really knocked them back. It seemed unbelievable. The reality was such a shock that the only logical explanation for them was that this normality was just a front – that there must be something behind it all, it was just well covered-up. What could anybody have done to prove their innocence in such circumstances ?

Most serious of all though, was that in 1987 Isabelle's strongly atheist parents attacked their daughter and son-in-law for allegedly not allowing them to see their three grandchildren (their fourth little boy, who was taken from them by force on February 10, 1993, had not then been born). In fact, UNADFI had devised a plan with the grandparents' lawyer to use the French law giving grandparents the right to see their grandchildren in order to attack Isabelle and her husband, Robert. In such hostile circumstances, they did not wish their children to visit the grandparents without being present themselves. At one stage Isabelle and Robert were arrested, while their three little children were whisked away by the police without warning. After they had spent eighteen days in prison, their lawyer persuaded them to comply with the examining judge's ruling and allow the grandparents visiting rights.

This led to these three little children being forced to leave their parents to go and stay with their grandparents every other weekend in an environment which was openly hostile to Isabelle and her husband. The grandparents eventually used these visits to state, without proof or witnesses, that the children had said bad things about their Daddy. Eventually in 1989, Isabelle and Robert, both dental surgeons, lost the custody of their three beautiful little children, and at the time of writing (November 2002) they still have not been able to see them, though there has never been proof of misconduct, or even an inquiry into these allegations. Their children were only 5, 4 and 2 years of age

The plight of this family touched me personally. I had been babysitting for Isabelle and Robert on the very day they went to the hearing at which it was decided that their three children should be given to the grandparents. Their three children were usually charming and quite quiet, but that day it was difficult for them to listen to stories or concentrate on colouring-in. I just let them run around and play games – it was as though they somehow sensed the tragedy that was about to befall them. These memories were made even more poignant for me because I was already five months pregnant with Victoria, and I was only too aware that such a plan could be used against us as well: Axel's parents could easily be urged by UNADFI to use the same strategy. In such a situation I think it is understandable that Axel and I chose to keep Victoria's birth a secret from Axel's family. These attacks against innocent children were just too much.

I had also just lost my Dad the month before from a double stroke he had while in hospital in New Zealand, ironically for a heart operation. After the first stroke he had been unable to talk, but had written just two words on a piece of paper: "Get ready", they said. My Mum, who was only in her early fifties, was shattered by his death. We all knew they had loved each other deeply. But what with me being pregnant for the first time and our situation in France being so dire, we didn't feel we could go to New Zealand for my Dad's funeral and had to content ourselves with sending a telegram.

So UNADFI, with the help of the French authorities and especially the French Judiciary, was ravaging our church. UNADFI openly rejoiced at the news that Isabelle and Robert's three little children had been taken from their care, publishing this 'success' story which showed the "strong effect" of UNADFI's action in their monthly magazine *BULLES*. The media continued to publish articles and broadcast programmes against us regularly. We protested against this unfair and extremely harmful treatment to the French authorities; the elders of the church went to see other Protestant pastors; we tried everything we could think of, humanly speaking, to make the truth known. Most people, even the 'pastors', simply did not want to hear. It was too easy to fall back on the old excuse that anyway "there's never smoke without a fire", etc. Job's comforters... The truth was, nobody wanted to become involved with us and risk coming under the media spotlight, UNADFI attacks, the accusations of the church's detractors and the power of the judiciary.

We had been stabbed in the back by former church members, morally assassinated by the media, and knocked around by police inquiries and judicial and administrative investigations. What was most distressing was the process UNADFI put in place to "prove" its false accusations in court.

Here UNADFI produced its *coup de grâce*. Their proof, produced as exhibits in court against the church, or rather against Richard, for he was their main target then, consisted of the newspaper articles that they had arranged themselves with the help of their media 'friends'! Whatever appears in the media in France can have an enormous influence on the judiciary, and since it was considered a "cult" case, it immediately aroused deep suspicion, even contempt, in the judges' minds. Basically, UNADFI & co. were saying to the courts, "What we say is true – look, the press says exactly the same thing!" We were dumbfounded. There seemed no end to the relentlessly destructive force of this organisation, and no limit to its influence in France. In fact, they were now announcing the elimination of our church, and were awaiting our public demise.

They were in for a surprise.

Legally cleared

After more than three years of investigations, all the inquiries launched came to a pitiful nothing. No financial fraud had been committed; no tax fraud had been committed; René's claims for money were rejected; and the legal investigations into the welfare of Michèle and other young people and children were closed with a non-suit order: the church was blameless. Despite all the pressure applied by UNADFI and the media, and the disdain of the authorities, there was simply no evidence to support the accusations. Only Robert and Isabelle's case for regaining the custody of their three little children was still on-going. We felt as if we were coming to the end of the tunnel – surely there was light ahead now.

In January 1990, our daughter Victoria was born – a gift from God for us, and a joy for the whole church, which was still meeting together at the time.

Over the years, while Richard in particular was being investigated so closely and rumours were rife about our church, we had all grown closer. We were all determined to defend the truth as we knew it – after all, we had lived it. When one member was attacked, the rest of us felt attacked as well, and we had prayed through so many ordeals together that a bond of common suffering had been formed. We had grown used to taking the contempt and ridicule patiently, just riding it out. Above all, we had been given a unique opportunity to practise what we preached: keep your faith in God no matter what. That had toughened us. Looking back, it was almost as though we were being prepared for what was to come – and that was far worse, totally unexpected and struck at our most vulnerable point: our children.

It is said that persecution strengthens a church in the long run – well it definitely did that for us. We had come through as a church, but now everybody's personal faith was also to be put to the test. In April 1990, with still others about to leave the congregation, we decided to close the church in order to prevent any further persecution. We wanted to live quietly.

Unknown to ourselves, many were determined not to let us live quietly. UNADFI had inflamed the media against us and built up such a monstrous image of a cruel, devious and perverse 'cult', that public opinion couldn't grasp why we hadn't all been locked away in the deepest dungeon in France a good while ago. UNADFI was extremely vexed that the judiciary had not been able to find something – anything – against the church. Their reputation was on the line. Even worse, the church's detractors and Mme Beauchamp herself, as President of UNADFI, were starting to look dangerously like false witnesses in court.

On the legal front, once the law machine was rolling, apparently nothing and nobody could stop it. The French Judiciary, who had been shocked into action by UNADFI and the media, did not appreciate looking like fools. We learnt that the case was deemed so 'sensitive' that the Ministry of Justice was kept regularly informed of all developments. To their way of thinking, they had either been completely wrong (but that was unacceptable and impossible to admit), or else we were even more tenaciously deceitful than even they had imagined, since we had apparently been able to slip through their fingers, as they saw it. It was in this spirit of "we can't be wrong so you must be much worse than we thought" that the police, judiciary and social services were to carry out the next stage of persecution.

Outright persecution

Persecution ? What persecution ? If we so much as mentioned the word we were immediately dismissed as trying to use it as a crutch to defend ourselves with, attempting to deceive the public,

and building up a false picture to dissimulate the 'atrocities' that
were supposedly behind it. Yet what other reason could there be for
such ferocious attacks on a small independent evangelical church
like ours ? Why else was all the proof in our favour pushed aside
and rumours upheld instead ?

With the rumours came aggressive attacks over the years –
physical and verbal aggressiveness from individuals, slander spread
amongst work colleagues, cancellation of contracts etc., threats and
intimidations by letter and telephone, friends and acquaintances
threatened and intimidated, houses under surveillance, and finally
acts of vandalism and violence (graffiti, petrol bombs thrown onto
property, stones thrown, etc.). The worst of these came after
slanderous television programmes were broadcast under the
influence of UNADFI.

Yet what could we do in such a situation ? We may have come
through the fire once and come out with a non-suit order, but it wasn't
enough for these people. They wouldn't be satisfied before we were
totally eradicated. It was no longer a matter of investigations, as it
had been in 1988 – it was an urgent need for elimination.

Sure enough, towards the end of 1991, a few months after the
non-suit order had been announced and in spite of the fact that the
church had been closed for more than eighteen months, UNADFI
started the whole vicious circle spinning again with another slanderous article in its own magazine, *BULLES*.

Our hearts sank. When accusations were made in the media, the
accusers' identities were always protected, their faces hidden and
their whereabouts never mentioned, but it was always just the
opposite for those targeted. Little did we suspect just how far it would
all go.

We hadn't imagined that any other accusations could possibly be
used against us, since everything had already been investigated the
first time round. However, behind the scenes UNADFI was jubilant
at having succeeded in keeping Robert and Isabelle's three children
from them. Why should they not use the method they had followed
in that case as a blueprint for attacking the other families ? The
children were the key – if they could separate the children from
their parents, then get 'confessions' from the children, hopefully even

'confessions' from the parents, or one of the parents, they could get convictions in next to no time. Dead simple. So that was how they attacked this time – with accusations of mistreatment in the aim of withdrawing the children. Then they would be free to use the children against their own parents. It was to take us completely by surprise.

That article in BULLES dashed all our hopes. We knew that the non-suit order had not wiped the slate clean – the French judicial system allowed the suspect to be treated as guilty, and once the case over, the damage could not be undone – but we had thought it would at least protect us from further harrassment. After all, nobody endures three years' investigations just for it to start all over again. And yet there we were, once again the object of the vilest accusations.

This time Richard and Anutza, whose names had been mentioned in the article, reacted legally. It was just too much - the time had come to stand up and defend ourselves. So they sued UNADFI for libel. When put on the spot UNADFI could produce 'witnesses', but of course no proof. The next step was to sue the 'witnesses' for producing false testimony in court. When pressed, two of these so-called witnesses finally admitted (in October 1992) that they hadn't actually been witnesses of what they had written in their testimonies. At long last we seemed to be getting somewhere.

In fact, our defence was showing up the weaknesses of the whole UNADFI set-up and increasing the unease felt in 1991 by UNADFI, our detractors and the French Judiciary.

The big cover-up

Unfortunately, far from calming the attacks, our arguments in defence brought everybody down on our heads in one gigantic joint initiative, as UNADFI and the judiciary sought to protect the detractors who were about to be proven false witnesses in court.

In May 1992, just when my Mum was visiting us from New Zealand, these false witnesses against the church had secretly agreed with UNADFI to write once again to the judiciary to slander the church and ask for legal action to be taken speedily. This time it was for "mistreatment of children", in spite of the fact that the judicial investigation had already gone into that from 1987 to 1991 – and found nothing against the church or any of its members.

UNADFI was of course backstage, pulling the familiar strings, activating their different contacts in government bodies and within the judiciary and bringing everyone into line. They also continued to arrange meetings between the false witnesses and UNADFI's own contacts in the media in order to continue to nourish public opinion with false testimonies.

This produced in particular a gravely libellous, prime-time television programme *La Marche du Siècle* (The March of the Century) on 29 April 1992, when our little church was placed on a par with the 'Church of Scientology'. Two star witnesses appeared on the show live : René and Mireille, backed by Mme Beauchamp herself, seated just behind them. There were also two books published about the same time on the 'cult' topic. The first, called *"Les Sectes"* had a whole chapter devoted to us, based on a full account of the wild accusations made against the church by Mireille. René himself wrote in the second, *"Le Grand Décervelage"* (The Great Brain Removal). So much for 'not doing us any harm'.

No accusation was too atrocious, nor were any pains spared to make the names and workplaces of our different friends and ourselves infamous to the whole nation. The only course left open was to sue the television channel and the publishers of the book for libel as well. The whole business was getting completely out of hand.

But the crucial factor in this legal war was timing, and on that point we were (humanly speaking) simply over-powered. With UNADFI acting as go-between for the Judicary and the false witnesses, they could coordinate their actions. With the Judiciary on their side they could also slow down the proceedings in which we were plaintiffs, and speed up those against us, i.e. fresh investigations into child mistreatment which we were not aware of.

When on 10 February 1993, everybody was arrested and the children removed, we were faced with a *fait accompli* – the deed was done and there was no going back. With our children brutally taken from us and subtly forced to turn against us, they had a weapon *par excellence*. The presumption of innocence, which is embedded in the French Declaration of Human and Citizen's Rights, and should have prevailed over any rule of law, was trampled underfoot. All they needed now was a little time to tighten the noose.

The pressure was off everybody except us. The church's detractors now only needed to point to the children's removal to vindicate their position and 'prove' that everything they had said in their false testimonies was true. All the legal proceedings we had undertaken against them were subsequently dropped or rejected by the Judiciary, so they had no cause for worry. At their side, UNADFI were the heroes of the day. And the Judiciary were seen by the public to have done 'justice'. After all, they must have had extremely good reasons to take such drastic action, mustn't they ?

It was understandably just a little difficult to explain all this long and complicated process in a few words to reporters phoning from the other side of the world, i.e. New Zealand.

We could only try as best we could to be short but clear, in the desperate hope that anything printed abroad would put pressure on the French authorities to return Victoria home quickly.

But could anything change the French justice system's bias ?

5

Into the fray
February - June 1993

Monsieur et Madame Schmidt ... meet the French Judiciary

Waiting outside the Judge's office for our first hearing with her on 24 February 1993, we were both extremely anxious.

The *Tribunal* was a huge, impressive-looking building, whichever side you looked at it from. It took up almost a whole block, stretching from one street, the *place André Mignot*, to the next parallel one, the *Avenue de l'Europe* and therefore had two entrances. The original *place André Mignot* entrance was stately and ornate, in the traditional Versailles style, whereas the *Avenue de l'Europe* one was modern and grand, with a wide flight of steps up to the huge dark-glass entrance doors, in a whole façade of dark-glass windows three or four floors high. Once inside, there were several different ways of getting to the judge's office on the 3rd floor... So many cases were connected with that *Tribunal* – Isabelle and Robert's case had been heard there, Michèle's case too, and finally Rebecca, Anutza and Axel had been indicted here, just a couple of weeks before. It had become an image of oppression for me. Now we were there to plead for Victoria to be returned home.

It had been impossible to eat that morning, we couldn't have stomached a thing. Richard's advice had been to be calm and reasonable, but the shock of Victoria being snatched, the worry of the last two weeks and the stress of having to face this judge had us both tense and my mind was a whirl. I had no idea what to expect.

"*Monsieur et Madame Schmidt ?*" Our lawyer, a Versailles colleague of the famous Parisian lawyer Axel had been able to engage, had already been in to speak to the judge and was now inviting us in. We had briefed her on the case a few minutes before and she had appeared indignant and advised us to use the word "abduction" to describe Victoria's placement. We had no problem with that – it was a word we had been using ourselves and exactly described the way Victoria had disappeared. But then she had gone in to see "if anything could be done" – and apparently it couldn't. Her submissive smile to the judge as we came in said everything.

The judge's office wasn't cramped, but it wasn't spacious either – just big enough for her large desk across the far corner, with her clerk's desk perpendicular to it at one end, filing cabinets behind her and around the room, and several chairs in front of the desk – for us. The lawyer placed herself strategically between Axel and I – dividing us again. The judge herself, Mme Durand, was a very ordinary-looking woman in the sense that you wouldn't really have expected her to be a judge, heavy, with straight, thick black hair in a sort of bob, held back by a large black hair band. On the judge's left sat the court clerk. On her right and our left was a wiry, elderly, slightly bent little woman with sharp, bird-like features and short-cropped gray hair – quite the contrast of the judge – who was introduced as the "*Substitut du Procureur*", the Deputy Public Prosecutor, Mlle Cornil.

The judge introduced herself and the public prosecutor.

"I know nothing about the whole case", Mlle Cornil murmured, as though inviting us to lay all our arguments before her.

Then the judge addressed us, leaning her heavy forearms on the desk with her hands together.

"You do realise that I can't return your child to you today, or tomorrow," she said.

In my nervousness my mind grasped at the shred of hope she seemed to be holding out. Surely then, in a week, or a couple of weeks…Victoria would be back with us !

Axel was presenting our submissions and file of evidence. The submissions carefully refuted the judge's reasoning from the February 12 judgement, concerning five main matters:

1. Axel was indicted – but he should be presumed innocent until proven guilty, and the accusations did not concern Victoria in any way;
2. The accusations targeted the church, which had been closed since 1990;
3. Some accusations concerned other people and had no connection with ourselves or Victoria;
4. The main accusers had been brought to justice for false witness (in some cases they had admitted in court that they had not told the truth) and decisions were pending;
5. Other accusers quoted had not been in contact with us for seven years and could know nothing of Victoria or our family circumstances.

The file of evidence showed that in every way Victoria was perfectly well cared for:

- She had never been "deprived of all family contact", as my Mum had testified, who had been to see us in May 1992, as well as one of my sisters;
- She was not "submitted to confinement" as photos readily showed;
- The only danger Victoria was in stemmed from her separation from us, as her paediatrician had written in the medical certificate;
- The last entry in Victoria's health record book, dated December 22 1992, summed it all up : "*superbe enfant*" (superb child).

The court clerk was noting down each document as it was presented. As well as all this, my family had that very day sent faxes directly to the judge stating their support for us and demanding that Victoria be returned home.

They were turning to me. What had I to say ? My mind went completely blank. I couldn't find my words. It was the first time I had come face to face with a judge – somebody who held such power over my family's future and Victoria's happiness… yet there was something oddly disproportionate between this woman's attitude and our situation. Was she not aware that our personal, private and family life was in total havoc ? And that it was in her hands to completely destroy or restore it ? For the moment I stumbled out something about Victoria needing us, needing to be back home.

"*Mme Schmidt*, you are in front of a magistrate," said our lawyer, as though reproaching me for not expressing myself well enough.

Bias in the place of justice

Meanwhile, Mlle Cornil had been leafing through the photos of Victoria. "*Qu'est-ce qu'elle est mignonne !*" (What a little darling !), she said, looking at me. Once again, for a moment my heart leaped – but then I remembered the police saying the same thing… and the look on that woman's face was not admitting our good care, it was … I could only call it cynical. She seemed to be actually gloating at the thought of such a darling little girl being torn from her family and placed into state care. Never had I seen anything like it. It remains engraved on my memory.

Axel was now mentioning the false testimonies given by former members of the church – some of them had admitted in January of that year that they hadn't actually seen what they had attested to.

"Well, I have asked that they be acquitted, Monsieur Schmidt," retorted Mlle Cornil. It was obvious whose side she was on ! Then I remembered her saying she knew nothing of the whole case, and suddenly found my tongue.

"I thought you said you knew nothing about this business, *Mlle Cornil*," I remarked politely, but pointedly. She glared at me, but didn't reply. I might have shown her up, but I had got her back up in the process.

Now Axel was asking why Victoria was being kept in state care when the court had full proof that she had been well brought up in a loving home, that we were both good parents, and that this separation would inevitably be seriously prejudicial to Victoria, as her paediatrician had written –

"He's probably a member of the 'cult' as well, I suppose" murmured Mlle Cornil.

"He has nothing to do with the church!" I exclaimed. She just smiled falsely at me.

Axel ignored her and continued on. If there had been anything at all wrong with Victoria, the Social Services doctor who had examined her when she arrived there would certainly have raised the matter. Why had she not been returned to us immediately ? It was a most disturbing question and the tone of the discussion was rising. The judge was becoming defensive. Anyway, her decision was already made, she said – today she was simply confirming to us in person the judgement of 12 February. In spite of the fact that this was the first time she had ever laid eyes on us, and that she had never met Victoria.

"But *Mme le Juge*, you can't just confirm a decision without examining the case!" protested Axel. The judge was speaking loudly in an effort to drown him out. "Nothing you can say will convince me!" she declared.

"But you don't have the right to do this," continued Axel.

"*Monsieur et Madame Schmidt* need to learn that they are obliged to submit to the authority of the Judge for Children," remarked the judge. There was a pause.

"*Mme le Juge*, if you don't mind me asking – do you have children yourself ?" asked Axel.

"That is a personal question!" retorted the judge heatedly, "and has absolutely nothing to do with my work ! You will refrain from asking personal questions!"

By now Axel and I were at boiling point. The lawyer in between us was desperately trying to keep the situation under control, turning from Axel to me and back again in an attempt to smooth things over. But this judge had no regard for concrete evidence, no human compassion, and *no intention of rendering justice*. "What you're doing is illegal!" exclaimed Axel.

And that hit the limit. The judge was on her feet, shouting at Axel (but strangely with one hand on her stomach, as though in some sort of pain). Before we knew it we had been ordered out of the office and found ourselves outside, joined a few minutes later by our lawyer. "You were wild in there," she told us. "Do you know what she's done now? Ordered psychological and psychiatric examinations for both of you!"

We gazed at her in disbelief. But what else could we have done in that office except protest, in the face of such blatant injustice ? Wouldn't anyone else have done the same if it had been their child ?

Still worse, as we were to find out on reading that actual judgement, we were still strictly forbidden to have any contact with Victoria or to know where she was in State care. It was the kind of punishment reserved for parents who had grievously harmed their child – half-blinded them, or something !

The hearing had left me crushed and yet still blindly clutching to the hope that surely these magistrates – they *were* magistrates, after all – would come to their senses and Victoria would be back with us soon. There was no reason for anyone to keep her from us, but the passing of time was to bring only disappointment. This cycle of mounting hopes and bitter disappointments was to become downright mental torture. What a waste of time and energy – and anxiety too, since the decision had already been taken before we even set foot inside the judge's office ! That was where the whole thing was completely out of proportion. No reason for Victoria to be kept from us – yet no possibility of her returning – not now anyway, not yet. And there seemed no way out.

Axel understood that day that they wanted to keep Victoria no matter what and that they were now mounting a file against us to justify her placement in care. The Judge for Children was going to take vengeance for our resistance: we were about to be delivered up to a judge-pleasing court-appointed French psychologist and psychiatrist.

A new judge ...

Towards the end of February Judge Durand was away "on holiday" – in an unguarded moment a court clerk mentioned a nervous breakdown – and Judge Bennichou, President of the Versailles Children's Court, had temporarily taken over the children's cases during her absence. We naturally jumped at the possibility of appealing to this new judge, especially one in his prominent position, in the hope that he might do justice to our children and return them to their rightful homes.

In spite of our repeated requests, we never did manage to actually secure a hearing with this judge, but a couple of incidents concerning Judge Bennichou were most revealing of the man.

Monsieur Vannier, a French Social Work Director, actually went to see Judge Bennichou especially on behalf of Isabelle and myself, since our children were so young – only 2 and 3 years of age. After talking to us on the phone Monsieur Vannier's brave intention was to go and see the judge in person and insist that we be permitted to see Victoria and Michael – as far as he was concerned it was "really too much" to separate them so abruptly and completely from their parents at such an early age. He had seen the children and obviously considered that the Judiciary had gone too far. Unfortunately, we were to hear no more from him after that, and on inquiry we learnt only that he had been moved or promoted to a different area. Judge Bennichou had got rid of him, being apparently of the same calibre as Mme Durand. But never did we speak with anybody else from French Social Services of the same calibre as Monsieur Vannier.

On another occasion one of our American friends had gone to deliver a letter to Judge Bennichou. After being directed to his office and knocking on the door, she was invited to enter. She slipped quietly inside – and froze. Sitting opposite the judge were René and his wife Mireille, Axel's brother and sister-in-law, and the atmosphere was most congenial.

"*Ex … excusez-moi …*" she murmured, left her letter inside the door and slipped out again. There seemed precious little sense in giving a letter of protest to a judge who was obviously working hand in glove with our accusers. So much for Mme Durand's accountability to her immediate superior – *he* was providing full cover.

Release from the detested Fleury-Mérogis prison

While we had been battling on the 'outside', Rebecca and Anutza were still detained in prison pending trial. 'Inside' they came across many cases of women who had already been there in '*détention provisoire*' (temporary detention) for months and even years, although strongly protesting their innocence. They were completely at the mercy of a slow, weighty and merciless judicial system.

Both had been placed initially in the Versailles House of Detention for Women, but Anutza had soon afterwards been moved to the hated Fleury-Mérogis prison, one of the biggest high-security prisons in France. If Anutza had been put in there, it was probably an attempt to obtain a confession.

Anutza had got on well with her cell-mates in the Versailles prison and had even been able to speak to them about the Lord and share the Bible with them regularly. But in Fleury-Mérogis she was put into a cell with a woman who must have been slightly deranged. I will never forget Anutza talking afterwards – only a long time afterwards, and tears were never far away – about being in the same cell as this woman, who had murdered somebody with a pair of scissors. That wouldn't have been too bad perhaps, except that during the day she actually had access to scissors in the cell. Anutza had always to be on her guard.

The effect of prison life on both Anutza and Rebecca was profound. Both suffered in their health. Only they could tell the extent of these and the depth of their emotional anguish. It was a miracle that these two mothers, whom I had known and admired for their devotion and commitment, did not become bitter from a sense of gross injustice. That was inevitably part of their pain – enduring accusations, even prison, while knowing their innocent children were in State custody and that they were innocent of the accusations against them. If the accusations against Axel did not stand up, those against Rebecca and Anutza were almost laughable.

The case against them had been presented as a serious criminal one. UNADFI and the church's detractors had come up with the accusation of 'confinement' (*séquestration*). Bernadette, the 13-year-old daughter of the last detractors to leave the church (who incidentally were facing serious charges of false testimony in court, and had actually confessed in January 1993 that they had not been witnesses of what they had attested to), had been used in order to accuse Rebecca of having confined her, or shut her up, in the cellar of Anutza and Richard's house over a period of several months in 1990-1991; and Anutza was accused of being an accomplice to this act by supplying the room used for the alleged confinement.

Actually, as several people including myself could witness to, Bernadette's parents had specifically requested that Bernadette stay with Rebecca and her family so that she could get help with her school work and music studies (she was a promising cello player). Rebecca, who was always ready to help when she was needed, took care of Bernadette as she did her own children. I lived in Sartrouville where Rebecca and Philippe and their family also lived and saw them daily. Sometimes during the day Rebecca would be round at Anutza's house with Bernadette, but they were always home every evening, so she definitely could not have been 'confined'.

The biggest joke, though, was about the cellar. The "cellar" was the room that had been specially prepared for church services from 1985 onwards, and that was where we were married in December of that year. Yet that was where Bernadette was supposed to have been "confined" ! They called a spacious room, with no less than three pairs of French windows opening onto the garden, a "cellar" ! I don't think any of Axel's family would have turned up at our wedding if we'd told them we were going to be married in a cellar.

Yes, it would have been laughable, if it hadn't been for the dramatic consequences of such ridiculous accusations.

At last, after five weeks of *vie carcérale* (prison life) Rebecca and Anutza were finally released, extremely thin after such an ordeal, and emotionally and physically drained. Their release only came after the French authorities had been bombarded at every level with letters from Christians and friends from France and abroad, expressing indignation at both women's imprisonment and demanding their release.

Even when it had at last been decided to release both our friends on bail, the Judiciary still insisted that security be paid for them both to ensure that they 'appeared in court' – although neither Anutza nor Rebecca were in any state to leave their homes and families after that prolonged stay in prison, and it was out of the question that they abandon their children in State care. Finally, thanks to help given from concerned Christian friends, the amount was at last collected, the formalities were gone through and the day of (temporary) freedom arrived.

Once these two mothers were out of prison, there was no reason for their children to be kept in State care. They were supposedly 'innocent until proven guilty', after all, and were now fully available to care for their children. But for the French Judiciary, legal theory and practice often do not correspond – *the children continued to be held without good reason.*

Bail conditions for Rebecca and Anutza included forbidding them to have any contact at all with the other indicted persons, i.e. they could not meet or phone each other or Axel. In practice, this meant we couldn't meet anymore, at least not all together.

The French authorities' official line

By now the whole case was making waves in New Zealand, and echoes were even reaching the United States. The French authorities found themselves more or less obliged to make some sort of response. So the French Embassy in New Zealand issued a press statement in which, as we might have expected, those who were accused were treated as though they had already been proven guilty. All the accusations were trundled out, with a few hearsay additions and exaggerations.

The removal of the children was supposed to have happened "without incident", began the French Embassy. One mother in hospital after four police officers held her down (and finally called a doctor to give her an injection so as to keep her quiet) in order to take her 2-year-old baby boy away from her – and they called that 'without incident'? Seven happy, intelligent children removed from loving homes to state care – how could that happen 'without incident'? They snatched Victoria behind my back – how dare they call that 'without incident'?

According to the French Embassy, the February 10 raids were also supposed to have happened "at the end of a perfectly regular court proceeding and after due hearing of all parties". But we only met the Judge for Children two weeks later, on February 24, and no hearings or any other normal inquiry preceded Victoria's removal on February 10.

The French Embassy in NZ also found it very handy to compare us to the Koresh group in Waco, U.S.A. (The events surrounding Waco took place shortly after the removal of our children.) In this case, the French authorities were certainly experts in the art of slander.

The Embassy stated that we had not appealed the 12 February decision – as though we were therefore admitting guilt and consenting to Victoria's removal. "It should be noted that none of the parents concerned lodged an appeal within the 15 days that were granted them. Moreover, the removal was an interim measure and the parents can request that it be altered by means of a simple letter to the judge". As though we cared so little about our daughter that we hadn't even made the effort to write a "simple letter" to the judge ! We had done far more than 'write a simple letter' to the judge.

On February 11, I had appealed to the judge by phone, pleading with her to return Victoria to her parents. On February 19, on our lawyer's advice, we had written a registered letter to the judge asking for Victoria to be restored to our care, since the custody order was obviously unjustified. When the judge answered a month later, reproaching us for our "numerous calls to the Tribunal" and indicating that we would be meeting with her at the end of April, we made sure that by April 1 we had written another letter to her to voice our concern for Victoria's well-being and ask her to receive us as soon as possible. However, although the end of April meeting had been confirmed in principle by the court clerk, Mme Durand wrote on May 6 to say that she "did not believe it necessary to fix the appointment her secretary had told us of by telephone".

Yes, she could have changed her decision at any time but constantly refused to do so and 'nothing we said would convince her'. If we had appealed, a "simple letter to the judge" would have been useless, since the case would have then been considered as the job of the Court of Appeal and Judge Durand would have washed her hands of all responsibility and told us to wait – for months – for the Court of Appeal hearing. We wanted Victoria back straight away (and there was no reason why she shouldn't be), so we had to ask the judge, and ask her we most certainly did.

Apart from these letters to the judge, we also wrote to the Minister of Justice, Monsieur Vauzelle, on 4 March 1993; to Monsieur François Mitterrand, the French President, on March 15; and on April 30 we wrote three letters, one to the newly-designated Minister of Justice, Monsieur Pierre Méhaignerie, another to the Minister for Health and Social Services, Madame Simone Veil, and the last to Madame Michaux-Chevry, Minister for Human Rights within the Ministry of Foreign Affairs. We were determined to do all we could.

As usual, the French Embassy mentioned that the Judiciary was "independent" and therefore the French Government and authorities were powerless to do anything. It was well known however that in practice the Judge for Children worked closely with the Public Prosecutor in this type of case. The inevitable link is the Public Prosecutor's Department , which works under the Ministry of Justice, and therefore under the Government, and at the same time has in practice a powerful influence on so-called 'independent' judges, especially Children's Court judges and investigating judges. It was as simple as *"bonjour"*, as the French would say, for the Government to intervene in proceedings through the Ministry of Justice and the Versailles Public Prosecutor's Department.

I also wrote personally to Mr Jim Bolger, then Prime Minister of New Zealand, who did pass my letter on to the NZ Minister of Foreign Affairs, Mr Don McKinnon, but he, like most of the others we wrote to, simply "passed the buck" to the French authorities and said he couldn't intervene. And the French authorities all passed it on to the French Ministry of Justice.

We happened to discover that Judge Durand's husband was working in the Ministry of Justice. Oh yes, the French Ministry of Justice knew all about our case. Their defense of Judge Durand and the blatant lies in the cover-up story they fed to the New Zealand public clearly show the position taken by the French authorities – and they certainly didn't consider us as 'innocent before proven guilty'.

The same line was taken by the French authorities both in France and abroad. Anybody who wrote to them got the same reply, always in French, though they must have known full well that this would cause delays and misunderstandings. From my family in New Zealand to Dr Trumper in Wales and us in France, everybody got the same story: Axel had been indicted (this was nothing less than an accusation of guilt, though he was supposed to be presumed innocent); everything had gone 'smoothly' on February 10 and was done solely 'in the best interests' of the minors concerned; we parents should use the legal remedies open to us; and it was impossible, in any case, for the authorities to intervene in a legal case. Stalemate: game to the French Judiciary; or so it seemed.

Unfortunately, a section of the New Zealand press latched onto the French authorities' line. An apparently sympathetic reporter from a prime-time TV programme came over to France to interview us and subsequently invited us to London for a live interview. We foolishly agreed, wanting to do everything possible for Victoria. It was only at the last minute that we were shown the whole report, and woe and betide it included interviews with our accusers, who with the usual gut virulence incited by UNADFI, accused us of almost everything they could imagine without the slightest proof to back it all up. The live interview was a disaster. Never having done anything of the sort before, I didn't even know where to look – all I had in front of me was something in the shape of a tiny microphone. This was in March 1993, my mind was still whirling from the catastrophes of the last month and the wild accusations I had just seen thrown at us by our accusers, the questions were double-edged, in short I felt I had been set up. It had been a good lesson in public relations. Never again.

As for the French Judiciary, they had not finished with us yet …

Not only considered "guilty" before trial

The judge needed some justification for keeping Victoria in State care, and psychological / psychiatric reports by judge-appointed 'experts' were a means of doing this. The official papers requesting a psychiatric examination for Axel and myself were based on the assumption that we were "maladjusted". That seemed to be what we got for protesting against injustice. With the pretext that we were 'maladjusted' and claiming to want 'expert' advice, the judge had ordered these examinations, going so far as to "consider that [we were] suffering from a state of dementia…" !

Then the request for psychological examinations was based on the pretext that there had been "incidents", which, it was claimed, needed a psychological 'explanation' and a 'remedy' so that we "would no longer display anti-social behaviour in the future".

Our daughter had been snatched from us unjustly, but the judge's message was clear: we were *not* to protest. What's more, both examinations were to specify any "professional or other contra-indications" – meaning that even our jobs could be on the line if these reports weren't favourable.

As if the accusations against us weren't enough, losing Victoria wasn't enough either, the Judiciary had to stick another knife into us. Now we knew why most people 'understood' fairly quickly that they would do better to "submit to the Judge for Children". Her powers were exorbitant. We still had more to find out, because most importantly the psychiatrist and psychologist were both personally appointed by the judge herself. And she was going to make use of it.

The psychiatric unit was one of the more modern buildings hidden away at the back of a huge hospital complex in a suburb not far from our own. I still felt rather nervous before meetings, though since being 'broken in' by the hearing with Judge Durand, and seeing that these people really had nothing to reproach us with, but were simply prejudiced, I had become more confident. We had decided to fight, hadn't we ?

Axel and I had been able to fix appointments one after the other, and he went first, at the psychiatrist's request. He was the one accused, after all. His interview must have lasted over an hour. The questions were sometimes quite surprising. One was about whether Axel sometimes had to recheck whether he had locked the door at night ! Others were frankly out of place. Axel was under no illusion. The judge had undoubtedly made it implicitly understood that the psychiatrist was to present him as some sort of paranoiac.

When my turn came I was rather embarrassed to see that as I walked down the long corridor towards the interview room, Dr Moreno, the psychiatrist, was studying me – the way I walked !

I learnt afterwards from Axel that he had done the same with him.

My first impression was that this man looked like the one who needed psychiatric care. He had a speech defect which seemed to bloat his mouth on one side when he talked, and at times his face would twitch in quite a distracting way. He looked old enough to retire – around 60-65.

He was polite and didn't seem to ask any particularly 'difficult' questions, so nothing special came up during the interview. After all, I had had a pretty normal childhood and life experiences in general, so I just answered all his questions. In fact, he didn't even seem to be very persistent except for a few pointed questions about disciplining children, fasting etc. He had obviously been 'fed' the story of accusations. When he spoke about Victoria though, I couldn't help becoming emotional. As he said goodbye, he promised that he would do everything he could so that Victoria be reunited with us!

I came out feeling quite positive about the interview, which couldn't have lasted much more than forty-five minutes. But by then (April 1993) we were both beginning to know better than to get our hopes up.

The reports came out in June. Basing his conclusions solely on the fact that we protested our innocence and had clearly stated our faith in God, Dr Moreno concluded that Axel was "psychorigid" and I "highly influencable" and that neither of us were therefore fit to be entrusted with the care of children. Thank you, Dr Moreno. Another waste of time and hope. How people like him could sleep at night, knowing they had been instrumental in tearing families apart, I did not know.

Axel did request a counter-examination later on, but when we found out that it would be in the same centre, by the same service, we just gave up on it. It would very probably have been just another cover-up job that would only make matters worse, as had already been the case for Anutza. She had been assessed by Dr Moreno as well because of the accusations against her – and the counter-examination she had requested had been carried out by a second psychiatrist from the same hospital and the same service – once again appointed by the judge – and his report simply backed up the first and was even harder against her than the first. The message was clear – nobody should ever dare question the findings of a judge-appointed 'expert'.

Being psychiatrically dissected after a traumatic family separation was bad enough for us as parents. But just a few months later we were to learn that during this period all the children except the two youngest (Victoria and Xavier) were examined by the same psychiatrists and psychologists, after repeated 'questionings' by policemen, judges, and social workers.

It was a subtle 'questioning' process which had the same effect as brain-washing. Gradually the children came to consider their past as a hideous experience of mistreatment and repression, and after some time, far from their parents, they were forced to believe it and to take it up as their own story. They could not be blamed, they were only children. When we at last got hold of a copy of the file the gradual change in their statements was clear, though some took longer than others, and some went further than others. It was extremely distressing to learn that to get them to that point, Richard and Anutza's twin boys had been made to undergo a long period of what the Ministry of Justice called "psychological rest", separated from each other and isolated

The means apparently didn't matter, the end result seemed the important thing to the French Judiciary. The five older children were all forced to accuse their own parents and friends and we were in no doubt that they had been placed under pressure to be made to do so. But we had no access to the children, and even if the older children were able to see their parents, it was always under strict supervision and they only ended up accusing them in front of the social workers – as had been planned, of course. Once again, there seemed no way out. *La boucle était bouclée*, as the French would say – it was a catch-22 situation.

However, both Derek Pearce in New Zealand and Dr Peter Trumper in Wales had published articles that clearly showed up the reprehensible actions of the French authorities. These articles were to provoke the full fury of UNADFI who, with the aid of the French authorities and, believe it or not, *French Protestant* organisations, set out to demonize us in the French press, discredit us before the

French Judiciary and destroy any support from abroad, and from New Zealand in particular. How ? By firing up the old accusers, of course !

6

Who will stand for us ?

July-August 1993

"There's no religious persecution in France" – a French 'Protestant'

Monsieur Rosenberg was a small, chubby man, with short, plump fingers that you noticed when you shook his hand. A chubby face with a small nose, small eyes, small, drooping ears. A cold, detached manner. The kind of man who seemed very difficult to get through to. Axel and Richard could probably have talked until they were blue in the face, he somehow remained untouched – or perhaps he simply did not want to hear.

As General Secretary of the Protestant Federation of France, he had an office in a big old apartment house in one of the older parts of Paris (near to the Gare St Lazare). It was fairly big, but also fairly bare – no books, no evidence of work underway, Monsieur Rosenberg didn't even have a pen and paper with him to take notes of any kind. He showed no concern for the plight of young children wrenched from loving families and placed in State care, no compassion for distraught parents, no desire to examine the whole affair "diligently", as the Bible commanded, to discover the truth of the matter, not even the slightest interest in the well-being of religious freedom in France. Monsieur Rosenberg did not want to know.

"But M. Rosenberg, do you realise the grave consequences of your actions ?"

There was simply no reply to Axel's question. Least of all in this man's heart did there seem to be any thought of putting right a wrong he had done.

Rosenberg's slanderous letter to the French authorities had sealed our children's fate. Now he was washing his hands of the consequences. He affirmed that he had met with former members of the church – "reliable witnesses", as he called them – and that his letter was based on what they had said. But, argued Richard and Axel, there were other reliable witnesses who maintained exactly the contrary to these accusations. No, M. Rosenberg's mind was already made up. After all, there had been articles in the press about this …

But this was more than just a matter of public or personal opinion. If Monsieur Rosenberg had based his letter solely on other people's words, how could he state that "it is not possible to find the features of a Protestant church" in our church, without ever having met the 'accused' himself or examining what he had been told ? How could he state so assuredly, without having checked any facts, that "the problems people from this group may have had with the law in no way proceed from any religious persecution, but from the application of the law" ?

If Monsieur Rosenberg had cared to look into the 'problems with the law' a little further, he would have found that according to 'the law' there was nothing against the church – no medical certificate had ever shown any harm done to children or anybody else, a non-suit order rendered in March 1991 had put an end to lengthy investigations into accusations of embezzlement, fiscal fraud, mistreatment of children and young adults etc. The whole case was built solely on slander, along with "statements" from children who had been brutally snatched from their parents and turned against them. But Monsieur Rosenberg *did not care* enough to look seriously at our case. He just let slander manoeuvre him onto the bandwagon.

He had granted Axel and Richard an interview, and that was it. He listened, said very little, and it was over in fifteen to twenty minutes. Monsieur Rosenberg had proved himself guilty, by his own hand, of breaking one of the Ten Commandments, reiterated by the Lord Jesus Christ himself in Matthew 19:18 :
"Thou shalt not bear false witness."
Talking to him about it was hopeless.

It seemed that such people were not interested in knowing whether those slandered were true Christians or not – that their priority was to keep their reputations publicly untarnished, and they cared little for how their actions appeared before God.

It is one thing for a judicial system to disfunction. But when 'Christian leaders' join up with non-Christian extremists and a band of malcontents to accuse other Christians and deliver them up to the fury of such a system, the responsibility for the resulting miscarriage of justice surely falls squarely on their shoulders – they should have known better.

In contrast, those who were determined to believe only hard, documented evidence of the accusations against us were fast coming to the conclusion that there was none. There were newspaper articles, yes, judgements based on the newspaper articles and on false accusations, yes, accusations without proof, yes – but these were often shown to be discordant with others, or unreliable, or obtained from children after they had been suddenly removed from their parents' care and placed in State custody, where they came under the influence of biased Social Services staff, etc. and were even secretly visited by our accusers.

The Editor of the New Zealand Beacon, along with the Rotorua Daily Post reporter, Dr Trumper, Editor of the magazine '1521', and Elisabeth Farrell from the American news agency News Network International, were among the few responsible news reporters who refused to write without having examined the proof.

Unfortunately, Monsieur Rosenberg was not alone in committing such felony. We were in fact up against the heads of the two main French Protestant organisations:

-   Monsieur Rosenberg, General Secretary of the Protestant Federation of France;

- Monsieur Lafont, President of the Evangelical Baptist Churches' Federation of France;
- Monsieur Morin, Vice-President of the same.

Disowned

Unknown to us, Morin was the first of these men to be approached by our accusers (in February-March 1993), amongst whom were René and Mireille. First these malcontents needed to sell the story of accusations against the church (not too difficult after the media campaign organised by UNADFI), then ask these Protestant leaders for letters of support (if they didn't they would be accused of supporting a 'cult'), and finally take the letters to the judges concerned. As a fully qualified doctor, thanks to the assistance he had received in particular from Richard, René was presented as a most 'reliable witness'.

The accusers' plan worked perfectly. Morin, with the full approval of his superior, Monsieur Lafont, President of the Federation of Evangelical Baptist Churches, fully and deliberately – even zealously – complied, just as Rosenberg was to do a few months later. Surely the proverb could be aptly applied to such men:

"For their feet run to evil and make haste to shed blood." (Proverbs 1:16)

So on 25 March 1993, we had the honour of being disowned by Monsieur Morin, in a letter of accusation against us written to the General Secretary of the New Zealand Baptist Union in Auckland, Mr Hunter. The support we had received from New Zealand Christians had provoked the fury of UNADFI and our accusers – and this was the result.

Monsieur Morin accused us of "claiming to be Baptists", perhaps because I had stated that there weren't any doctrinal differences between my family's Baptist church in New Zealand and our church in France. In any case, his letter vehemently denied that the Evangelical Baptist churches had any link with our church and also contained the usual wild accusations concocted by our accusers.

Monsieur Morin also took special care to send a copy of his letter to the French Embassy in Wellington, and then wrote to the examining judge on 25 April 1993, again disavowing any link between the Federation and our church and calling us a "dangerous cult". The French Judiciary naturally made full use of these fresh denunciations.

We could not sit back and hope this was going to go away. In May 1993, one of the elders of our church phoned Morin to discuss the letters he had written and tell him what the real situation was, and he afterwards slightly modified his position. A formal "clarification" written on 27 May 1993 for all legal intents and purposes stated that the Evangelical Baptist Federation had perhaps gone too far in calling us a "dangerous cult", and now only wished to affirm that our church did not belong to the Federation, that "the other considerations contained in our document are merely testimonies which have been supplied to us" – and that Baptists had at no time been persecuted for their religious opinions in France.

Ironically, on this last count Monsieur Morin (and Monsieur Rosenberg, who was also to ridicule the idea of religious persecution in France) was to be proved wrong by the French National Assembly themselves, when the Parliamentary Report on Cults produced in 1996 numbered Baptist churches on its hit-list of groups labelled 'cults' ! What these men had callously condoned and allowed to be used against us was eventually to be turned against them and their own churches.

As far as we were concerned though, the damage had already been done, and none of Monsieur Morin's 'clarifications' were taken into account by the French Judiciary. Lafont and Morin both resigned from their posts rather than truly make amends, e.g. admit they had misled the Judiciary by writing about things they knew nothing of. So we were left to pick up the pieces.

Our accusers could not content themselves with Morin's back-down, half-hearted though it was, and therefore turned to Rosenberg. Playing directly into the hands of the accusers and UNADFI, Monsieur Rosenberg wrote his false statement to Judge Durand on 29 July 1993, the very day before the judge was due to take a new decision concerning the children. The little chance our children stood of going home shrank to practically zero.

Not only did none of these men ever attempt to interview us, or check the facts to see whether there was evidence of misconduct, but it never once came into their minds to check the motives of our accusers, who were in fact blackening us in order to protect themselves or their friends from being proven false witnesses in court. Just a little research would have uncovered this, but *no questions were asked*.

What's more, any mature Christian would have noticed that these former church members cared little about glorifying God. Their testimonies held no encouragement for other Christians, no account of a personal struggle to do what was right, no testimony to deliverance by the hand of God. They were incapable of testifying to the goodness of God. They had known His goodness in the church and had betrayed it. Their mouths could utter only foul, base accusations. And Messieurs Rosenberg, Lafont and Morin were only too ready to join forces with them rather than take the trouble to defend people who had been wrongly accused.

One thing was clear: these three 'leaders' had no Biblical basis for their actions. From a Biblical point of view they were deceitful and dangerous men. It was not much of a surprise to discover that they were prepared to lie themselves, as we were about to find out.

Repercussions in New Zealand

Incalculable damage had been done to our cases and vicious rumours had been spread on the Baptist 'grapevine' – all the way to New Zealand.

Seeing such injustice being done, the editor of the New Zealand Beacon spent forty-five minutes on the phone to Monsieur Morin in an attempt to get to the bottom of his venomous letter to Mr Hunter, Secretary of the New Zealand Baptist Union, on 25 March 1993. When asked why he had made a legal statement on 27 May 1993 saying that his letter to Hunter had been "of a strictly private and confidential nature … [and] cannot therefore be used in public for other purposes", when on 25 March 1993 he had already sent a copy of it to the French Embassy in New Zealand who made a press release to the New Zealand public out of it, Monsieur Morin 'was not able to furnish the Beacon with an answer'.

There was to be no wriggling out of it for Monsieur Morin. He had also falsely asserted that court cases brought against our accusers and enemies such as UNADFI etc. had all been lost by us. This was simply a matter of court record, as the Beacon pointed out, as precisely as ever, and proceeded to give an exact account of that record, which included several court cases won against our accusers.

I wish I could say that there was some spiritual soundness in the reaction of Mr Hunter, but this was sadly and glaringly lacking. My family minister from Rotorua, who had been to visit the church in France, had given Mr Hunter a very favourable personal testimony to our genuine faith. My mother, who had also worshipped with us in the church as well as visiting us personally, had also told Mr Hunter that we were genuine Christians. Mr Hunter had nevertheless sent a damning circular to all the Baptist Union pastors in the country, containing some of Morin's false accusations which he presented as the truth. Our family minister even received a letter from Hunter telling him to back off supporting us.

Once again the editor of the New Zealand Beacon, with a copy of Mr Hunter's circular in hand, courageously confronted the man. When questioned, it appeared that Mr Hunter was content to rely on the hearsay he had been told and, as the Beacon put it, "did not seem very perturbed that none of his informants had personally verified with the believers in France any of the accusations made against them. They relied solely on the testimony of malcontents who had previously left the church, plus the articles in godless news-papers and TV reports (whose allegations have been disproved in court!)". Mr Hunter refused to read the 100 mm-thick file that the Beacon had so painstakingly put together.

Base lies and corruption amongst 'Protestant' leaders, and their collaboration with evil-doers was crucial in prolonging the seven children's agonising separation from their parents and worsening the situation in France for all Bible-believing Christians. These men had to be denounced, and the 'New Zealand Beacon' and '1521' both bravely did so.

So support for us from churches in New Zealand gradually caved in, as Mr Hunter had known it would. The line taken by the French Embassy, based on Morin's denunciations and encouraged by Mr Hunter's blind support for them, discouraged the general press from inquiring further. The general New Zealand public lost interest, or put the whole story down as "cult".

When the French Embassy in Washington gave out the same sort of report, articles were published in Christian publications in the USA and some even appeared in certain British publications.

From grievance to fantasy

The articles published in the New Zealand Beacon had evidently caught the attention, or rather the imagination, of a public far beyond the shores of the land of the long white cloud[1], as can be seen by the reactions to them.

There were threats of legal action against the Beacon from UNADFI themselves.

Then another Baptist pastor, this time of the Evangelical Alliance Mission (TEAM) – contacted the editor of the New Zealand Beacon, stating that he lived "only a few kilo-metres from the church", that the Beacon report was "false" and that the editor had been "misled".

The editor of the Beacon was of course only too happy to follow this lead up, especially as this pastor boasted a PhD in occult studies and had stated that what went on in our church was "the same as in the occult seances"! It sounded foolproof. Unfortunately, when asked if he could kindly furnish the Beacon with documentation about the occult practices of the group, "as that would clearly identify them as being of the Devil", the pastor replied: "I don't have any documentation, it is hearsay".

Once again, the theme of his letter was an echo of the words of Rosenberg and Morin: "there is no religious persecution in France". Why were all these deceitful pastors so anxious to deny religious persecution in the French Republic ? The same cry had been heard before, long and loud, in the communist countries of Eastern Europe, where it represented the typical "official church" line. While

[1] Aotearoa: the Maori name for New Zealand.

the real church was forced to go underground, such churches collaborated with the state, became "show churches" to be displayed to the outside world, and their pastors always vehemently denied that there was any religious persecution in their country. The bottom line was – these pastors had a cowardly and unChristian fear of being persecuted themselves.

Catholic France

In the years that followed we were to meet with some Protestant pastors in France who did grasp the gravity of the situation and were prepared to denounce it, but unfortunately, they were few and far between. One day in June 1993, not long after the run-in with Morin and Lafont, and while our accusers were working on Rosenberg, we came across someone totally unexpected.

From time to time we had got into the habit of listening to a Protestant radio station called *Fréquence Protestante* (Protestant Wavelength). They in fact shared the radio station with the Catholic *Radio Notre-Dame*. So around one o'clock on a Saturday there was a switch from *Radio Notre-Dame* to *Fréquence Protestante*, and we happened to hear – I think it was Isabelle who put us onto it – the last Catholic programme before the switchover. It was a systematic Bible study, starting in the Old Testament, led by Abbé Hamelin, accompanied by a panel who would ask questions about the text studied. Abbé Hamelin's knowledge of the Bible and insight into its characters and events was impressive, and we were often encouraged by his comments. So in June 1993, Axel and I decided to go and visit Abbé Hamelin, and talk to him about what had happened to us.

The Abbé lived in one of the wide, busy, outer boulevards of inner Paris, lined with leafy green chestnut trees and high stone walls. Parking wasn't too bad that morning and we managed to find a space not too far from our appointed meeting-place. After we had rung the buzzer, the huge wooden gate swung open to reveal a tall, fairly heavy-set man in his late 60s, with a slight stoop. Receding grey hair, neatly combed back, framed a regular-featured face. His voice was gravelly and his manner reserved, but his eyes were kindly and discerning as he welcomed us in. The apartment was small, but meticulously clean and tidy. He received us warmly, though he must have been wondering what we could possibly be coming to see him about, as I had only said that it was 'personal'. We knew our phones were being tapped and didn't like saying too much.

From behind his desk, Abbé Hamelin got straight to the point.

"Well, now, what can I do to help you ?"

Axel did the explaining while Abbé Hamelin listened intently. When Axel had finished there was a silence. The Abbé had his head down and seemed to have withdrawn as far back into his armchair as he could. We didn't quite know what to make of it. Had we come to the wrong person? Were we being naïve to think a Catholic priest would help us when it was obvious that the Catholic church itself was implicated in this business because of the backing it provided for UNADFI ?

The Abbé told us on a later occasion that he felt as though a dark blanket of fear had descended upon him and all he could do was pray. Axel's story had reminded him vividly of the Jews being rounded up in the streets of Paris in 1942.

When at last he broke the silence, his voice was graver than before. He told us that he had no illusions about the situation within the Catholic church. He had no confidence in his hierarchy. What struck Axel was that all this confirmed his own impressions and conclusions from his involvement in the Catholic church.

Abbé Hamelin had a thorough understanding of the mentality of the 'ruling classes' in France, too. He had followed the war in Algeria closely, and had spoken openly against the use of torture by recruits in the French Army. Although he was deeply affected by what had happened to us, he did not doubt that such things could happen in France today. He had a few stories to tell about incidents that acquaintances of his had had with the French police in particular... Experience told him that our situation was a sad reality.

After some thought, he said: "The very way they took the children away, by surprise and without investigations first, just goes to show that the whole thing is wrong." For him, it was clear.

We also mentioned that we had heard him on the radio, and appreciated his programmes. He told us that his own father, who he remembered had close Jewish friends, had read him the Bible from when he was only 4 years old and taught him to respect it, Old and New Testament alike, and he had grown up with it. This was our common ground. We told him all about reading to Victoria, how she loved her Bible stories and would often sing choruses aloud to herself while she played; how we prayed with her every night, and then she would sing herself to sleep... This was the child they had taken away from us and were holding still.

Abbé Hamelin looked at us in silence again. Then, suddenly business-like, he leaned forward and said, "What can I do then ?"

We discussed whether it would be worthwhile appealing to the Catholic hierarchy, i.e. the Archbishop of Paris. Abbé Hamelin wasn't too hopeful about this. According to the Abbé, it would be in the Catholic church's interests to pull out of backing UNADFI and stop involving themselves in cases like ours, because the whole thing could well be turned against the Catholic church herself one day.

"Look," he said in the end, after another short silence, "Just leave it with me and I'll see how things go with the Archbishop. How does that sound ?"

We thanked him warmly, and also gave him our lawyer's contact details, as he said he would be interested in speaking to him. It was encouraging just to be able to talk sensibly about the whole case to someone in France, who knew and understood the shortcomings of French society. This man left us with a definite impression of honesty, uprightness and compassion, which until then we had only come across among those we called "true" Protestants. Unfortunately, the deceitful, uncaring and worldly French Protestant leaders we had encountered, such as Rosenberg, Morin and Lafont, made for a very poor comparison.

In fact, over the coming two years Abbé Hamelin was to meet with politicians, organisations and individuals in an effort to bring their attention to our case and request the release of the children. He also painstakingly prepared many documents analysing the situation, which we produced in court. He was even to accompany us to a meeting with the New Zealand Ambassador. He remained convinced and steadfast in his analyses and opinions, and constant in his encouragements. We were going to appreciate them in the days, weeks and months that followed.

Back in the judge's rooms

On July 16 1993, we were back in the huge labyrinth of the Versailles *Tribunal de Grande Instance*.

That very same day President François Mitterrand commemorated for the first time the 'Vel d'Hiv" round-up of 16 000 Jews in Paris on 16 July 1942 by French police under orders from the Vichy Government. Arrested with their families at 4 o'clock in the morning and held at the Vel d'Hiv (a winter cycle-racing track) before finally being sent to Auschwitz, only eighteen of the 4000 Jewish children survived. Ironically, 50 years later it seemed that the spirit of the Vichy Government was still alive in France.

For this hearing Mlle Cornil and Mme Durand, both present as in February, had a few cards up their sleeve. First of all, the judge received us separately. She stated that this was "the normal procedure" – so why hadn't she done so in February ? We didn't ask the question aloud. In fact, she told us both separately the same story: that Social Services had described Victoria as a "rag-doll" with an "expressionless face, eyes empty and staring, gaze distraught", "as though she had fallen from another planet", she seemed "shut up immobile in a shell", "pale", she sometimes "lies down in the guinea-pig cage".

This was obviously designed to increase our distress. It was nothing less than emotional torture. We knew that such reports (if true and not just concocted to please the judge) could only be the result of the traumatic separation between Victoria and ourselves. But the Public Prosecutor, Mlle Cornil, immediately stopped us from presenting this argument by affirming, as though she were some authority on such matters, that this was "acquired behaviour", and therefore Victoria must have been like this with us. Of course – torture chambers never allow for honourable exits. Under the shock, neither of us thought of pointing out that our family photos showed a completely different little girl.

There were some issues which the judge obviously wished to discuss with us separately. In particular, she suggested to me that if I "separated" from my husband, I might possibly regain custody of Victoria. Never had anyone put pressure on me to turn against Axel in such a blatant way. I protested that no way would I consider it, Axel was a good husband and father and I wanted none other ! I think the judge got a little more reaction there than she had bargained for, but at least my position was clear. I knew that in fact what she was talking about wouldn't be half as simple as what it sounded like. 'Separating from Axel' would mean testifying against him, and then against the church, in short I would end up having to do anything the French Judiciary asked of me in the hope that they would return Victoria to me. They would be calling all the shots. The torturers had turned to blackmail. As for me, I simply could not turn against people I knew were innocent.

Once she got Axel alone, the judge informed him in pitiful terms that she had not been absent because of a nervous breakdown – it had been a miscarriage. Axel (though rather embarrassed at a woman telling him this!) could not but feel compassion for her as he remembered her suddenly putting her hand to her stomach when she stood up to shout at him, back in February. It tied in with something someone from the Ministry of Justice had told him on the phone: stop putting so much pressure on the judge. Now he understood the whining. Well, why doesn't she return Victoria to her rightful home and put an end to the pressure ? was the obvious question. He had asked it over the phone, without getting an answer.

Anyway, however distressing the situation might be for the judge, Axel wasn't going to let them stop him with a plea for compassion – let them show some themselves. After all, Mme Durand was fully responsible for her actions and their consequences, but we were fighting for a little 3-year-old girl who was feeling bewildered and abandoned and completely traumatized because of this judge's actions, and *we* were responsible for her !

It is strange that the English word "miscarriage" has both meanings as applicable here. Judge Durand was responsible for a miscarriage of justice that had deprived us of our child, but she herself had suffered a physical miscarriage and lost her own child to death. What terrible justice life had served up to her.

After we had both been in separately we had to wait outside together while the judge, the prosecutor and our lawyer "discussed" the case. We had a different lawyer this time, a slick young man who came out after a while and sat down to wait. The judge apparently now had other business to attend to. This gave him time to tell us we should try to compromise – agree not to be in contact with our friends, for example, just a gesture to show the judge we were trying. We just looked at him blankly. He would probably have liked us to write a letter of accusation against our friends right then and there. We had never heard of a judge for children deciding which friends you could be in contact with ! By the time we were taken back in, our position had not changed, though the lawyer had done his utmost to persuade us to. We were becoming disillusioned with our lawyers – they were more like the judge's auxiliaries than anything else.

"I am prolonging the placement," declared Madame Durand, when we were finally back in her office together. "And you will be allowed to visit."

My heart jumped. When would this be and where and how often… They were exactly the questions going through Axel's mind, but when he asked, the judge would not give an exact answer. She wanted us to say then and there whether we accepted visiting rights or not – and what parent would not want to – but refused to say when, for how long or how often visits would take place. Axel was being very careful about this. I kept quiet to see why. The judge was becoming irritated.

"Do you want to see your daughter or not ?" She was back to torture again.

"We not only want to see our daughter, *Madame le Juge*," said Axel. "We want her back home with us. If she is upset, as you have said she is, it is because you removed her from a secure, loving home, and she needs to be returned to us."

"We can't just take Victoria out of the home she is now in and return her to you from one day to the next," said the judge.

"Why ?" I asked. "Isn't that exactly how you took her away?"

"That was different," I was told. "That was part of a judicial investigation. There were reasons for us acting that way." A judicial kidnapping, more like it, I thought to myself.

"Well, there is certainly every reason for you to return Victoria to her home immediately," I replied. "You have all the proof you could ever need."

"But Victoria needs a gradual, staged return," explained the judge, as though I didn't understand what was best for my own child. "Now, I need to know whether you agree to visiting rights or not."

She was insisting on these visiting rights so much, all of a sudden, after having forbidden us all contact for six months... It was obvious that if we refused them she would say that we were unworthy and unfeeling parents. But if we agreed – yes, of course, now I understood why Axel was being so careful. We had seen it with some of the other families. The visiting rights would be set up in such a way that Victoria would arrive with a negative attitude to the whole thing, we would be observed by social workers and social work psychologists, and anything they could possibly twist or use would be immediately turned against us. Victoria would be manipulated between visits and gradually turned against us, and our family wouldn't have a chance in between it all. It was a *machine à broyer* – a crushing machine. Axel knew it only too well – he had seen it all already with Isabelle and Robert and their children.

"Oh, come on, Monsieur Schmidt," took up our lawyer. "Visits are a must – it's the only way forward!" So much for our lawyer arguing *our* case.

"You decide whatever you think is right, *Madame le Juge*," Axel finished by saying. "We shall then decide what we will do about it." We had to be very careful not to commit ourselves to anything. Once we set a foot in this mess, there would be no getting out of it.

So we left the judge's office for the second time, disappointed once again, but convinced – once again – that there had been nothing else we could honestly do.

As the lawyer was standing in the corridor talking to us about the outcome of the hearing, the three women came out of the office – the wiry little prosecutor, the ponderous judge and, a little further behind, the big-eyed court clerk.

"So," Mlle Cornil, the prosecutor was saying, "Shall we have lunch together then ?"

"Yes, of course," replied Mme Durand.

And away went the independent judge – practically arm in arm with the Public Prosecutor who worked under the orders of the Ministry of Justice. Oh, the independence of the French Judiciary !

7

True colours
September 1993 – February 1994

Help on the way – or was it ?

Suddenly there seemed to be light on the horizon.

"I am very hopeful, in fact I am confident your children will be back with you very soon – if not before we leave France," Reverend Snyder was saying to Axel with assurance.

There were four of them in the 'team of Christian investigators' sent to find out "the facts". The American minister, a middle-aged Swiss woman who was to interpret for the team if necessary, a Jewish-American 'legal advisor' from Massachusetts, and a young American woman who had come as an observer on behalf of the American congressman Christopher Smith.

It had been thanks to the news releases made by the California-based News Network International (NNI) reporter Elizabeth Farrell that Richard had come into contact with this American pastor, Steven Snyder, President of a Washington-based human rights organization, Christian Solidarity International. In an article entitled '*Disinformation prevents affirmative action*', Rev. Snyder had protested strongly in the United States against the treatment we were being given in France, insisting in particular on the danger of a precedent being set which would "be disastrous to the Christian family".

Our hopes rose. This was in July 1993, just after we had been betrayed by the main French Protestant organizations, and we were encouraged. We gave the team all the details about our children's sudden disappearance as well as all the documented evidence of how healthy and well-developed they were while with us, including health certificates, testimonies, photos, etc. The facts of the case concerning the children were so clear, the French State intervention so unexpected, unwarranted and brutal, that it was clear nothing could possibly justify that they continue to be kept in State care.

Unfortunately, after meeting with our accusers and UNADFI, this 'Christian' organisation simply lost all interest in helping us. Worse, they even published the accusers' and UNADFI's story. It seemed that the words of the Lord Jesus Christ in Matthew 24:24 had been proved right: "they shall deceive the very elect".

Snyder's report, when it appeared at the end of October 1993, was not only damaging because it promoted the slander campaign against us, but it was also immediately used by our accusers, who sent it to the Judge for Children and the Court of Appeal in Versailles (we had all appealed Judge Durand's rulings on 30 July 1993 to keep the children in care, since she was obviously not going to respond to our written requests to her). So the slanderous CSI report was used against us in an effort to keep the children from being returned home by the Court of Appeal. Mr Snyder also personally sent a copy of his report to René, who was to use it in his own cases as he was due to come before the Paris Court of Appeal on 24 January 1994 for slandering Anutza and Richard on French TV back in 1992.

Once again, our hopes had risen only to be smashed. Amidst my personal turmoil of the loss of Victoria and the ups and downs of legal proceedings, I didn't fully register the gravity of what this organisation had done straight away. But the atmosphere of oppression that I had been only too aware of over the past few years, and which had climaxed in February 1993, darkened yet again. There seemed no way out of this dark tunnel of persecution which was closing in on us. The whole case had been too well set-up against us. Whatever help we had was twisted and turned against us. Bitterness became a danger. We *had* to keep trusting in God and loving Him.

Nevertheless, there were certain facts that the 'investigative' team could not just brush under the carpet. The report had to admit that there had been no opportunity for cross-examination or even any hearing before the February 10th dawn raid. The first hearing was two weeks after the raid and this was confirmed to the team by an assistant to the Minister of Justice. So there had been admittedly no evaluation of the children's well-being *before* they were brutally removed from their parents' care, which in fact made any subsequent reports absolutely invalid, as was confirmed to me later by British psychological experts.

The accusation about the children not being schooled was strongly refuted by the team, since they were in favour of home schooling – and so they made much of the fact that Philippe and Rebecca's four children, as well as Richard and Anutza's twin boys, had been enrolled in a State-run correspondence course.

Unfortunately these sparse positive points were completely outweighed by the negatives. Lies and slander had brought Rev. Snyder full circle. Now he had been taken in by the 'disinformation' himself and 'prevented' from taking 'affirmative action'.

Once again, revealingly, people calling themselves Christians had shut their eyes to the facts and blindly denied that there could be religious persecution in France. Once again, there was a huge gap between what people said or suspected and the reality we knew and had explained at great length, but to no avail.

Going home to our empty flat, feeling let down and abused by these 'Christians', memories of Victoria came flooding back as though to underline their callousness.

Just a normal, happy little girl

When Axel and I had learned that we would be expecting a new addition to the family in January 1990, we had both been delighted. I had just obtained my degrees the previous year and Axel had started into regular work the year before. There had also been a lull in the attacks on the church. She had almost been named Debora Victoria, but we changed at the last minute to Victoria Debora. The name Victoria was our way of saying that we were placing our faith in the victory of the Lord, both for our own family and for the church at that time. We trusted He would provide peace and happiness for the child He had given us.

We were of course enchanted by this rosy baby girl, who was calm and peaceful and even slept all night through practically from birth. I was blissfully ignorant of what it was to be woken in the middle of the night by a hungry baby – our Victoria seemed to have an acute sense of day and night!

By the time she was two she was also very active and imaginative. Anutza dropped in one day and was charmed to hear Victoria wake up from her afternoon sleep with her usual sing-song "*Bonjour, Maman !*" That was her morning routine too, which was usually followed by : "*Il est là, Papa ?*" ("Is Daddy there ?"), and if he was (sometimes Axel left early) she would be through onto his knees in a minute, and usually try to "work" like him. He would often get a little stroke on the cheek from time to time too.

Her 'work' brought her results– at two and a half she knew all the letters of the alphabet! Other children were very impressed and played with her at writing the letters and making her say them. One young boy said to her in amazement : "Victoria, you're going to be a genius !" Stairs were great fun for counting – sometimes a little too much fun. She was very fast at copying others, from pretending to play the cello (with two bits of wood) and singing songs, to giving her dolls baths, and meals which she cooked in her own little play oven.

I remember her at three in the bath, singing away to herself and playing around with words. The sound "ay" as in "hay" is very common in French (often spelt "er"), but she used to add in an "oy" before it just for fun, transforming "nager" (pronounce "najay", meaning "to swim") into "najoyay" etc.

Then there were the stories, which she never tired of, like most children; after which she would sit on the sofa and tell them to her dolls. She soon began writing letters too, as well as doing colouring-in and puzzles etc. Circles were her great favourite and she often covered whole pages with them, lots of little ones, or little ones inside big ones. And she never got too old to enjoy an exciting game of hide-and-seek with her Daddy.

In short, she was a very busy little girl. Never indifferent to our comings and goings, she would always be there to enthusiastically wave goodbye or welcome home. She loved going out to the play-ground too, and we were regular users as the nearest one was only fifty metres from our front door. The cat at home also kept her fit – I'm afraid Victoria was expert at teasing it until it chased her round the house, clawing at her ankles. She would squeal with delight and then turn around and tell it off !

"*Méchante Minette* !" she would exclaim ("You wicked Minette !"). Always nice to have someone to pick on when you're the littlest...

I will never forget the day we went to the doctor's for a regular check-up and he was checking the glands on her throat. All of a sudden Victoria's little voice piped up in the silence:

"You have to be careful of people's necks, you know – they're very fragile."

I don't think she appreciated having her neck poked and pressed! The doctor was highly amused.

"You'll go far in life, won't you, *Mademoiselle* ?" he said, smiling at her.

And of course, there was that day in November, 1992, when I took her to the doctor's again and she (a different doctor, replacing her regular paediatrician while he was on holiday) was very taken with Victoria and wrote "*superbe enfant*" on her health book. I didn't notice Victoria doing anything special, just taking her time to size up this new lady doctor, as she usually did with strangers, and answering her questions. She certainly had a particular reserve which she used so as to keep people at a distance until they were accepted – and too bad for them if they weren't, they just had to put up with a permanent reserve...

As I looked round our empty sitting room at the big cupboard where we kept Victoria's toys, the comfy armchair where she would sit with the kitten, the large L-shaped sofa where she would tell her dolls stories, or sit to play on the coffee table, or play her imaginary cello, there were so many happy memories... How could this tragedy have happened to my little girl ?

There was one man, however, who had truly taken Victoria's plight to heart, and he wasn't one to let himself be put off by smooth-talking French officials or false accusers.

True solidarity

While the representatives of this 'Christian solidarity' organisation had been busy trying to find reasons not to help us, the editor of the "New Zealand Beacon", whom we had invited to come to France at the same time as the CSI team, was preparing to put the plain truth of the matter before the French authorities.

Although he didn't manage to see the judge, by Wednesday October 6 Dr Pearce had obtained a rendez-vous with the President of the Children's Tribunal in Versailles, a certain Monsieur Jolivet, who was Judge Durand's direct superior. Monsieur Jolivet occupied a spacious office on the ground floor of the enormous *Tribunal de Grande Instance*, where we had attended the hearing in the Judge for Children's office. He was a respectable, fit-looking man, with a tanned, regular-featured face and glasses. After a brief introduction, Dr Pearce got straight to the heart of the subject.

"In this affair, Monsieur Jolivet, there was no inquiry whatso-ever preceding the judge's decision. Can you tell me why that is and how it is possible ?"

"Why, it's totally impossible," answered Monsieur Jolivet. "No, no, it can't be true."

"But the parents have clearly told us that there was absolutely no prior investigation," insisted Dr Pearce.

"Oh, you cannot take everything the mother says as the truth!" There was contempt in Monsieur Jolivet' voice. I was present as Dr Pearce's interpreter – I just bit my tongue.

"At any rate," he continued, "I know nothing of this case, only the judge does, and even if I did I wouldn't be able to tell you anything."

"But Monsieur Jolivet, surely the judge must be accountable to somebody ...?"

"Dr Pearce, in France, as in New Zealand I'm sure, judges are independent, this is the judge's responsibility, not mine or anyone else's. Perhaps the judge did not carry out an inquiry beforehand. If certain elements were brought to her knowledge, it may have been decided to investigate afterwards. It is possible. The judge can make her inquiry either before the withdrawal of a child, at the same time, or immediately afterwards. Anyway, if the mother is not happy with the judge's decision, she should appeal."

"So the judge can do more or less whatever she likes?" Dr Pearce raised his eyebrows.

"There must be other factors in the file which you are not aware of, Dr Pearce," replied Monsieur Jolivet, looking slightly hot under the collar. "This is not a file open to the public, only to the parents and their lawyers. It is useless for foreigners to come and see me or write to me, because they cannot know the essential facts of the case as only the judge can."

Now it was obvious why our lawyer had advised CSI to name a lawyer who could go and see the file for himself. But Dr Pearce was not put off. He could play this game too.

"We have the file, Monsieur Jolivet, and we aren't going away."

Jolivet was rattled.

"Hold on… what case is this now… oh, yes, now I know what you're talking about… In fact, I have a whole stack of letters about it from California, Australia and New Zealand which have been sent on to me by the French Ministry of Justice, the French National Assembly and the French Senate."

Now he spoke slowly and meaningfully.

"They are all piled up in the corner of an office somewhere and the judge knows nothing about them."

He leaned forward.

"You see, Dr Pearce, the only way forward for the parents is the legal way. If they appeal the judge's decision, their case will be heard by three magistrates who are older and more experienced."

He didn't say how long that would take or that it was highly likely that the appeal judges would cover up for the first instance judge. In a case like this, where the French Judiciary knew they were at fault, they certainly also knew how to protect themselves.

Dr Pearce took up again.

"This case has been labelled as one of religious persecution, Monsieur Jolivet."

Monsieur Jolivet waved the argument aside with a gesture.

"That's what parents in a cult always claim when their children are removed."

"But in this case there must be evidence for it – its their lawyers who are stating it," Derek insisted.

"Well surely that's obvious – a lawyer's job is to defend his client."

"Monsieur Jolivet, if I told you the name of the lawyer in question, I doubt you would talk about him that way," replied Dr Pearce.

Jolivet waved his hand again dismissively, but was silent.

"Monsieur Jolivet – do you know that this little girl was called a "superb child" by her paediatrician but now has been described as a rag-doll baby, who lies down in the guinea-pig cage and only draws straight lines ?" Dr Pearce's voice was quietly emotional.

The stark reality of it seemed to hit home. Monsieur Jolivet hesitated.

"Well… of course, when a child is taken away from its parents it inevitably has negative psychological consequences," he admitted. Then perhaps he felt he had said too much. He was in fact saying that Victoria's appearance and behaviour were due to her sudden withdrawal – and was not "acquired behaviour" as the Public Prosecutor Mlle Cornil had said. At any rate he stood to his feet, suddenly brusque.

"Dr Pearce, I received you purely out of courtesy, now I consider I have given you quite enough of my time and I do not wish to see anybody else about this case. Is that clear?"

But Dr Pearce was already on his feet too, thanking Monsieur Jolivet for his time.

Rumours in the corridors of power

Next morning we had a meeting with Monsieur Masson, a representative of Mme Michaux-Chevry, Minister of Human Rights, who worked under the Ministry of Foreign Affairs on the famous Quai d'Orsay in Paris, near the Place de la Concorde. I was acting once again as Dr Pearce's interpreter.

After finding our way to the old, impressive-looking Ministry of Foreign Affairs building on the bank of the Seine called the Quai d'Orsay, we were disappointingly greeted with the news that Monsieur Masson couldn't see Dr Pearce after all. From the reception desk I spoke to Monsieur Masson's secretary, Mme Guerin, over the phone, who spoke contemptuously of Dr. Pearce, saying that she had left a message on his answer phone cancelling the appointment and couldn't understand that he hadn't got it. Perhaps news of the way the meeting in Versailles with Monsieur Jolivet had gone had already made its way to the Quai d'Orsay – faster than the mail. I explained that Dr Pearce was staying at a hotel – perhaps the message had been overlooked. She suggested that he change hotels…

"Well, it certainly is a very embarrassing situation," I continued. "Monsieur Masson fixed an appointment with him just yesterday, and now he's here only to learn that it has been cancelled – after flying all the way from New Zealand."

Dr Pearce was determined to see the man. He was standing just outside the office which I, as "interpreter", had been allowed to enter.

"This is a case about a little New Zealand girl who has been removed from her parents' care here in France," I informed Mrs Guerin.

"Oh, yes, that's old news," she assured me. "I've even spoken personally to Monsieur and Madame Schmidt myself, several times in fact. But Monsieur Masson really cannot receive this man now."

My heart missed a beat. She had spoken to us on the phone! I couldn't remember. If she realised who I was… I put on my best real French accent and took on a confidential tone of voice.

"Well, I have to say it is very embarrassing for me – I don't know what to tell the man. So why did Monsieur Masson give him an appointment in the first place ?"

The secretary also lowered her voice confidentially.

"I'll tell you what happened: after Monsieur Masson fixed the rendez-vous, he inquired into the matter and found it was one of those cult cases, you know... and then he inquired further – and discovered there is sexual abuse involved !"

"Really ?"

I must have sounded horrified – I really was. So these were the lies being spread round official corridors behind our backs !

"Yes," she went on. "And the parents want their child back – can you imagine ! It's out of the question of course."

Reeling from the enormity of it, I put my hand to my head, my fingers tracing over my eyebrows, trying to clear my mind. Looking down, my eyes suddenly lit upon the reception's "entries" register. It was very clearly laid out:

APPOINTMENTS	WITH	INSTRUCTIONS
Dr Pearce	Monsieur Masson	Warn the bailiff straightaway

Above all don't let him through

What kind of a country is this ? I wondered – yet again – to myself. And this was the representative of the Minister of Human Rights - what a sick joke.

The secretary was still on the line. I managed to keep talking.

"Well... couldn't Monsieur Masson see Dr Pearce for a few minutes at least ? ... Seeing he's here?"

My subdued voice perhaps made her think that her remarks had done the job – that she had at least got round the interpreter.

"I'm afraid Monsieur Masson is at a meeting with the Minister at the moment," she replied, business-like again. "But... if you can wait a little, I'll ask him as soon as he comes out."

"Thank you. We'll wait then."

We must have waited about 20 minutes.

I was still trying to take in what I had just heard. No wonder everyone was against us, I was thinking. But how could lies like that spread without there ever having been even any *accusations* of sexual abuse ? It was an extremely malicious rumour. I wondered how many people had been stopped from helping us by these sorts of lies being spread by French officials ! The very idea was chilling. Could this possibly explain why the international Christian organisation's recent inquiries had come to such a sudden halt? Anyway, it was obvious that the French authorities would stop at nothing to put an end to any support for us from outside of France.

Then Monsieur Masson was on the office phone, asking to speak to the 'interpreter'. He was dismissive of the whole case and obviously just wanted us to go away.

"I really do not have time to receive Dr Pearce now," he explained. "I know I did make an appointment with him yesterday, but that was only because he was very insistent, and as I had some difficulty understanding his English, it was easier to fix an appointment with him when he had an interpreter."

"It will look very bad to the New Zealand public, Monsieur Masson," I warned him, though trying to sound as detached as possible.

"That's not my problem!" retorted Monsieur Masson.

"But after flying all the way from New Zealand – 24 hours in a plane – to see you," I reminded him. After all, I had to do my duty as an interpreter who wanted her client to have the best possible impression of France!

"Dr Pearce has asked for interviews all over the place and he will get some, don't worry," Monsieur Masson assured me. "We know by the way he writes his articles that he is not on our side, anyway."

Really. So there had been sides taken in our case – that meant that all the French authorities involved in the case would be against us – I filed that one away for future reference.

"The thing is, Monsieur Masson, that Dr Pearce was told at the beginning that he would have no problem at all in getting an appointment. You do understand my difficulty."

"Yes, yes, I am quite aware of all that. Look, tell Dr Pearce that in any case this affair does not concern human rights, all right ?"

There was a pause while I conveyed the message to Dr Pearce, who had now been allowed into the office area. The reception register had disappeared from sight. Dr Pearce took the phone.

"This is definitely a case concerning Human Rights, Monsieur Masson: a little girl has been taken away from her parents without any preceding inquiry or any valid reason, and after 8 months she is now becoming a vegetable." I winced at the thought. Our Victoria! Dr Pearce certainly was getting straight to the point once more.

"Dr Pearce," replied Monsieur Masson, "There has been a judicial decision taken in this affair, so it concerns the Ministry of Justice and not the Ministry of Human Rights."

The usual buck-passing again. These French officials seemed to be trained in it. Dr Pearce was not stopping there, though.

"Monsieur Masson, we are talking about a child's life here. For 8 months a young couple have been in agony, deprived of their child…"

"Dr Pearce, this is a law-respecting country…" Monsieur Masson seemed to be weakening.

"Oh, and it's a law-respecting country that blew up a ship peacefully harboured in New Zealand waters, and killed an innocent person, was it?"[1]

That finished Monsieur Masson off. The lid blew.

"Well, if you're talking like that, it's just as well I'm not seeing you!" And he hung up.

While Dr Pearce was on the phone to Monsieur Masson, the receptionist came over to me.

"Could I ask what interpreting company you work for?" she asked.

"Oh, I'm working in a private capacity," I answered with a smile.

"Oh," she said, "Are you not from the *Quai d'Orsay*, then ?"

"No, no," I assured her. They had thought I worked for the *Quai d'Orsay*, i.e. the Ministry of Foreign Affairs, on which the Ministry of Human Rights depended. Perhaps Mrs Guerin had only passed on to me such confidential lies about "sexual abuse" because she thought I was part of the system ?

At any rate, that was Monsieur Jolivet and Monsieur Masson: two down… and the French authorities were not appreciating being faced with the truth.

---

[1] Reference to the "Rainbow Warrior" incident in 1985, when a Greenpeace ship of that name was blown up by French army personnel in Auckland harbour, and a photographer on board was killed. Greenpeace had been demonstrating against French nuclear testing in the Pacific.

And so into the very heart of the French Judiciary

Out of all the calls we made to different French Ministries asking for meetings for Dr Pearce about the case, and although they were directly concerned by the issues raised in Victoria's case, they were all, like Monsieur Masson, excellent at directing us to someone else "who could help".

We had either personally delivered letters about Victoria's case or faxed letters through to the Ministries of Foreign Affairs, of Health and Social Services, of Human Rights, as well as to representatives of President Mitterrand, Mrs Mitterrand and Prime Minister Balladur, and they had all been contacted by phone afterwards. Some of them, like the Minister of Health and Social Services, said they couldn't give us a meeting, but would be following the case; others just referred us to the Ministry of Justice, as did the Ministry of Foreign Affairs (they had probably had some fairly strong feedback from Monsieur Masson, who worked in the same building); others, such as the Prime Minister's office, simply refused to give us a meeting. The doors were closing, and the shutters were coming down. Nobody wanted to even admit there was an issue here.

Interestingly, the representative for President Mitterrand, Monsieur Louis Joinet, intelligently told us that we could have a meeting there if we were refused one by the Ministry of Justice. This meant that the Ministry of Justice was obliged to give us a rendez-vous to avoid us obtaining one with the President's assistant!

We spent hours trying to sort out meetings over the phone. The person we needed at the Ministry of Justice was away *en province*, i.e. in one of the *provinces*, where we attempted to contact him but to no avail. When we tried the Ministry of Justice again, we were told someone would ring us back. Eventually we were called and given a rendez-vous with a certain Monsieur Gaeremynck for Thursday, 5:30 p.m. A strange time for a meeting... This appointment was confirmed, but then changed: it would no longer be with Mr Gaeremynck, but with a Monsieur Carnot. And not at the Ministry of Justice, but at one of its annexes, no. 57, rue Saint-Roch.

We were starting to wonder when they would stop throwing us round and whose court the ball would end up in.

We had a meeting in the afternoon at the New Zealand Embassy with Ambassador Chris Beeby. The Ambassador was very good at listening to us and telling us that we should do what the French authorities were telling him, but he never seemed to be able to get across to them the urgency and distress of Victoria's situation. Derek tried his utmost to fire things up and get things moving, but unfortunately – as usual – there was a lot of talking done and no action taken.

Then we were due for the meeting with Monsieur Carnot, a representative from the Ministry of Justice with competence in international law…

Situated in the back streets of Paris not far from the Ministry of Justice itself, no. 57, rue St-Roch looked respectable enough. Inside though, it was cold and kind of silent, in spite of the fact that there were still quite a few people at work. Some were leaving. A secretary asked us to wait – Monsieur Carnot was just upstairs. It was strange, but while we waited I got the uncomfortable feeling we were being watched. People would eye us as they went past. The wait seemed to have a purpose in it. Perhaps just an attempt to unnerve us, and Dr Pearce in particular. He must have felt it too, because when I started talking to him in a low voice, he signalled that it was better just to keep quiet. I resumed my 'detached interpreter' role. This was our third meeting that day…

My unease only increased when Monsieur Carnot did not come downstairs at all, but out of a door just opposite where we had been sitting. I could only guess at the meaning of all this. Were there hidden microphones near us so Monsieur Carnot could listen to our private conversation in the room next door? Or was there a judas hole in that door? What's more, Monsieur Carnot's manner was also almost sinister. He was a small dark man with dark, practically black, eyes and dark, slicked-back hair.

We were invited coldly, but politely, to come in and sit down. As he closed the door we suddenly became aware that there was someone sitting behind it, whom we had not been able to see as we entered. A thin, older, balding-gray man, who gave us as warm a

welcome as Monsieur Carnot: chilling. He didn't say a word throughout the whole interview. He just watched, and listened. It was very
intimidating. I don't know what kind of business usually went on in
that room, but it felt as though we were on trial for some heinous
crime, and someone was set on obtaining a confession from us.

Monsieur Carnot started off the meeting by launching into a long
explanation of the French judicial system and in particular the
difference between civil and criminal procedures – nothing to do
with Victoria's case. In the end, Derek had to more or less interrupt
him, or I think he would have continued on in the same strain for the
whole of the meeting.

"I am aware of all these details, Monsieur Carnot. My question
is this: why did the French authorities lie to the New Zealand public
in a press release, saying that the decision to remove little Victoria
Schmidt had been taken after a normal inquiry ?"

"Dr Pearce, there must have been some sort of inquiry, the judge
must have had some grounds to act on," replied Monsieur Carnot
confidently.

Dr Pearce had his facts all ready.

"The French Embassy in New Zealand has stated that the
decision was only taken after several months of long, debated
inquiry, but in fact neither Social Services, the police or the judge
had investigated anything to do with little Victoria before February
10 – so they effectively lied to the New Zealand public."

"I don't think you have your facts right, Dr Pearce," answered
Monsieur Carnot, though in a quieter tone.

"Well, tell me then," carried on Derek, "Why, after seeing a
paediatrician's excellent report and comments on a child, would a
judge declare that nothing would convince her?"

"Look, Dr Pearce, if the parents are not satisfied with the judge's
decision, they should appeal and the case will then be heard by the
second degree judges."

He was starting to sound like Mr Jolivet all over again.

Dr Pearce expressed his concern that there could be nothing to
hope for from the second degree judges: what was to stop them
saying the same thing as Mrs Durand ? that nothing would convince
them ?

"Dr Pearce, the only way open to the parents is to appeal – and that is entirely normal, since France is a law-respecting country."

Why did everybody feel they had to insist on that so much ? After all, in a 'law-respecting country' everybody can usually see that the law is respected.

"Yes, and French 'respect for the law' led to the explosion of the 'Rainbow Warrior' in New Zealand waters," remarked Dr Pearce.

"No, no, no – come on, Dr Pearce, the people involved in that episode were in fact a very good example of France's respect for the law: they were penalized afterwards!"

"Monsieur Carnot, you and I know full well that that is simply not true – on their return to France those people were not penalized, they were decorated," Dr Pearce stated, quietly forceful.

"Well… there have been controversial legal decisions taken in New Zealand also," retorted Monsieur Carnot.

"That's not the question here," replied Dr Pearce calmly. "You are not going to make us go away, Monsieur Carnot. Are you aware that Monsieur Jolivet, the President of the Versailles Children's Tribunal, has received letters of protest from all over the world about this case and that he has simply stacked them up in a corner and forgotten about them?"

Monsieur Carnot waved his hand dismissively and seemed to suddenly remember that he had not finished his long-winded explanation about the different French judicial procedures…and finally made the point that the judge was independent, that she could not be allowed to be affected by outside influences, and that the file was totally confidential.

"I know the file, Monsieur Carnot," stated Dr Pearce, "and nothing justifies this judge's actions because there is nothing to substantiate the accusations and on the contrary abundant proof of the child's good health."

He leant forward.

"A little girl who was called a "superb child" by her paediatrician is now reported as being a 'rag-doll baby' who lies down in the guinea-pig cage… No, I will not leave this business alone, Monsieur Carnot."

"Dr Pearce, I think you are letting your feelings interfere too much," said Monsieur Carnot, patronizingly.

"Well, you may have heard of the parents' famous lawyer," said Derek. "He has clearly stated that this case is one of religious persecution and that he has never in his whole career seen such hostility on behalf of the French Judiciary. Do you really believe that such a lawyer is inclined to have flights of fancy, or let his 'feelings' get in the way of his work, Monsieur Carnot?"

"Oh, a lawyer is still just a lawyer, not a judge," replied Monsieur Carnot. "At any rate, French judicial procedures are supposed to be confidential and I do not know how you came to be in possession of the file…"

That was the second time he had made that comment and it was starting to sound like a threat.

"You aren't giving me any answers to my questions, Monsieur Carnot," Derek said finally. "In which case I have nothing more to ask you."

And we had to leave it there. Derek's plane was leaving the next day.

8

In desperation
November 1993 – February 1994

Let our daughter go !

By November 1993 we were feeling desperate – Christmas was looming. Easter had been bad enough, now we were having to contemplate spending Christmas without Victoria.

We had been writing to Victoria regularly since shortly after she was taken. It always had to go through French Social Services of course, since we didn't even have an address for her, and we never knew what actually got through to her. I had sent her gifts and chocolate at Easter, and now we had to start thinking about sending Christmas presents to her in State care. It was like sending them to someone in prison, except that we never heard anything back. Apart from the reports we had received through the Judge for Children we knew absolutely nothing about how Victoria was coping with all this. Worst of all was not being able to comfort her. I could only weep to God for her at night, as I thought of her amongst strangers, inconsolable

It was at times like these that we really felt our need of the church, the need to pray this whole situation through together – that had always been our strength in the past. Now, though, the French Judiciary had seemed to try to split us on purpose: one member of each family had been indicted and forbidden contact with the others. So it was impossible for us all to meet together, and difficult to meet at all, since it split the families. We were all very much on our own. On top of this was the sad reality that we didn't have another church to go to. So many had already turned against us, and we knew that any church belonging to or associated with the Evangelical Baptist Churches Federation or the Protestant Federation of France would only be turned against us sooner or later, and the situation had not been made any easier by the American CSI intervention. The betrayal of these so-called Christians was still very raw in our minds, and in the extreme situation we were in we preferred to simply stay away.

Only one American pastor in Paris who had known Richard and Anutza for some years was courageous and faithful enough to continue supporting and helping us as much as he could in spite of strong pressure. He had been in meetings with other ministers who had all been against us and had still kept to his stand. He had also suffered much himself in France over the years, and would not have chosen to return there except he felt bound to answer God's call. He had even mentioned our situation to churches in the States when he was home on furlough. So we attended his church in the centre of Paris a couple of times, and some of our friends went there regularly. It wasn't the same of course, but at least we could have fellowship with other Christians who understood our situation to some extent and some of them were praying with us – praying for the children's release.

Meanwhile, we were still hoping that the New Zealand Embassy might help us obtain Victoria's release, but they had recently told us that because Victoria and I were French citizens as well as New Zealanders, we came under French domestic law, so they couldn't intervene. So were we just expected to bow to the tyranny of the French justice system ?

If being French meant the State could take your child away for no valid reason and you couldn't do anything about it, I didn't want anything to do with it. I made inquiries about renouncing French citizenship, and it turned out to be less complicated than I had thought. According to law I could renounce French citizenship for myself, and Axel and I could renounce it for Victoria – we still had parental responsibility for her, and they couldn't take that away without very serious, proven reasons. And they had nothing.

After providing several documents and making several visits to the *Préfecture* in Versailles, just across the street from the "old" entrance of the *Tribunal de Grande Instance*, we eventually received a letter asking for one final document from the New Zealand Embassy providing proof that Victoria and I were both New Zealand citizens. That was apparently all they needed, and then we would be fully and only New Zealand citizens, and then – who knew what we could do ! We impatiently awaited the outcome of our request.

Meanwhile, we had been expecting to hear from the judge about the visiting right she had given us in her last judgement rendered on 30 July 1993. We were still very cautious about such an idea, but realized it was a matter we were going to have to deal with. It was too easy at the moment for the judge to fob off our requests for Victoria's return by saying that we refused to agree to visiting rights. The problem was, the judge had not given any specifications as to where, when and how long visits could take place (we had still been forbidden to know where Victoria was in State care).

For the month of August 1993 the judge was away on holiday. I don't know how she managed to enjoy her holidays – we were just going through the motions, enjoyment and relaxation were almost impossible. Victoria's absence left a void, and our thoughts were always going to her. The absence of the other children, who were usually together during the holidays, only made it worse. And then there were those tormenting moments when something reminded me poignantly and painfully of Victoria: a song, a saying, a situation, a child. The only consolation, if it could be called that, was that there were several of us in the same situation, deprived of our children – we could at least try to encourage each other, talk things over, pray together…

September saw everybody back to work, including ourselves, but only silence from the judge. Axel's work, training bank employees in fiscal and banking law, was demanding more of his time, and I was away a couple of evenings a week teaching English night classes, as well as continuing to apply and interview for jobs in secondary schools as an English teacher. Axel was doing quite a bit of the legal work both for ourselves and the other families as well, preparing documents for the lawyers, and I was getting into the typing of it all. And then there were the letters we wrote to any and everybody we could think of, from French associations against mental torture to the Queen of England herself.

When October came and we still hadn't heard anything further, we decided we would have to contact the judge ourselves. But the letter we wrote on October 8 wasn't answered until November 23 – one and a half months later. Even then, all she said was that we were to contact Social Services to make arrangements. So we finally arranged appointments with Social Services representatives.

We will not let her go...

First came the meeting with the people who were supposed to be "educating" us, i.e. suggesting changes in our lives which would supposedly allow Victoria's return home (*Aide Educative en Milieu Ouvert* – Educative Assistance in Neutral Surroundings). Their problem was that they had nothing to reproach us with ! They had to admit that Victoria was in excellent health, ate well, was clean, had a considerably large vocabulary for a child of her age, knew how to hold a pencil and colour in properly and already knew her alphabet. They were agreed that they had nothing to reproach us with materially speaking, and that there was no doubt as to our healthy morals.

At that point, Axel and I could only ask, well, what else could we possibly do ? Why wasn't Victoria being returned to us ?

We were amazed to hear that according to these 'professionals', the situation could change "if our life took a different direction". When pressed to specify exactly what that "direction" should be, Social Services refused to explain themselves, but told us that this was what the Judge for Children was also waiting for in order to be able to return Victoria to our care. In reality, it was blackmail. This whole 'judicial kidnapping' had been arranged to force us to change our choices, choices we had made according to the freedom that French law and the French Constitution bestow on every French citizen. It was nothing less than taking a child hostage until her parents decided to change their religious beliefs! And this was France in 1993. 200 years after "Liberty, equality and fraternity" had become the country's motto and France had become known as the "country of human rights". The anti-"cult" policy had penetrated all Government and administrative bodies in France by now, and we were more than ever considered as second-rate citizens, "cult" adepts who had to be forced into a "proper" way of life and "proper", acceptable beliefs.

After the meeting with AEMO, we were not surprised when the ASE (*Assistance Sociale de l'Enfance* – Social Aid for Children), who were supposed to arrange the visits with Victoria, took exactly the same approach. Yes, Victoria was perfectly well developed; no, we could not be faulted for her education and upbringing, but... The injustice of it was crying out loud. If they had something against us, why not come out into the open with it ? Were they just playing head games with us, trying to imply that in spite of having nothing to reproach us with openly, there could still be something wrong – wrong enough to keep our child away from us ?

Visits in such a context were impossible, as Social Services' only aim was to prove that they did have something against us. The ASE proposed giving us one visit only, without any guarantee of further visits or any hope of Victoria's eventual return home, and it was to be for a half an hour to an hour long. They did not want us to know where Victoria was living, so she would have to be brought to their offices for the visit.

We reminded them that Victoria had already been deeply traumatised by being brutally separated from us back in February, as well as by the fact that the separation had now gone on for so long. Such a short meeting, followed by another separation, without any reassurance that she would see us again, was absolutely inhuman. I asked to be able to visit Victoria daily – that was what she needed.

Though the ASE representatives had claimed from the beginning of the interview that they were there to consider our wishes, they then proceeded to lay down the law to us, with no regard for what we had to say. We soon understood that they had no intention of returning Victoria to us after a series of visits. All they wanted was the chance to get us involved in a system of visits that they would entirely control. The suffering of a child separated from her parents for ten months without any contact with them whatsoever, who would perhaps be feeling abandoned and bewildered (and who knows what they had told her in State care, if they were being so insidious with us) – it all mattered little to them, except as a means of bringing pressure to bear on us. We had no doubt that they would try to twist anything that happened during visits in order to have something to accuse us with. The other families had seen it done.

We weren't prepared to do that to Victoria, especially at her young age. Better for her to live apart from us, but untouched, than to be torn apart emotionally and psychologically for the sake of a few tense minutes with us. But it was a difficult decision to take. Any mother or father's heart just aches for a sight of their child, a hug, a chance to give comfort. Yet I was convinced, as was Axel, that we had to do what was right for Victoria.

I clearly remember being struck at the time by Solomon's wisdom when the two women came to him claiming the same child, and he ordered the child to be divided in two. How I could identify with the mother whose "bowels yearned upon her son, and she said, O my lord, give her the living child, and in no wise slay it. But the other said, Let it be neither mine nor thine, but divide it."[1] We could only trust God to render justice just as Soloman had, to us who truly loved Victoria and refused to see her torn apart.

We explained in writing to both the AEMO and the ASE, clearly giving our reasons, that there seemed little point in continuing contact with them in such circumstances. They could not deny the fact that they had no valid reason for keeping Victoria away from us, and we had no hesitation in reminding them that in these circumstances their duty was to reunite Victoria with her family, but they refused to envisage her return. We knew they would probably still accuse us of "refusing visits" with Victoria, but we had our reasons and were convinced that we had no other option. We continued to write to Victoria regularly, and prayed God that the bond between us would be preserved.

[1] 1 Kings 3:26

Then in December 1993 we received news from the Citizenship Service in Paris that our request for renouncing French citizenship for Victoria and myself had been refused. No explanation, no reasoning, a blunt refusal in spite of the fact that we had provided all the necessary documents according to law. The French authorities obviously wanted to keep us in their clutches and have complete control of the case right to the bitter end. We seemed doomed to continue to suffer at the hands of the French judiciary.

Making appeal

Christmas 1993 came and went. We didn't want to know about it. We had sent Victoria presents in early December and then preferred to forget what time of year it was. We were so preoccupied with the fight for Victoria that normal life seemed to pass us by.

Meanwhile our appeal was coming up and we didn't have a decent lawyer. These lawyers that we had seen side with the judge against us during the hearing were no good. Axel made appointments with one lawyer after another. The problem was that most of them asked for provisional fees of about ten thousand francs (£1,000), and even then we never knew if they would really defend us properly. Several times we had lawyers take up the case only to drop it again very quickly, which was both expensive and damaging. In fact, every time a lawyer of any reputation or importance showed an interest in the case and went to see the judges (as lawyers do in France), we invariably found that they eventually backed off, dissuaded by the judges from defending us, leaving us high and dry and strengthening the Judiciary's position against us. The date for the appeal was 13 January 1994, and it had already been postponed once. Finally we managed to have it postponed again until February 24.

Appeals for the other three families were going ahead. Isabelle and Robert's case was the first to be heard by the Appeal Court. Social Services were there and were adamant that their little boy, who had just turned three, should stay in State care. Isabelle and Robert had a little more experience than us in the matter of Children's Court cases, what with their three elder children's removal and placement with Isabelle's parents in 1989. They had wisely taken the precaution of having a court-approved child psychiatrist assess little Xavier back in 1992. They now produced this very positive report to the Court of Appeal to show that there were absolutely no grounds for continuing to keep their young son in State care. They were well rewarded for their pains – on January 20, the Versailles Court of Appeal reversed the Judge for Children's placement order and granted Isabelle and Robert full care and control of their son once again, without prolonged visits or any other preliminaries! Needless to say, we were all delighted. Perhaps there was hope for the rest of us before the Court of Appeal after all…

A week later Isabelle and Robert joyfully arrived to pick up their son from the Social Services venue in Versailles. To their consternation, there were newspaper reporters, photographers and television cameras there, anxious to get a shot of the "child returned to a cult". Obviously, UNADFI had been at work again, making use of its numerous contacts in the Judiciary and the press – how else had they been able to find out when and where this little family was to be reunited and get the press onto it so quickly ? The story was in the national media that night, and UNADFI was quoted sure enough – and there was wrath against the Versailles Court of Appeal for ever letting little Xavier back home with his *papa* and *maman*, however many good legal and humane reasons there may have been for the court's decision.

Young Xavier may have been home – but was he safe home ? In the days that followed, the Public Prosecuting Department themselves appealed to the *Cour de Cassation* (Supreme Court) for his return to State care. Robert and Isabelle were astounded. Reunited only to be torn apart again in six months time ? Would God allow such a thing ? Besides, they were seriously concerned that Xavier's stay in State care had been gravely detrimental to his development. They hastily contacted the child psychiatrist who had examined Xavier in 1992. His subsequent report, drawn up on 28 February 1994, showed that little Xavier had in fact regressed developmentally during his year in State care. Whereas he had been a normal, bright little two-year-old before his removal in February 1993, he now, at three, had the mental age of a **one-year-old**. We were all devastated

– and scandalized at the same time. Where would this stop ? What about Victoria – was her whole life and future being destroyed as well ? And Philippe and Rebecca's three lovely children ? And Anutza and Richard's boys, who had been such intelligent, curious and cultured young livewires…? We could only trust that God would keep them.

Then a former lawyer for Robert and Isabelle whom Axel had become acquainted with, recommended a certain Versailles lawyer to us – a Maître Lamont. So Axel fixed an appointment with him and to his surprise this man didn't ask him for any money at the initial interview. He seemed to take in Victoria's case at a glance and told Axel at the end of the meeting that he was convinced our daughter should be back with us. As simple as that – and he was a well-known and well-reputed lawyer, actually a former Head of the Versailles Bar.

Before the hearing, Maître Lamont needed to know what was in the file – what could possibly be used against us. Under French law, the Judge for Children's file was inaccessible to us as the parents of "the minor" in question. The judge, or in this case the Court of Appeal, keeps the file in their office and it is available to the Public Prosecutor, Social Services and court experts such as pscyhiatrists, psychologists, etc., but on the parents' side only their legal representative, the lawyer, can have access – and he isn't allowed to photocopy anything. Any documents he wants a record of have to be noted down by hand or voice-recorded, which is extremely time-consuming for the lawyer and expensive for his clients, the parents. Naturally, this puts parents off consulting a Judge for Children's file, and means that the lawyer usually ends up picking out certain documents from the file which he thinks may be of interest or importance to his/her client. The result is that most parents only have a vague knowledge, if any at all, of what is actually in the judge's file against them.

After the initial interview, Maître Lamont therefore made it his business to go and consult the file, and Axel went to see him afterwards to discuss the contents. There was of course the psychiatrist's negative report saying both of us were "psychorigid" because we had religious beliefs, and that Axel was "paranoiac" because he denied the accusations against him. For these reasons, the psychiatrist wrote that Axel could not be given custody of Victoria at the moment, and that this situation could only be modified if he admitted to the accusations against him. This report did not seem to surprise Maître Lamont, nor unduly worry him.

The file also revealed that Axel's parents had been given the right to see Victoria every week right from February 1993, without us knowing anything about it. Even Axel's brother René had been given access to Victoria while we were forbidden to see her. He had taken full advantage of the opportunity to spill all the usual accusations against us into the ears of Social Services, who included them – without the slightest proof, of course – in an offical report which was sent to the Court of Appeal.

Worse, Axel's parents had written to the Court of Appeal to dissuade them from even thinking of returning Victoria to us. At the time they were still working hand in glove with UNADFI. Their lawyer – who incidentally was UNADFI's lawyer also – had written to the Court of Appeal as well, to ask them to designate a lawyer for Victoria, i.e. someone the Judiciary would choose to represent Victoria, speak for her, and state her wishes and opinions. From the other families' experience we knew that such lawyers were never impartial – they were carefully chosen by the Judiciary to in fact misrepresent the children, prevent them from expressing themselves freely, and influence them against their parents.

There were several Social Services reports in the file which the lawyer described as *bouillie* ("incomprehensible nonsense"), generally against us, yet often contradictory. Although it was said that Victoria never asked for her Mum or Dad, she would "cry often and sometimes inconsolably", which could only be a sign of the deep distress she felt. She would certainly never have cried like that at home – simply reading about it made us cringe. It didn't make sense either that Victoria could have abnormal "acquired" behaviour yet suddenly behave normally with "other adults" (i.e. her paternal grandparents on visit). When she received cards or letters from us the report said she would sometimes ask for them to be read to her but would usually put them away in a drawer; but then it was later said that she would carry them around with her and even keep them with her during mealtimes. The list went on...

Basically then, we were up against three united opponents: the Public Prosecuting Department, the 'experts' and Social Services who were under the orders of the Judge for Children, and UNADFI and its band of slanderers. They were all working together against our lawyer and ourselves – all "fighting the cult" as they saw it.

We were given a glimmer of hope when Maître Lamont rang to say that he had been speaking to the President of the Court of Appeal, Monsieur Bauer, on the phone, and that he had seemed positive about the outcome of Victoria's case. Perhaps we would soon be picking Victoria up and taking her home, just like Isabelle and Robert had been to take Xavier home just a few weeks before ?

The stage was set for the hearing before the Versailles Court of Appeal, and the date was fixed for 24 February 1994.

Into the corridors of the Court of Appeal

The Court of Appeal was a much older building than the huge, impressive *Tribunal de Grande Instance*, in fact it used to serve as the *Ecurie du Roi* (the King's Stables). Tucked away in a smaller Louis XIV-style street of Versailles, we walked over a cobbled court-yard on that wet, blustery February morning before climbing a wooden staircase to the first floor. The stairs were worn and unvarnished, and the paint on the walls was coming off in places. We were surprised to find an American pastor from a church in Paris there, who we had come to know over the past year. It warmed our hearts to find him there and we prayed together briefly in the stairs before going in. Chamber no. 9 was a wood-panelled court room, though a little forlorn-looking because it was totally empty. The hearing was taking place in *huis clos* (a private hearing) that day, so we were shown into a little, long, narrow, back room where the three judges awaited us behind wide desks, Monsieur Bauer, the President, in the centre, and his two counsellors on either side, taking up most of the long back wall opposite us.

Monsieur Bauer was in his fifties, with a very red face and some sort of blistery skin problem. He also had a very distracting, irregular tic which screwed up one eye and made him look as though he were either winking or wincing. The counsellor on the

President's left, just opposite us, was a strict-looking woman in her mid-fifties, with black hair pulled tightly back and worn up in a bun. She never spoke. The other counsellor really looked past retirement age, a very elderly gentleman who seemed to sleep through most of the hearing.

The only other people present were two Social Services representatives whom we had never seen before, seated immediately on our left opposite the elderly counsellor: the Director of Versailles Social Services, and Victoria's pre-school educator within Social Services. Finally, at the far left-hand end of the room, with the Social Services on his right and the judges on his left, was the Public Prosecutor.

Maître Lamont was asked to speak first. I had not met him before: a kindly-looking man in his mid-fifties, with a gravelly voice and a quietly discerning way about him in spite of his business-like manner. We knew that as far as he was concerned, it was an open and shut case. All the evidence of Victoria's well-being was there, and he would be arguing it to the full. The fact that we had not let ourselves be pulled into the traps set by Social Services actually made his job easier, though it had undoubtedly set Social Services against us.

He spoke of Axel being innocent until proven guilty.

"May I respectfully remind the court that although he is indicted, M. Schmidt must at present be presumed innocent of the accusations against him. As his lawyer, I see no reason why the investigations underway should lead to his conviction. Above all, nobody has ever reproached M. Schmidt, or anybody else for that matter, with any misconduct regarding his daughter Victoria."

Everyone was listening in silence.

"As for the psychiatric report by a certain Dr … Moreno," continued Maître Lamont, "the term psycho rigid has been applied to M. and Mme Schmidt, which I can well understand, since that is how a psychiatrist views anybody holding any kind of faith. What astounds me, though, is that Dr Moreno allows himself to make a judgement about M. and Mme Schmidt's religion, in spite of the fact that France is undoubtedly a democracy, where everyone has the right to their personal religious beliefs. What's more, when M. Schmidt defended his religious beliefs and refused to deny them, or to say he was guilty of the accusations of misconduct which he has constantly denied, Dr Bitoun called him a "paranoiac". These, your Honour, are judgements brought against my clients solely because of their religious beliefs, and are therefore unacceptable."

The judges were making notes. I was beginning to feel a little more at ease. At last here was someone who knew how to cut through the Judiciary's speculations and prejudice!

"The file I present to you today, Your Honour, proves that Victoria was perfectly well brought up by her parents and in excellent health, and also shows their good character. I have testimonies here from many different people – including neighbours, a doctor, an army colonel, a priest – as well as from Madame Schmidt's family in New Zealand – which all testify to this. More concretely, M. and Mme Schmidt have produced a set of photographs of Victoria from since she was a baby until her withdrawal shortly after her 3rd birthday, showing how healthy and happy she was and the loving care her parents gave her –"

"Are these originals, Maître Lamont?" the President of the Court interrupted him. "Photocopies won't do, you know, we've had problems with photocopies…" But how could we have given them the originals – we wouldn't ever have been able to use them again in our defense !

"These are perfectly valid colour photocopies of the originals, Mr President," answered Maître Lamont authoritatively, and continued on. "Even more importantly, little Victoria's health book shows that she had been given regular health checks by her paediatrician and that all vaccinations were up to date. Now, I have seen a great many health books in my time, Mr President, but never have I seen "*superbe enfant*" written in any of them – yet that is what the paediatrician wrote concerning Victoria on 22 December 1992. And finally, we have the medical certificate and testimony written by Victoria's paediatrician on 23 February and 23 July 1993, stating his stupefaction at Victoria's withdrawal and his concern at the prolongation of her placement in State care. I therefore submit that all these are extremely important pieces of evidence showing little

· Victoria's excellent living conditions and up-bringing, and I request that she be immediately and unconditionally returned to her parents' care."

Then it was our turn. I had so many things I wanted to say about Victoria, but the President of the Court asked me a legal question – why we hadn't appealed the Judge for Children's first decision on 12 February 1993. I was feeling too emotional to think legal.

"Victoria was… she was so special, like a gift to us," I said. "We are absolutely horrified that at only three years of age she has been made to go through what no child should suffer – being torn from a normal, loving family from one day to the next and plunged into a totally foreign environment. For three years we did all we could for her, we gave her our love, our care, and all our attention, and this is how we are rewarded! It is urgent that she be returned to us, Mr President."

Axel briefly explained the legal situation, especially emphasizing that because we were anxious for Victoria to return home as soon as possible, we had decided against lodging an appeal in February, which would have taken four to six months at least, and in favour of applying directly to the Judge for Children for her return, as the law allowed, with the proof of Victoria's excellent up-bringing in hand.

At one stage the very elderly counsellor on the far side of the President seemed to liven up, nudging the President with his elbow.

"He has a point there, do you not think, Mr President ?"

"What ? What are you talking about, Counsellor?" asked the President.

"His legal argument," persisted the old man. "He's got a point there."

"Oh. You think so," muttered the President. Obviously, the old counsellor's opinion didn't count for much. The old fellow looked away and dropped his head again. He must have been invited just to make up the numbers.

The question of visiting rights came up, but when we explained that it was for Victoria's sake that we had refused them, the judges stopped asking questions.

Our defence swept aside

They turned to the Director of Versailles Social Services.

"I received Victoria when she arrived with us on 10 February and I have followed her progress since then," he started off. "On her arrival she was like a child from another planet. Her face was pale and expressionless, void of emotion, she was limp as a rag-doll, she never reacted to anything, she didn't even defend herself, she was incapable of playing with other children or showing affection, and she never asked for her parents: all of which are signs of acquired behaviour. Yet she becomes a very normal little girl with her paternal grandparents. We have had her for a year now and she is doing very well. I think she should stay with us. We *must* think of her psychological well-being."

Victoria's teacher took up where he left off.

"At pre-school, Victoria is not very bright. She only draws sticks and bars… If she spills paint on the floor she gets into a panic. She delights in pinching the other children, and she is obviously used to telling tales on others. She even lies down contentedly in the guinea-pig cage. Yet she does talk very well for a three-year-old and has a good range of vocabulary. The strange thing is that she never mentions her parents, never asks for them. When she was asked if she wanted to see her Mum and Dad, her exact words were: 'I want to see Mum and Dad but not at home.' "

Maître Lamont strongly contested that such behaviour was 'acquired'. Axel said that nothing Social Services had said corresponded in any way to what Victoria was like at home.

"You talk about the year she has spent with you," I said, "What about the three happy years she spent with us, her parents! With us, Victoria knew her letters, she was great at drawing and colouring-in and was almost reading words before she was taken. She loved playing with her kitten and would never have hurt anyone. As for wanting to see her Mum and Dad, but not at home, it just doesn't make sense – for a three-year-old child, 'Mum and Dad' and 'home' are simply one and the same thing!"

"Exactly," brought in Maître Lamont. "And I can perfectly understand why a little girl like Victoria cannot bring herself to speak of her parents – it is obviously the most painful subject for her to talk about and hurts far too much to even mention unless she has to. It was natural that she appeared lost at first and didn't react like other children. Most children in care come from broken homes and are probably happy to be there, but imagine what it is like for a little girl who has always been happy with her parents: she was in a state of shock – pained and bewildered at being separated from her Mum and Dad who had always been there for her."

But the President was suddenly impatient to hear the Public Prosecutor. All eyes turned to the far end of the room. The Prosecutor spoke slowly and deliberately.

"Victoria was not in physical danger with her parents," he began. "But we must think of this case within the context of the "cult", where children are kept inside and cut off from the world, resulting in an educational imbalance... Victoria was therefore in grave psychological danger. Moreover, Monsieur and Madame Schmidt have shown no respect for judges' decisions – they refuse to understand that they are not on the right path, that the Judiciary is there to help them and that they should therefore submit to the Judiciary. The Court should confirm the Judge for Children's decision and keep the child Victoria in State care."

Maître Lamont asked how a child could have been kept inside all the time when there were many photos of her outside, as well as corroborating testimonies... but the hearing was obviously considered to be over. The Court were set to issue their ruling on 17 March 1994.

Axel made a last appeal:

"Mr President, we are a normal family, and all we ask you is to return our child to normality."

Maître Lamont was indignant at the way we had been treated. On the way out, handing the file to the President of the Court, he said with force:

"Monsieur and Madame Schmidt do not wish to visit their daughter in *prison*."

He had grasped the heart of the matter: our daughter was a prisoner in State care.

9

In limbo
March 1994 – January 1995

The Court of Appeal accuses

In spite of Maître Lamont's apparently positive telephone conversation with Monsieur Bauer before the hearing, we were not too optimistic about the outcome of the Court of Appeal hearing. We couldn't bear to give up hope, but we felt it would take a miracle for anything worthwhile to come of it. The Court had not seemed interested in hearing what we had to say or the evidence we had to give them, and the Public Prosecutor and Social Services were formidable opponents. UNADFI's lawyer, acting for Axel's parents, had already intervened in the case, and after Isabelle and Robert's success with little Xavier and the ensuing outcry in the media, we had little doubt that UNADFI would be doing everything possible to prevent Victoria from being returned to us. Then there were people like Axel's brother René, who had done everything he could to persuade the Court to rule against us.

It was hard to imagine those three judges holding out against all that pressure. The odds were strongly against Monsieur Bauer, a lady judge and an old counsellor standing up to the Public

Prosecuting Department, Social Services and pressure from a lobby group like UNADFI and their associates. The Court had already been severely criticized in the press for returning little Xavier to his home and family, however right that decision was – it did not fit in with the French Government's policy on "cults", as expressed by the Public Prosecutor at the hearing.

On March 17, the day the ruling was due to come out, we rushed to the Court to be able to see it straight away, instead of waiting to receive it by post. I vaguely remember that it was a rainy end-of-winter day, but in those days we hardly noticed. Time itself seemed to have stopped for us since this legal battle had begun for Victoria. Even the seasons seemed to pass us by like the scenery in some enormous theatre. We were too busy with the action to notice.

This time we were directed to the administrative centre of the Court of Appeal, just inside the cobbled courtyard, where two secretaries were typing away full time. We weren't allowed to make any copies, just read and take notes. Although we had known the decision could go either way, we read it in disbelief, and in spite of the two secretaries being there we couldn't help a few incredulous exclamations. Then these gave way to furious writing as we worked together to note down the important passages.

Far from giving us any hope, the Court of Appeal went even further than the Judge for Children, to the point of questioning even whether Victoria was our own child, since Social Services alleged that she had never asked for her Mum or Dad, and that her mind was "unclear" as to her immediate family ! Just what were they accusing us of ? Once again, we were tongue-tied by the injustice of the French justice system. We could not believe that they could rule so wantonly against all the evidence.

I went home in a daze. It seemed that every judgement, every psychiatric or Social Services report was something like being hit repeatedly over the head with a stick. My mind was groggy to start with but when it started to sink in indignation took over. That evening we arrived home exhausted to the big, silent apartment where we had spent so many happy moments with Victoria. The world seemed completely upside down. In the days that followed we were once again turning the whole thing over in our minds, talking it out, praying. We now had a Court of Appeal decision against us. Had we really gone wrong somewhere ? Why was God allowing this to happen to us – and to Victoria, an innocent child caught up in the tangle of the French judicial machine ? Axel, for his part, was determined to show up the injustice of it, and spent his spare time writing a 10-page commentary of the court judgement as well as a comparative analysis of Robert and Isabelle's ruling and ours. The Court had criticized us for any and everything, whatever the reasons behind our actions; they had used anything they could against us even if it meant going against the law, on the presumption of innocence, for example; and nothing of all the proof in our favour was taken into account.

There was an enormous contradiction between the Court of Appeal judgement rendered on January 20 for Robert and Isabelle, and ours on March 17. The original accusations in the 12 February 1993 judgement against Robert and Isabelle had been the same as those against us, as were the accusations about little Xavier being "pale, limp, expressionless" on his arrival in State care (no mention was made of the fact that he had been taken from his mother by force that day while at least four policemen held her down and kept her quiet). Robert and Isabelle had also refused to "collaborate" with Social Services or even a psychologist, but like us they had excellent health certificates and other proof. The Court had simply taken the evidence of his well-being with his parents into account and ruled fairly and logically for Xavier's return.

In our case, the magistrates had decided to set aside almost identical evidence because they simply did not want to return Victoria to us. The 'cult' theory had to be upheld, and be seen to be upheld.

The Court of Appeal had unwittingly given us one important piece of information: we now knew where Victoria was being held in State care. Axel's parents had happened to mention it in their letter to the Court President, Monsieur Bauer. So why shouldn't we try to contact her ourselves somehow, or even attempt to just take her and get out of the country ? We felt compelled to go and have a look at the place, but all you could see was a huge front wall and an immense building, quite a distance back from the road. Most importantly, there was a guard patrolling the entry. Well, what if I tried to get a job in the place – as a cleaner or something, anything…but then they would of course check who I was and find out. Crazy ideas, but we were in a crazy situation.

Now we truly felt in limbo – the Court of Appeal had torn our hopes of winning the legal battle for custody of Victoria. Our nerves and emotions were being stretched to the limit. It was very difficult to carry on with the normal everyday tasks of life. The shops were a place I only ran in and ran out of – who cared what we ate. I remember the feeling of horror when I saw once that they were giving out roses for Mother's Day. I could feel the tears building up, but thankfully Axel was with me that day and I hid behind him. He took the rose for me and I got out of the shop without even looking at the man behind the counter. I put it in a vase beside the typewriter, to remind me that I was still a mother…

Time after time we were brought back to the need to simply persevere and believe that God would not leave us "desolate"[1]. Along with the other families we encouraged each other over the phone with such promises. Many of us had read books by the Romanian pastor Richard Wurmbrand, and one of the lessons he learnt had stuck in my mind: when your situation really seems hopeless, that's when you can really start to hope that God will intervene

Where to after the Court of Appeal ?

We asked for a meeting with Maître Lamont. After finding our way to his small but comfortable consultation office in a leafy little street in Versailles, we were welcomed by a disappointed Maître Lamont. His experience of Versailles judges had told him that we could have had either an excellent judgement, or a very sick one. Monsieur Bauer was well known for being unpredictable.

Maître Lamont was very much aware of the emotional rollercoaster we had been on since February 1993. He was also convinced that Victoria should be returned to us, and he was still determined to do anything he could about it. The humanity of his approach was a welcome contrast to the many cold, impersonal interviews with lawyers we had faced over the last few months. It was no small

[1] Psalm 34:22

consolation to have a lawyer we felt we could trust taking charge of Victoria's case. However, we now had a Court of Appeal decision against us. Where could we go from here ?

The Judiciary had set the case up in such a way that it made our struggle to regain custody of Victoria extremely difficult. Maître Lamont's view was that unfortunately he could not see how anything more could be done for Victoria until Axel's case had been heard. The Court of Appeal had used the fact that Axel was indicted as a reason not to return Victoria to us (legally he should have been presumed innocent until proven guilty), and this meant that in practice, Victoria's case now depended on the outcome of Axel's case. In other words, they were using the accusations against Axel as a reason to keep Victoria. We had had no news of how the *instruction* was progressing, or of how long it would be until there was a hearing, so Victoria's case seemed to be indefinitely postponed.

However, we did have some news that day for Maître Lamont from a very different direction. My mother's New Zealand M.P., Mr Max Bradford, was due to travel to France on business, and had said that during his stay he would be willing to meet with different people concerned with Victoria's case in an attempt to make some headway. Would Maître Lamont be able to meet with him, give him information about the file, his opinion on the case and answer any questions he may have ? It was agreed that we would meet at the New Zealand Embassy on 22 March 1994. Abbé Hamelin had agreed to be there too, to present his knowledge of the situation in France to Mr Bradford.

The meeting with Mr Bradford at the New Zealand Embassy lasted around two hours, mostly because an interpreter was needed for both Maître Lamont and Abbé Hamelin. We felt that Mr Bradford should be pushing for Victoria to be returned home, but it was evident from the outset that Mr Bradford, unsurprisingly, was following his party's line that we must start implementing our visiting rights. It was a line the Ambassador had been feeding us (directly from the French Ministry of Justice) for a considerable time already. Such insistence sometimes made us wonder whether perhaps we were wrong after all, perhaps it really was just as simple

and straightforward as the French authorities were making out...
We wouldn't have been opposed to the idea of visiting rights if it
had been clear that they were intended to eventually lead to
Victoria's return. Unfortunately, from our meetings with Social
Services we knew that the idyllic picture of a happy, return home
after a series of visits was only a mirage.

As far as visits went, the other families' experiences were a
reality that brought us down to earth with a bump. They had seen
their children after they had been set up and turned against their
parents by Social Services. They had seen them contemptuous of
their parents and their Christian up-bringing, vindictive because their
parents wouldn't "do what the judge said", i.e. abandon their
religious beliefs. The children were obviously under enormous
pressure themselves to do and say exactly what they were told
by Social Services or the judge. These were the people who ruled
the children's lives now – what choice did they have ? Their
parents were powerless to help them escape the clutches of the
State.

Attempting to explain this to Mr Bradford was hopeless. He
seemed to think we were just being difficult. He had been told by
the French Judiciary that the case would only go forward if visits
were started. In fact, they were hoping he would put enough
pressure on us to get us started into a process which would really be
the beginning of the end as far as Victoria and ourselves were
concerned.

Mr Bradford did obtain one thing for us – a promise that the
Judge for Children had a "solution" to propose. It sounded like the
"final solution" ! It was true that there had already been cases where
UNADFI had pushed people to commit suicide or some such
desperate action, and I'm sure that would have suited the Judiciary
only too well. Imagine the newspaper headings: "Cult member
suicide", for example. Well, we wanted to be able to tell Mr
Bradford exactly what "solution" was on offer here. So we returned
to see Mme Durand – again. It was 6 May 1994. You never knew,
we told ourselves – that judge could change everything with just
one piece of paper.

Mme Durand was not so disposed.

"If Monsieur and Madame Schmidt are not prepared to change their life-style," she said, "nothing else will change."

"Exactly how do we need to change our life-style, *Mme le Juge* ?" I asked. "Victoria was perfectly well looked after physically, and I don't believe you are accusing us of having bad moral standards."

"No, no, no," the Public Prosecutor Mademoiselle Cornil dismissed this with a gesture.

"Monsieur and Madame Schmidt, you are not fourth-world citizens," the judge took up again (she meant we weren't among the poor and destitute). "You are intelligent enough to understand me."

We understood all right – first of all that it was the poor and destitute she was used to dealing with. We had heard how the French Judiciary was in the habit of removing children from the homes of poor people, usually immigrants, who had nothing but their children left – making their situation even worse.

And we understood all right, what she didn't want to spell out. We were supposed to give up our religious beliefs and turn against our church, our friends and the truth. We tried to ask her to be more specific – what *exactly* was it that we had to change in our life-style? But she refused to answer the question and we were sent out while she looked at other business – to give us time to think it over.

Since when did any judge have the right to criticize someone's personal life-style, if there was nothing legally wrong with it ? How could the Judiciary keep Victoria from us for a reason they were not even willing to spell out ? We seemed to be once again at a dead end.

Back to work ?

Meanwhile, I had had a successful interview with the Private Schools Administrative Centre in Versailles around the beginning of May, and had been told by the interviewer, himself a secondary school principal, that if any vacancies came up, he would not hesitate in contacting me. As it happened, he rang me himself a few weeks later, to ask if I could replace an English teacher in his own school who was off on leave. Although I did have two other job offers which would have kept me in work for the rest of the term, I felt a little obliged towards Monsieur Arboux, and decided I would help him out. As a private school, I hoped it would have good discipline and I was not disappointed. I had been broken in to secondary school teaching and was determined not to let myself be walked over ! I was welcomed and shown very courteously round the school by Monsieur Arboux himself, everything was arranged for me to start the following day and I tried to settle down to the teaching routine.

However, I arrived on the morning of my third day of teaching to find the principal's secretary waiting for me. I had left home at around 7:30 a.m. to get to school on time, allowing for traffic jams. My route lay along the edge of the Seine river for a good way and I enjoyed the drive, although it could sometimes become a bit tedious if the morning traffic was bad, and there was an old stone bridge to cross which was beautiful to look at but created a considerable bottleneck.

The traffic had been bad that morning, and when I finally arrived there were only ten minutes or so remaining until the start of class, so I was rather surprised (and a little annoyed) when the secretary informed me that Monsieur Arboux wanted to see me. I could only hope that he wasn't going to keep me for long. I was shown into his office where he introduced me to a Madame Tessier, the vice-principal, whom I had never seen before. I was starting to worry. Why were there two people to see me ? Had something serious happened?

Monsieur Arboux must have noticed that I was becoming concerned.

"Madame Schmidt," he started, "We need to talk to you about a rather annoying matter."

I could only wonder what on earth had happened. His next words froze me.

"We have just learned that you belong to a 'cult' and that your child has been removed from your care by the Judiciary. In such conditions, we regret that we cannot keep you in our establishment."

I was shocked. I didn't really take in the meaning of his words. I had been made to feel very welcome in the school and felt I was integrating well. I was putting care and effort into my teaching and doing the best job I could, although with Victoria's situation constantly in the back of my mind, it wasn't always easy. And then Monsieur Arboux himself had specifically wanted me to do this job. They couldn't really mean it...

I asked them who had told them *that* story. Mme Tessier seemed to be more convinced than Monsieur Arboux about what they were doing.

"*Obviously*, we can't tell you that, Mme Schmidt," she said with an ironic smile.

I went cold all over.

"It's not true, you know," I said. "I can show you proof that my daughter was perfectly healthy and well-developed. It was wrong to take her away from us. Her paediatrician, who had followed her since she was a baby, wrote in her health book that she was a "*superbe enfant*", and has drawn up health certificates stating that he was "stupefied" to learn of her removal. The judge had absolutely no good reason to ..."

"Mme Schmidt, a Judge for Children is never wrong," said Monsieur Arboux, with a condescending little smile.

"Travesties of justice do happen, Monsieur Arboux," I insisted.

"But not in children's cases," declared Monsieur Arboux. "Children's services always do everything they can to keep children with their rightful parents. No, no, there is a court ruling against you removing your child from your care. Given that, I cannot keep you here as a teacher."

"But you haven't any proof of all this," I exclaimed. "I contest the judge's decision and you can't dismiss me, since I haven't done anything wrong ! All this is a purely private matter, and has nothing to do with my work. At least let me show you the proof in my favour. Then you will be in a position to judge for yourself."

There was a short silence. Mme Tessier was looking at me with a show of pity. There was, *obviously*, no help to be had in turning to her.

"It's no use showing me what you call proof, Mme Schmidt," continued Monsieur Arboux. "That is a matter for the Judge for Children. And I am not questioning your ability as a teacher, or your work, or your conduct. Before I was informed of this matter, I had the highest opinion of you. But I cannot risk being accused of supporting a 'cult'."

Mme Tessier took over.

"You talk of proof," she said. "But in fact you were putting your child at risk of psychological danger."

"What psychological danger ?" I asked, rather heatedly.

She just shrugged in response, ignored me and went on.

"Everybody knows that cults send their adepts to places like schools to infiltrate them and proselytize those you come in contact with. I have information from unquestionable sources. What's more, your husband is accused of ill-treating two boys... if you want to keep your job, you should separate from him."

I knew then that they weren't going to change their minds. Mme Tessier had obviously been in touch with UNADFI or the judge or someone like that. The way she talked sounded exactly like the judge for children herself. It was too much. My emotions spilled over.

"So not only has a rumour taken my daughter away from me, now it's taking my work ! I can't believe this is happening..."

I couldn't hold back tears, and Monsieur Arboux looked embarrassed.

"All you have to do is withdraw," he said. Of course he didn't say what I was supposed to withdraw from – withdraw from a church to get my job back ?

"If your child is returned to you," he went on, "I will be able to reconsider the situation."

He may have intended to sound reconciliatory, but he was only making things worse. I couldn't believe how his attitude had changed so completely, so hypocritically. To think I had gone to that school at his request

I stumbled out of the school to the car. I had been fired, and in such a harsh, abrupt way that I was left absolutely stunned. I couldn't stem the tears, even as I drove. Never had I been treated in such a way. Humiliated, tormented by these false accusations, pressured from every direction to give in and do what was wrong. I felt very sore and bruised about it, but strangely, I felt no inclination to give in. God alone must have kept me – or made me naturally very stubborn. It was still a painful experience. Once again I was learning not to count on people, however pleasant they may seem. Unless moved by God, our human nature is very fickle.

I did telephone the following day to ask Monsieur Arboux for a letter stating his reasons for dismissing me. He was even more contemptuous on the phone than he had been in person. He bluntly told me that I would never get another job in the private school sector anyway, and finished by hanging up. It would have been useless and expensive to take him to court – Maître Lamont told us he would be judged by his own colleagues, the *Conseil des Prudhommes*, and nobody doubted that they would rule against me. We could do nothing about it. I would just have to concentrate on my evening classes.

In fact, my experience in work was only a reflection of what we all suffered to a greater or lesser degree. Richard was among the worst affected by slander, losing thousands of pounds in lost contracts, and contacts who suddenly didn't want to hear from him anymore. René especially had been introduced to many of Richard's contacts for his own benefit, and knew who to talk to so as to cause maximum damage. He also used the press to the full to slander Richard. It got to the point that Richard and Anutza's home in the Paris suburbs was actually sold by auction because they lost so much work and were no longer able to pay their mortgage. Their daughter Lydia and her friends, who had formed a chamber music quartet and trio, were constantly harrassed by slander that seemed to follow them wherever they went. As soon as publicity went out with their names on it, they seemed doomed to eventual refusals or cancellations. One lawyer that Axel met with later confirmed that this was a common strategy employed by UNADFI to destroy those that they were opposed to. Apparently the slander business was doing well.

One child disappears, another appears, and several disagree

With persecution mounting and media attacks continuing, Robert and Isabelle decided they were not going to risk having a *Cour de Cassation* (French Supreme Court) decision against them. They disappeared towards the end of May, before the hearing even took place, taking their youngest son Xavier with them.

We only knew that it must have been a hard decision for them to take: their three elder children were still placed with the maternal grandparents, and fleeing France meant that they might not see those three again for years. Yet how could they stand by and watch the Supreme Court rule that their fourth child should be taken from them yet again and placed back into State care in spite of the harm that had already done him ? We could only sympathize with their concern and with their action. There was no mercy to be had from the French Judiciary, we were certain of that. As we had expected, the *Cour de Cassation* rushed the case through and overturned the Court of Appeal decision, which meant that Xavier should legally have been returned to State care.

By June we were also facing a dilemma. I was expecting our second baby, and in our circumstances we knew that it was extremely risky to have her born in France, where she could be snatched from us practically as soon as she was born on the same grounds as Victoria.

We were not attempting to replace Victoria – she was our first child and her own special person, impossible to imitate or replace. It was true that suddenly being deprived of being a mother was extremely distressing : the empty arms, the listening for noises that no longer came, the gradual shelving of all our plans and projects for Victoria… This little one would never be Victoria, but she would still be our child, special in her own way. And we could not help feeling that perhaps in some way this new little baby might be able to help us bring Victoria home, though we had no idea how or when.

We decided that it would be better for me to move to a completely different area of France during the pregnancy, and we were very glad when I was able to find work with a private English language-teaching company in Annecy, a well-to-do town in the French Alps of Haute Savoie in the east of France, not far from a well-known ski resort. We found a quaint little apartment with French windows facing the Alps, and I could walk to and from work or take a bus if the weather was bad, and still earn enough to pay my way and save a little.

Axel couldn't leave his work commitments in Paris, so it did mean a fair amount of coming and going between the two (we were 300 miles apart), but the express train only took two or three hours, and we usually saw each other at the weekend. Both of us were very taken up with our work, but when we could be together we tried to make up for quantity with quality time. The old part of Annecy was charming, and we have beautiful memories of strolling through the old town, over cobbled pedestrian streets lined with stone arches, behind which the shop windows appeared even more appealing. After a meal we would walk around the canal or down by the lake, often thinking how Victoria would love it there. If only…

I was thankful that I had other friends not too far away. Anutza had in fact moved to the Ain district two years before – also in an attempt to get away from the harrassment in Paris. Another friend had found teaching work in the area and a flat in the Jura mountains (though she was teaching school children) and we were all able to get together fairly often, even if it meant an hour's drive. Circumstances meant that we had all drifted apart geographically, though in every other way we were still very close.

Meanwhile, back in Versailles Judge Durand had resigned in September 1994 and had been replaced by a Judge Barnier. Since we had never met this new judge, and also because we were expecting another child, which would usually have been considered an important new development in a Children's Court case, we immediately asked for a hearing with her. Mme Barnier refused categorically though, simply telling us we would have to wait until the next hearing was due, in June or July 1995.

Everything depended on the outcome of Axel's case. He had been questioned only once by the examining judge in August 1993, and then "confronted" with the children in May 1994. Both times he had clearly denied any wrong-doing, and during the confrontation the children had contradicted each other and themselves. One minute Axel was supposed to be a monster who beat other people's children mercilessly (so the story went), and the next the children were saying that he would have often made them laugh, or answered that no, they weren't afraid of him, etc.

Although the confrontation with the children had seemed to prove that there was nothing against Axel, we now learnt that their statements were getting worse, and that the accusations were growing even wilder. Things were building up and we knew the climax was liable to be extremely twisted, if the French Judiciary had their way.

The trial approaches

In the month preceding the trial, we had noticed that UNADFI was intensifying the media campaign against us. Articles appeared in national newspapers and even a telefilm was specially prepared with the assistance of UNADFI, concentrating on the issue of children in "cults" and broadcast on prime-time national television.

Suddenly Axel received a summons for 18-19 January 1995, less than a month before the hearing was due to take place, and there was not enough time to summon witnesses for the defence. The Judiciary was now rushing the case into the trial stage.

The examining judge had never granted me a hearing, so I wrote to ask her for one (I was a vital witness to the case concerning Axel, since I could testify that the accusations against Axel were false), but the judge dismissed my request and pressed on for the case to be referred to court for trial.

By this stage he and Anutza and Rebecca had engaged two lawyers, brother and sister, to represent all three of them. These lawyers were supposed to confront the media efficiently so as to oppose the slanderous campaign which had been orchestrated for years by UNADFI as well as fighting the case in court (Maître Lamont had agreed to this change of lawyer).

Christmas 1995 came and went. We once again sent Victoria her presents and were continuing to write to her regularly. I worked through Christmas except for Christmas day, and almost preferred it that way, since work at least took my thoughts off the pending cases and Christmas itself.

I had thought I was putting on a fairly good front at work, but the secretary there asked me one day if I was OK – she said she had lost her little daughter to cancer a few years ago, she knew what it was like to live through something difficult, and that if I wanted to talk about it, she would be there to listen. I just thanked her, but I was really touched. I couldn't have said a thing, the tears were too close.

And I didn't want this monstrous thing to get into my life at work – I was hanging on to the idea of being able to keep work as a place where I could pretend that everything was normal. Yet apparently to observant eyes, it was obvious that everything was not…

As January 18 approached, tension levels rose. Though I knew that God had His hand upon all these proceedings, I was anxious not to fall into any of the French Judiciary's traps as we seemed to have done in February 1993. Concerned for the little unborn one I was now responsible for, I finally decided to take the day off work on the 18th and travel to Geneva by bus – about an hour-long trip. If the worst came to the worst, at least I would be outside France and out of reach of the French Judiciary. I kept in touch with what was going on in Versailles by phoning friends who were themselves getting news from Lydia in Paris from time to time. All very complicated…

Not only had the Court left very little time for the defence to call their witnesses, but they had also not summoned Axel according to law. He informed his lawyers of this and they decided that they would ask for the hearing to be postponed.

The hearing was to take place at the *Tribunal de Grande Instance* in Versailles once again, but this time in the old building, on the opposite side to where the Judge for Children's offices were. The Court was full, with over 100 people present, including a few reporters, though no cameras. It was obvious that the majority of those present had been assembled by UNADFI, since Mme Beauchamp, UNADFI's president, was coming and going amongst them constantly. Only one television journalist had come at the request of the defence lawyers. She remarked to Abbé Hamelin, faithfully present once again, that she had "never come across such an atmosphere of hate". It must have been very obvious that the supporters of UNADFI were determined to rout the 'cult'. This crowd were not going to like it if the hearing was postponed. They were like the spectators in the old Roman amphitheatres, when they watched Christians being thrown to the lions – they wanted blood, and they wanted it straight away.

While the lawyers were being kept in suspense about the post-ponement question, Axel was called upon to come forward to the front of the court and asked to give his home address. He had moved out of our flat shortly before and had been staying in a friend's flat whenever he was in Paris. He had already given his professional address in Paris, but he did not want to give our home address in Annecy because of the harrassment we had experienced in the past from people spying on us, ringing the doorbell continuously, or late at night, etc. He didn't want me, alone and pregnant, having problems in Annecy, so he had given the court his professional address in Paris. The Public Prosecutor Mlle Cornil was now objecting that this address was not valid because it was not a residential address. It gave Axel a golden opportunity to denounce publicly, in front of the Court, the activities of UNADFI.

"I refuse to give my personal address because we have been constantly harrassed by UNADFI at home over the past years. If I give my address, there is nothing to stop UNADFI from harrassing us once again."

The President of the Court was left speechless. Mlle Cornil stared at Axel with rage in her face, furious that Axel had dared to denounce UNADFI.

From their places just behind him, Axel's lawyers were pressing him to comply and give his address anyway (they didn't want anything to prevent a postponement).

"Well, I will give you my address on the condition that we are not submitted to renewed attacks, and I hope the Judiciary will take all necessary measures to protect us in the future," Axel finished by saying.

Eventually the defence was not denied the right to call witnesses, and the trial was postponed until February 8-9.

I returned home to Annecy from Geneva exhausted from the stress. The climax of our battle with the French justice system was just three weeks away, but at least it would be in the presence of witnesses in favour of Axel, Rebecca and Anutza.

10

A parody of justice
February 8 – 9, 1995

The trial

If the atmosphere of the courtroom had been discouraging on January 18, it was openly biased on the afternoon of February 8. There wasn't even an attempt towards an appearance of justice. From the very beginning, the President of the Court Monsieur Breton, set the tone for the whole proceedings.

Monsieur Breton was supposed to summarize the case and allow for a contradictory debate between the prosecution and the defence. Instead, he launched into a series of accusations against the defendants as though he were a Public Prosecutor, presenting the accused in an extremely odious way. For example, according to this judge members of the church used to give food to their children "just as you would throw bananas to chimps". Nobody knew where he got such an outrageous accusation from. Maître Louis Devillecourt, for the defence, immediately interrupted the President and requested that the President's words be noted verbatim by the court clerk. Monsieur Breton hesitated for a moment before asking the court clerk to comply.

After the President's "introduction" it was time to call the witnesses for the prosecution. None of them had anything relevant to say, since most of them were ex-members of the church whom we hadn't seen for several years. Watching them outside the court, where I as a witness also had to wait before testifying, I was acutely aware of a strange hiatus, a missing link between these people who had enjoyed and benefited from their time in the church, and the accusations they were now bringing forward. Of course, they did all say the same thing, UNADFI had seen to that. But it still didn't add up, and of course there wasn't the slightest proof of any misconduct. Nevertheless, not only were their statements accepted by the court without cross-examination, but Monsieur Breton welcomed their "testimonies" and gave them full liberty to once again pour out their slanderous accusations against us. The children who were at the heart of the case against Axel (Paul and David) were strangely absent from court that day, but Monsieur Breton never even questioned this.

When it came to the witnesses for the defence, the whole proceedings really began to look like a farce. As we went in, we didn't have the slightest idea what to expect – like sheep going to the slaughter. It was only once we were inside that we discovered that the trial was being conducted in such a way that the defendants had no hope of trying to prove their innocence, and that we were only there to be made fun of. That was literally what happened.

We all entered by a side door in the left-hand side of the courtroom, on the judges' right. As each witness came in they had to present ID to the court clerk before taking the stand.

Being nearly eight months pregnant, I requested that I be allowed to sit during questioning, which was granted me. As soon as I sat down though, before I had been able to say anything as a "witness", the judge started accusing me of giving false information to the New Zealand press. I asked him what exactly had been said that he was objecting to. Of course he didn't have the exact documents there, so he gestured to the Public Prosecutor to produce them. He fumbled about looking for the bit he wanted to accuse me about, and at last drew out a paper.

"Aha!" he said. "Here we are... Bible-believing church in France that is under severe persecution...no, that's not it..."

Well done, Mr Prosecutor – he could go on reading that all he liked.

But then he pounced. "*Voilà*... 'In a dawn Gestapo-like raid'. You compared a French police intervention to an operation worthy of the Gestapo ?"

My indignation and my voice rose together. "They kidnapped my three-year-old daughter and I haven't seen her since !" Everyone in the room must have heard it.

As I spoke I turned towards the public, a little defiant. And there, only a few feet away from me, were René and Mireille, quite at ease, even looking as though they were enjoying themselves. Apparently whatever I said, whatever anyone said, it was useless.

The rest of the day was like a nightmare. Once we had taken the witness stand, we were permitted to join the public for the remainder of the hearing. The way it was being conducted was unbelievable. One by one, the defence witnesses were called: friends from outside the church, music teachers, other acquaintances. Whatever they said, even if it was just a matter of having played tennis or football with some of the children during the summer holidays, it was systematically denied by the children, in particular Richard and Anutza's twin boys.

I watched them as time after time they left a rowdy crowd of young people at the back to come to the front of the courtroom with apparent bravado and simply say the opposite of what had been testified to. No, we never played tennis with this person. Our witnesses were dumbfounded. And because none of them could know how the hearing was going before entering the courtroom, each one was taken at the same game. It wasn't difficult for the youngsters to do, though I wondered what kind of blackmail had got them to agree to it.

It was heart-rending. I knew those witnesses were saying the truth. I had seen the boys go off to play with them several times myself, joking, questioning, talking about their latest discoveries, whether a film, a book, maths or history. The day they were kidnapped in February 1993, both boys had said they wanted to return home, that all the accusations were lies and that we were just a group of friends who wanted to live our Christian faith. They had been rewarded for that by being separated from each other as well as from their family, and put through a period of "psychological rest" for a month or so. "Brainwashing" would be more like it. By the end of six months they had been turned against their parents, against their Christian up-bringing, and enthusiastic for all the smoking-drinking-plus culture of the French Social Services set-up – as well as being influenced by their own parents' accusers, whom they even went on holiday with. And their statements had gone from bad to worse to wild. This was the end result of the process and it was chilling

Some of our witnesses were quicker to recover and react than others, but whatever they said was then ridiculed by the President. Monsieur Popov, a Hungarian music teacher who had known Lydia and the twins well, stated that he had never seen anything abnormal with the children, that they played very well for children of their age...

"I believe there were people who played beautiful music in Auschwitz as well," remarked the President. The room was silent.

"But I wasn't at Auschwitz, your Honour," replied Monsieur Popov, without batting an eyelid. There were titters amongst the public, in spite of themselves.

When it came to Richard's turn to witness, the crowd of teen-agers practically mocked him out loud and cheered loudly when his own sons lied against him. I turned to Abbé Hamelin.

"What can we do, Abbé ? They've got the children lying against us!"

He shook his head and was silent. Several times during the breaks in proceedings, Abbé Hamelin had been able to speak with the lawyers, and had been astonished at their lethargy. They had made no attempt to reveal any weaknesses or incoherence in the statements made by the witnesses for the prosecution. The President was constantly making references (for all different sorts of reasons) to the tapped telephone conversations, and though there was nothing incriminating in them, the lawyers were doing nothing to point out the insignificance of his remarks. It was frustrating for Abbé Hamelin, who had been told by a magistrate from the Ministry of Justice that there was nothing of any importance in the file – the very same red file that was sitting on the bench in front of the President of the Court. And how could Maître Devillecourt content himself with remarks related by a children's lawyer when Paul and David weren't even there themselves to corroborate it ? For some reason, the lawyers seemed to be holding back. They were paid to do a job and they weren't doing it.

The judges had several times asked Axel, Rebecca and Anutza questions in an attempt to trap them in their words. Consequently both Rebecca and Anutza spoke as little as possible. Axel spoke slightly more in his defence, and with his legal background he was more able to make sure he didn't say anything that could be turned against him, and that the questions were kept to the matters in hand, i.e. the accusations he was being tried for. As the judges realized they were not succeeding in catching him out, they became exasperated.

"We can't get him talking!" the President of the Court complained to Maître Devillecourt.

"You have nothing against me," Axel replied.

Monsieur Breton was nettled.

"Monsieur Schmidt, if we had anything against you in this file, you would have been in prison long ago !" he exploded.

There was a short silence as his outburst resounded through the courtroom. Axel spread his hands with a slight shrug.

"So there is nothing in the file against me," he repeated quietly. His tone seemed to calm the situation a little, and the judge sat in silence for a few moments. But he had admitted what Abbé Hamelin had been told at the Ministry of Justice – there was nothing against the defendants. They should have been released.

The first day of the trial had been reserved for hearing witnesses from both sides, and the second for the different lawyers and the Public Prosecutor. After a wearying, sickening day, the trial was adjourned around 11:00 p.m.

Deliberations

We were staying overnight at a friend's flat in Paris, since the trial was to continue the next day. I had the sofa and Axel had a camp-bed – in the circumstances we hardly noticed where we slept. We had scarcely eaten all day either, but hardly even felt hungry.

It seemed that Axel was almost certain to be convicted. It was a night of weeping for me: weeping for the children, made to condemn their own parents as the world looked on; weeping for the parents, betrayed and condemned by other professed Christians who had once been their friends, who had "walked unto the house of God in company" with them[1]; weeping to God for the injustice of a system that called itself 'just' in the name of 'liberty, equality, fraternity' and for those who pitilessly carried out such iniquity in the place of justice; weeping for Victoria, the unwitting victim caught up in such a system; and for Axel, who tomorrow seemed certain to bear the brunt of these malicious attacks against a Christian church...

Of course, we prayed. Axel was determined to see the thing through to the end, but he didn't want the baby and I in danger. If the worst happened, we decided it would probably be better for me to go home to New Zealand for the birth. At least there I had family and the support of other Christians. It all sounded rather distant to me, like a vague possibility far away in the future. I didn't want to think of where Axel would be if I had to go to New Zealand.

We had the chance to talk things over a little with Anutza (now the *instruction* was over, the defendants were again allowed to be in contact each other). She was apprehensive about the coming day. The lawyers were hoping for suspended sentences, but Anutza was wary. She and Rebecca had been kept in prison for a month back in 1993, and would probably have stayed there much longer if the French Judiciary had had its way. She felt they would get her back there just as soon as they could, and tomorrow they would stand a pretty good chance of doing just that, the way things were going. She was thinking she should perhaps flee the country. How often Christians had done that throughout history. Anutza had fought this to the end, and not been done justice. The only tug at her heart was her boys; but with what we had seen today, there seemed little hope of a reconciliation in the near future. It would only be worse if she was imprisoned... There was the question of how and where to, which nobody had an answer to. The main thing she wanted to know was whether it was the right thing to do.

[1] Psalm 55:13

In the end we had to each make up our own minds. It was clear to Axel and I that we needed first and foremost to protect our unborn child. And that meant leaving France. The kind Parisian gynaecologist, who had been following the pregnancy had told me clearly that he could guarantee the safety of the baby as long as we were in the hospital, but after that, knowing Victoria's story, he could do no more. He was disgusted, but realistic. He was also adamant that whatever the cost, we should protect our second child *and* continue to fight for Victoria. That was where the problem lay. How could I continue to ask for Victoria to be returned to me if I wasn't even in France ? And what would happen to Axel ?

Axel was most concerned about the baby. If he was imprisoned, he said it would be better if I was away in New Zealand, then they couldn't put pressure on him, or on me, and above all they wouldn't be able to touch the baby. We could only pray and trust God to keep us right.

I must have got some rest that night in spite of my weeping, for I woke refreshed. A verse that an American friend had given us some time before came back to me in a new way:

"Thou wilt keep him in perfect peace, whose mind is stayed on thee: because he trusteth in thee." (Isaiah 26:3)

My job was clear – simply trust in the Lord. As for Axel, he had had a word the morning before from Proverbs 1:10 – "My son, if sinners entice thee, consent thou not." He didn't know what this trial held for him, but he was definitely going to be on his guard.

Eleventh hour decisions

There were cameras and photographers all over the entrance hall to the courtroom in Versailles when we came in a little before 2:00 p.m. when the trial was due to start again on 9 February 1995. Axel went straight over to talk with the lawyers.

As I moved away from the crowd down the quieter corridor leading from the older to the newer part of the building (it did help knowing my way around that place), I unexpectedly caught a glimpse of Maître Lamont. He was coming out of a side door of the courtroom where the trial would be starting again in a few minutes, and crossing the corridor to go into another door on the opposite side. We hadn't seen him for a while, since the two Devillecourts had taken over our cases. I only saw his face fleetingly, but it was enough. He was white as a sheet, and haggard. That look told me everything. There was no hope for Axel.

It was perhaps from that moment that my mind was fully made up. Anutza was there, and she had been talking to Axel and the Devillecourts already – whenever there weren't too many journalists around. One of the lawyers had hinted to Axel that he had enough time to get to the border if he wanted to, and Axel had mentioned this to Anutza. All three defendants had been warned several times that the trial would undoubtedly result in prison sentences for all of them. Now Anutza was more sure of what to do.

"Shall we go ?" she asked me.

"I'm for it," I answered.

"I don't know where to," she said.

"Neither do I," I smiled at her, amazed at my own calmness.

Anutza made sure Rebecca was aware of the situation, but Philippe was against the idea of fleeing the country. Anutza talked briefly to a couple of friends. They came very naturally towards us – soon to be our companions in flight.

In the general hubbub I found Axel with the lawyers and Abbé Hamelin. Maître Eveline Devillecourt was talking about the pressure we had told her had been placed on the lawyers we had engaged before them. She hadn't believed us at the time, but now she admitted to the three of us that as soon as she had agreed to defend us, she had come under considerable pressure, such as she had never before known in her career. She obviously didn't want to say where this pressure had come from or what form it had taken.

I was able to tell Axel very quickly what we were thinking of doing. He nodded. We had agreed together that I should get out of the country anyway. It was all decided in a matter of minutes, and all I knew was that Axel and I were both convinced about it. It was not the time for tears or kisses or goodbyes. In fact, it had to look anything but that: we didn't want to raise anyone's suspicions. It all seemed to have been cried over the night before, in anticipation. At the time Anutza and I left, the hearing hadn't even started and our minds were more on getting out of there – and more exactly, where were we to go ?

We walked out through the new part of the building, the opposite side to where we had come in. There was no-one to stop us, not even a police officer on duty. One of our friends had the car waiting just a little further down the street. We stepped in and were gone.

The getaway might have been fast, but the trip seemed to take ages. We didn't really know where we were going, except that it had to be the eastern border somewhere. We talked as we drove, discussing the different possibilities open to us. In the end we phoned a contact who lived just over the border, someone who knew our circumstances and had been sympathetic. We were still going to be very cautious - the memory of betrayal by so-called "friends" was still very fresh in our minds. It was a little difficult meeting up, we were tense and had to be extremely discreet. Eventually, though, this contact helped us over the border at a place where there were no border police, and very kindly took us out for a meal. Once over the border, our tension levels dropped enormously. I was left with a sense of adventure that made our flight quite exciting in a way. That night though, as Anutza and I tried to relax in a quiet little hotel room by ourselves, tension and anxiety hit us again. Where were we to go from here, and what had happened back in Versailles today ?

We couldn't get any news about France ourselves, but during the evening we got a phone call to say that a French radio channel had announced that three members of our church had been convicted. Then it mentioned that two members of the "cult" had fled. That must mean Anutza and I, I thought. So what has happened to Axel ? The next morning we were told that there had been an article in *le Figaro* stating that two women had been convicted. It added that Axel Schmidt had been sentenced *without material proof* – a small consolation that a national newspaper had at least acknowledged that. Sentenced without proof, fine, but he was still sentenced…

Cat and mouse games

Back in the hearing, Monsieur Breton the President had wanted to get proceedings speedily underway. Rebecca and Axel had come in and taken their seats in the courtroom, but somebody remarked that Anutza Antonescu wasn't there.

"We shall start even if Mrs Antonescu is not present," he announced. "I just passed her in the corridor, no doubt she will be in soon."

How God works these things out is amazing ! The man was so sure of himself – and understandably so, in a way, for who would come for the beginning of a trial and then flee the country ? It would have made much more sense to leave the night before.

The trial continued all that afternoon. The Public Prosecutor spoke at some length, our lawyers spoke also, as well as those "representing" the children.

The Public Prosecutor was obviously infuriated with Axel. It was Mlle Cornil, the same woman who had faced us across the Judge for Children's office, when Axel had told them that what they were doing was illegal; and she really had it in for him. She started off by asking the court to imagine what it must have been like for poor little David to find himself at the mercy of Axel Schmidt...etc. The woman should have been a novelist. The job was made even easier for her by the fact that little David wasn't even present at the hearing to back up or question what she said or to be questioned himself.

The defence lawyers' pleading didn't amount to much, nor did they speak even once to the media outside the courtroom in support of the defence (the pressure applied had obviously been effective), but at one stage a young colleague of the Devillecourts started to point out some of the contradictions on different pages of the investigation report. After listening to her for three or four minutes, Monsieur Breton, the President of the Court, interrupted her angrily and upbraided her for even attempting such a thing.

"You are wasting our time," he told her furiously. It seemed that all he wanted to do was get on with this farce of a hearing and get the defendants convicted.

Maître Eveline Devillecourt intervened, but instead of invoking the rights of the defence, she humbly excused her young colleague, on a tone of servile submission.

"Please excuse her, Mr President, she is a very young lawyer, and today is the first time she has ever pleaded in court."

The only argument the defence raised was to ask for an alleviation for parents who had "undoubtedly been demanding but never brutal with their children."

It was the lawyer for the civil parties (also the official lawyer for UNADFI) who strangely enough seemed to have the most to say, and the most freedom to say it. Maître Azoulay-Romanov (the name is undeniably quite a mouthful) was "all mouth" that day in every sense. A small, wiry woman with a shock of bright hair, large buck teeth and a large, well-lipsticked mouth which she articulated with much expression, she was certainly in fine militant style, as became a "professional" who had formerly been the lawyer of the French Communist party.

She first made much of the special honour which the association UNADFI had apparently just received from the Ministry of Justice for "services rendered", and pointed out that the court was bound to take into account the fact that UNADFI was a civil party to the case.

Here the President interrupted her oration to say politely, but with some authority,

"Maître, we are not here to discuss this."

"But we are, *Monsieur le President*," insisted Madame Azoulay-Romanov. "This is exactly the place and the circumstances for discussing this, when UNADFI is intervening to preserve the rights of families threatened by a cult…"

And so the President gave in and she was allowed to go on to dictate to the Court what its duty was: simply to convict the members of the 'cult'.

With Axel standing firm, the Judiciary were unleashing their anger against him, determined to crush him.

While Axel was trying to enjoy a moment's peace inside the courtroom during a break in proceedings when everyone usually went out, his brother René came over to him along with a couple of others.

"Come on, Axel, it's all over, you may as well give in."

"Things are going to end badly for you, Axel…"

"You've got to think of your wife and daughter and the little baby, Axel."

"All you have to do is confess, Axel – it's simple, just say it."

"We're ready to help you out if you confess..."

"Come on, Axel... come on... confess... it'll be easy,.. better... we'll help you..."

But Axel had the Bible in his hands. He didn't say a word, didn't even turn his head to look at them.

"My son, if sinners entice thee, consent thou not."

The verse from the previous day came back to him clearly and filled him with a calm confidence.

Suddenly Maître Azoulay-Romanov was there with them, telling the accusers to back off.

"Now you really are harrassing him," she said, obviously worried about appearances, but also slightly embarrassed. Axel was surprised to see it.

But where did God want him to go from here ? That was the question upmost in his mind. Until then, the Lord had always given him an open door, a means of defending himself, a way forward. At the moment, all the doors seemed to be closing and a brick wall lay up ahead.

The trial recommenced, the closing remarks were heard, and then it was time for the judges' deliberations.

"You still have time to get away, Monsieur Schmidt." That was a possibility, he shouldn't rule anything out. But was it good advice ? Perhaps it would only make the situation worse. Perhaps it was even a trap. Axel needed time to think – needed to get away from this place a little.

When the judges retired to deliberate, he headed outside. In the entrance hall he met up with Lydia, very concerned for her mother, sympathizing with her father, pained for her brothers. It was an extremely harrowing situation for a young girl of twenty. She told him that she had spoken to the press... Axel listened as he walked, suddenly feeling in a hurry to get away, out the open doors and down the broad steps of the old Tribunal building. It was already getting dark outside on this cool February day. Probably around 6:30 pm. He left Lydia there on the steps and she turned and went slowly back inside. Axel set off and didn't look back, striding along with his briefcase in hand. He needed a bit of fresh air...

11

Dispersed
February 9 – 28, 1995

God's answer, God's way

Back at the flat in Paris, Axel decided to wait until someone else came back from Versailles – waiting to learn his fate, but out of the Judiciary's grasp for the moment. He waited. And waited. Nobody came. Only Monsieur Popov called, but he had not stayed till the end of the hearing so knew no more than Axel himself. Finally, he took the car again and went to Abbé Hamelin's home in the east of Paris, but he wasn't home yet either. He dropped in to get a coffee in a *café* down the road, phoning from time to time to check whether he had got in.

It was very late by the time the phone finally answered.

"Come on round, Axel, of course," said the Abbé immediately.

Once they were comfortably seated in his study, Axel asked what had happened.

"Oh… you were all convicted, I'm afraid," said Abbé Hamelin steadily. "Eighteen months for yourself and Mme Legrand, and three years for Mme Antonescu. You should have heard the noise in there - people shouting, protesting !"

"Who protested ?" asked Axel quickly.

"Your worst accusers — especially your brother and that woman who made her daughter lie against you, you know... They were both screaming that it was unjust, the woman was lamenting you, crying out your name – quite mad !"

At last their conscience had spoken, thought Axel. They knew it was all lies, but everything had gone much further than they thought it would and their conscience couldn't take it.

"What are you thinking of doing ?" asked Abbé Hamelin.

"I don't know," replied Axel.

"Your choice is pretty clear," went on the Abbé. "You either have to go back and give yourself in, or flee the country. Only you can make the choice."

Axel was silent again. Which direction should he take ? Where did God want him to go ? To prison, just so that the Judiciary could immobilise him, mock him, make him a helpless prisoner of a corrupt system ? He certainly wouldn't be able to do a thing for Victoria from there. In this war that he had been fighting, had God led him this far just to be imprisoned?

"I'm leaving," he said.

"Are you sure about it ?" Abbé Hamelin asked, looking at him carefully. He wanted him to be quite certain.

"I'm leaving France," repeated Axel.

The Abbé stood up.

"Do you have any money ?" he asked.

"A little..." Axel started to say, but the Abbé didn't let him finish. He was gone, rummaging through the flat and gathering as much cash as he could find, loose change, notes, anything he came across. When he came back he pressed it into Axel's hand.

"There, take that," he said dismissively. Axel took it thankfully. He had no idea what was ahead of him.

"Thank you very much," he said, moved by the Abbé's generosity.

At the door, Abbé Hamelin jammed his foot in the big wooden door to keep it open while he said goodbye, as was his custom.

"Goodbye, Axel," he said simply, putting his hand out for Axel to shake. Axel wanted to mark his appreciation for everything the

Abbé had done, with such constancy and thoroughness. He almost put his arms round the man, but in the end only grasped his hand and embraced it. When he looked up again, there were tears in Abbé Hamelin's eyes, he was smiling but seemed unable to speak. Axel stepped away and was off, without looking back.

Once in the car Axel put the money away properly. Abbé Hamelin had rounded up a very tidy sum – 1,300 francs or so. It must have been savings of some sort, because Axel knew he didn't have much to spare.

"God bless that man," he thought to himself, as he started the car up and headed for the *autoroute*.

There was only one place Axel knew he could get over the border without being controlled by customs police, and that was down towards Annecy. He had a good 400 miles to go. The reality of what he was doing was sinking in little by little. He was no longer a charged man, he had been convicted. That made him a runaway convict. It was a scary thought. The police would have every right to attempt anything to stop him, and at that moment he felt as though he would go crazy if they stopped him. For a few frightening moments he could just see himself trying to escape the police, fighting and running and … He stopped the car in a petrol station beside the motorway and went in to get a cup of coffee.

It was probably the strain of these last few days beginning to tell on him. At any rate, he reasoned with himself, if the police stopped him, it would be absolutely useless to run or attempt heroics. He would just have to accept it. It would only happen if the Lord allowed it. And if the Lord allowed it, it would be His will. There was nothing to get all heated up about. One way or another, he would discover what the Lord's will was for him. With that thought, he was able to go on in peace. In a very practical way, he was more than ever aware that his whole life, and this situation in particular, was entirely in the Lord's hands.

He drove throughout the night, arriving in the Alps at around six o'clock in the morning of February 10 – exactly two years since the police had arrived on our doorstep to take us in for questioning and eventually remove Victoria. Driving through the mountains, at about half an hour from the border, the road mounted in zig-zag.

Suddenly, after a couple of sharp bends, there was a police check-point in front of him – and a line of cars, of which he was now already a part. Never had he seen police stopping cars on this part of the road before.

"This is it," he thought to himself. This would be the test. Now he would know what God wanted for him. He waited calmly, at peace with God and confident in Him.

"Passport, please," asked the police officer. Axel handed it over, an almost brand new one that he had been able to obtain in just 48 hours (which was quick for French bureaucracy) about ten days before the trial.

"Where are you heading ?" asked the officer.

"I come through here regularly on my way home to Annecy from Paris," Axel explained. He could easily have been stopped – he later learnt that his arrest warrant had been issued nation-wide by the Court in Versailles immediately after the verdict had been pronounced the night before. The officer and his colleague looked the car over and checked the contents. Then he handed Axel's passport back and waved him on.

For Axel, that was God's answer. How much more real could it be ? He had been stopped unexpectedly and yet told to go on. He thanked God for His answer and kept going.

When he got near the border there was so much fog that he decided to park the car and go and see if there were any French police on duty. He found no-one. He returned for the car and drove past the French border post. One kilometre further on was the Swiss customs post, but he couldn't remember exactly where it was. The road came to a T-junction and he had to turn right. Then suddenly there it was – thankfully unmanned as well. Now at last he was truly over the border. He looked at his watch : 7:30 a.m., February 10, 1995. And he was out of France. He stopped for a rest as soon as he could – now he was really tired.

No man's land

Around ten o'clock that morning the phone rang in a house in France.

"*Allô* ?" Bernard, one of Axel's friends in the church, had answered it.

"Hello, how are you ?" It was Axel calling but he didn't want to give his name over the phone.

"Oh, hello," repeated Bernard with surprise, recognizing his voice. "I never thought I would be hearing from you today ! Where are you ?" He hadn't stayed for the end of the trial either, but had to be careful what he said on the phone. We had become used to conversations like this where things were only half said – though it had sometimes led to misunderstandings. What Bernard meant was: you were supposed to be in prison, what are you doing out ?

Not long after, the phone rang again, this time in our hiding place in no-man's-land. Anutza sounded pleased.

"Extraordinary !" I heard her say. "See you soon."

What good news could she possibly have, I wondered. With Axel probably in prison and Victoria even further out of reach than ever, I could only imagine that it was something to do with one of the other families.

Anutza's eyes sparkled. "Axel's coming," she told me joyfully. "He crossed the border last night and he will be arriving here this afternoon."

However did he get away ? I thought. Amazement and joy brought tears to my eyes again as I shook my head almost in disbelief. The Lord had brought Axel back to me again ! I certainly needed him at this time, God knew – and the French authorities had been confounded. They must have been furious. So when the radio news had said that two people had fled the country, it must have meant Axel and Anutza, of course. Surely this was a token for good to us in our escape from France. We would be needing the Lord's protection more than ever now. The situation was still very unpredictable.

Sure enough, Axel arrived in the afternoon, weary but relieved.

"Welcome, 007," Anutza said to him with a spark in her eye.

Our contact also congratulated him on having "played a good one on the French authorities". We got the impression they weren't too popular in the eyes of people in no-man's-land.

It was quite a reunion, and we were very kindly taken out to dinner – by our contact again. It was starting to feel like celebration time, instead of the total defeat that the French Judiciary had planned for us, especially when Axel told us about the way he had come out of France. How good it was to be together again, especially out from under the weight of that oppression we had felt in France for so long. We thanked the Lord together.

Then came the time for decisions. Where were we to go now ? How would we be able to live ? Especially Anutza and Axel, fugitives from French Justice. We had much to pray about. It was decided that the most pressing business at hand was to get our files out of France. As it happened, most of them were in our apartment in Annecy, because Axel was the one who consulted them most. But who was to go there, and when ? We had learned during the day that Anutza's home had already been visited at 6 o'clock that morning because of the warrant out for her arrest. No doubt our apartment had also been checked to see if Axel was there. It might even be under surveillance. Getting the files out could be a tricky job.

Obviously, neither Anutza nor Axel could go, and in my state it wasn't very advisable either – being so far pregnant made me very easy to recognise and not much help! One of the friends who had accompanied Anutza and I out of France volunteered, knowing it was very important to have the documents with us in order to be able to continue to fight for the children however we could. Our contact from over the border also offered to go and bring along a friend with a walkie-talkie system which they could put to good use. So it was decided. They left late one afternoon, hoping to arrive in Annecy sometime in the evening. We waited, in considerable suspense.

One thing we did have with us, thanks to someone who had smuggled it out of France, was a typewriter. So I spent most of my time in 'no-man's land' typing out Axel's notes from the hearing for future reference, or whatever else we needed to type: a letter to the lawyers, for example, asking them to file an appeal against the decision on February 9. They were a quiet few days, and we drew strength and peace from this calm after the storm.

We had had no word about Rebecca, except that she had been immediately surrounded by police as soon as the verdict had been pronounced, and marched off, back to prison. It was all so wrong, but we were helpless to do a thing about it now except pray. She and Philippe had taken their decision, and for them it could well have been the right one. Still, even thinking of Rebecca in prison for at least a year was distressing. With her blue eyes and amber-gold hair, you could have guessed she was originally from the Alsace area in the east of France near Germany; a tall, naturally slender woman, almost wiry, for she was strong, unlike Anutza. She would be able to stand the prison régime physically, whereas it would have been extremely difficult for Anutza, with her special diet and fragile health. Philippe undoubtedly had the family in mind, wanting to get them back together as soon as Rebecca was out of prison. We could all hope and pray for that.

Back in no-man's land, we were more or less confined to the small two-room flat that our contact had kindly found for us temporarily, and hardly dared show our faces outside in case the French authorities had issued an international arrest warrant. When we did go out once (we had a few urgent things to buy, since we had of course come out of France without anything) I felt very conspicuous, in spite of the big winter coat which concealed my figure a little. We were beginning to discover the difficulties of living in hiding. Sometimes we felt we had had too much peace and quiet and just had to get out of those two rooms for a while. It was a kind of prison…

Our salvage team got back very late that night, exhausted. They had managed to take three or four big suitcases full of documents, plenty to allow us to continue the fight for Victoria and the other children. All the proof in our favour was there – the originals, thank you, Monsieur Bauer. We received the three of them back like heros – and so they were. It was no easy thing to go into a place they weren't familiar with and remove whole suitcases of belongings, when at any time the neighbours could have become suspicious and raised the alarm or the police could even have been watching the apartment.

Once the documents had been sorted out and filed, we made a list of the contents of each suitcase. They were our lifeline, legally speaking. We tried to tie up as many loose ends as possible. I sent my key back to work along with documents that had been lent to me and a short note, and Axel sent invoices for the work he had done and not been paid for. We couldn't do much more.

Then there was the question of where to. Axel and I had already agreed it would be best and safest for me to go home to New Zealand, in spite of the distance and cost that would involve. But if I went to New Zealand, it would have to be by myself, it was unnecessary and useless for Axel to go so far. Where would he go, then – and what about Anutza ?

We spent about ten days in this in-between place, this quiet, hidden, no-man's land, before our plans were made. On February 20 Axel was to leave for Great Britain, the long way round, travelling through Europe to Amsterdam, taking a ferry across to England, and on to Wales, hopefully to see Dr Trumper. Since our friend Dr Derek Pearce from New Zealand had introduced Dr Trumper to us, he had published several up-dates about our case in his quarterly magazine, "1521", and we knew that had started many people praying for us. He was the only person Axel could think of going to. Then on February 26 it would be my turn. I was to take a plane to London Heathrow and then continue on for the 24-hour trip to New Zealand, where Derek Pearce and his wife Lilian would be waiting to meet me. Anutza wasn't yet sure of her plans... At least we would all be less noticeable by ourselves, and in New Zealand I wouldn't have to hide, and could perhaps even ask for Victoria to be returned to me there.

It was difficult parting. We had been through so much with Anutza, and she had been such a faithful friend over the years. Now none of us knew when we would see each other again. Expecting a baby and knowing that Axel would not be there with me for the birth or to see this little one's babyhood was the hardest. What could be done now for Victoria ? Would Axel manage to get to Britain without being stopped ? Life had never been so full of uncertainty, yet we all sensed that we were embarking on a new part of our lives, a step further with the Lord, an adventure that was only just beginning...

Fleeing to Britain...

Many disenchanted French citizens had fled to England down

the centuries, from the many, often anonymous, Hugenots in the 17ᵗʰ century to the famous *Monsieur le Général* De Gaulle during the Second World War. It was Axel's turn.

In Cologne, Germany, he spent the night in the waiting room at the station after just missing his connecting train. He ended up sharing it with a few drunks, which brought with it the uncomfortable side-effect of an early morning visit from the German police.

"I... I have nothing to do with them," stammered Axel, half asleep, in his broken English, for he knew no German, and started to try and explain that he was waiting for the early morning train. But they weren't really interested in him anyway – just doing their rounds. Axel remained ill at ease. He couldn't help feeling conspicuous, and uneasy. The Judiciary had issued a nation-wide arrest warrant for him, but he didn't know yet whether they had issued an international one or not.

When he arrived at the ferry he knew he would have to show his passport to be able to board. Well, now he would find out about that warrant. He could see them checking names on a computer list as people filed past. If his was on it and he was stopped, God would have closed the door, and it would be His will once again. Axel could stay calm and peaceful in that knowledge.

He nodded to the officer and held his passport out. And he was waved on ! Another open door. They apparently hadn't done anything on an international scale – well, not yet anyway.

In spite of feeling ill during a rough crossing, he arrived safely in England around noon the next day. On arrival though, an immigration official stopped him.

"Where are you going, sir ? What are you doing in Britain ?" Her insistence was a little unnerving.

"Oh, I'm visiting a friend for a few days, in Wales," Axel answered. Even if Dr Trumper may not have any idea he was coming ! He was glad of his French passport – at least the immigration authorities couldn't stop him, he was a European citizen. He arrived in Gatwick towards the evening. First things first – he bought a telephone card and phoned me to say he had arrived in London OK. Before looking for a B&B for the night, he wanted to get something to eat, and sat down to have a bite in a fast food place in the station.

Suddenly his eyes lit upon a newspaper heading: "Declaration of War" it read, or something similar, and there next to it was a photo of Dr Ian Paisley, taken from behind just as he was turning around, as though someone had just shouted something at him. Instantly Axel recognized the type of photo. It was a still take which had absolutely nothing to do with the headline, but had been used to make the person look designedly aggressive and intolerant. The technique had been used many times against members of the church in France. Someone is photographed opening their mouth to speak, for example, and they appear in the paper next day looking like an ogre about to devour someone! Axel's interest was kindled.

The next day he reached Chester in the afternoon and phoned Dr Trumper.

"Hello, Dr Trumper ? This is Axel from France. I'm in England, not far from where you live, and I was wondering ... could I come and see you ?"

He could hear the surprise in Dr Trumper's voice, but it certainly didn't change his welcome.

"Yes of course, Axel, that would be no problem at all. Come on over this afternoon."

Mrs Trumper opened the door to him, and Axel discovered the reality that Derek had mentioned to him: Dr Trumper lived in a wheelchair.

As they talked together about the recent events in France, Dr Trumper had a question for him.

"Do you not think, Axel, that it could have been the Devil who put the thought into your head to leave the country ?"

Axel had to think about that one. He had had doubts about it himself.

"All I can say is this, Dr Trumper, I didn't leave France just to run away from a prison sentence. I left so that I could keep on fighting and help my wife to keep on fighting for Victoria. And then, well, I put it all before God, you know, and God opened the door, and has kept opening them all the way."

He told him how he had come out of France, and Dr Trumper nodded. He understood.

After that, Dr Trumper must have sensed that Axel had just come out of an extremely trying time and went out of his way to cheer him up, getting him laughing with all sorts of stories about a great variety of people... Dr Trumper and his wife very kindly offered Axel a room for two nights and provided him with everything he needed.

When he came back to the matter in hand, he frankly admitted that apart from writing articles in his magazine, he couldn't really do much more to help.

"If anyone can help you, Axel," he said, "it'll be Ian Paisley. Go and see him is my advice."

Axel had heard of the preacher-politician from Northern Ireland – had read about him in that paper in London – but had never thought he could just go and see him like that. He phoned anyway and was agreeably surprised that he was able to make an appointment with Dr Paisley for the following Sunday evening. He remained skeptical, however. He didn't know if this man was first a politician and then a preacher, or the other way round. If he was first and foremost a politician, then he would probably be a compromiser, and no use. He had been disappointed too often in the past not to be wary. Whether they were police officers, politicians, journalists or Christians of one sort or another, he had learnt the hard way not to hope too fast.

Before Axel left the next day, Mrs Trumper provided him with the address of a good B&B in Belfast and offered to give him a lift to the airport. Dr Trumper also prayed with him that God would lead him as he entered unknown territory. Axel would not forget what this faithful man had done for him.

... and on to Ulster

A flight from Manchester got Axel into Belfast on Saturday afternoon. All he knew of Northern Ireland was the image the French press had been giving of it for years: a dark, sombre corner of the world made of dirty bricks and dirty streets and people shooting at one another. It had made him wonder why people didn't just leave the place for good...In short, he knew and understood nothing about it at all, and the French press certainly hadn't offered many explanations, even if the subject came up fairly frequently in the news.

This was February 1995, and the ceasefire in Northern Ireland had only just been declared. There seemed to be a high level of security at the airport, which was of course a little unnerving for Axel, but he soon realized that the police here definitely had bigger fish to chase than an innocent fugitive from French justice.

Driving past manned police barriers in his 'London' taxi, Axel's first impression was that he had come out of one battlefield only to enter another.

"Are things peaceful these days, then ?" he asked the taxi-driver.

"Yeah," he said, holding up crossed fingers. "Just hope it lasts."

"Well," Axel said casually, "You should trust in God – He's the only one who can really give you peace."

The man uncrossed his fingers on the steering wheel. "Yeah," he grunted.

Mrs Trumper had given Axel the address of a B&B that was fairly handy to the church where he was to meet Dr Paisley. As the taxi pulled up, a cheery-looking little man with a beard and a big smile was just coming out of the guesthouse and, seeing Axel getting out of the taxi, came over to give him a hearty welcome and take him straight up to his room (clean, comfortable, restful – lovely) although it hadn't been booked. Axel's ideas about Northern Ireland were changing by the minute.

A good night's sleep and a good Ulster breakfast (one of those Ulster fries that keeps you going until 3 o'clock in the afternoon) served by the little man's little woman a warm-hearted, homely, perceptive little lady who kept the place in perfect order – and Axel was ready to start out for the morning church service.

The church itself was an impressive size – the biggest in the United Kingdom at the time of building – and distinctive, with front arches and a high tower breaking the austerity of its four-square shape, with the words "Martyrs Memorial Free Presbyterian Church" written in gold Gothic-style letters. A big clock on the tower had the words "Time is short" above it. Inside, a corridor ran around the back and two sides of the church with large windows on the outside and busts and plaques between them, commemorating Britain's

Protestant martyrs. On the front wall, behind a high pulpit, were the words "We preach Christ crucified" in the same gold Gothic letters, under a simple but beautiful rose window. The height of the building allowed for a good-size gallery, and the church when full must have held a few thousand people. He was encouraged by the warm welcome he received as he went in.

Axel had been praying much that day. This was his last chance, really, and if this Dr Paisley turned out to be a 'broken reed'[1] he didn't know where else he could turn to. There he was, without work, only a little money, without his wife or his daughter, cut off from his family, his friends, his church, his country – a refugee who couldn't even declare himself as such. Only God could help him now. Was this church going to be full of nominal, wishy-washy Christians who back away at the first sign of trouble ? He hoped Dr Trumper had sent him to someone with a little more backbone. How little he knew about this man Paisley !

Three things struck him that morning. First of all, he heard solid Bible preaching, no flimsy, lacy embroidery round a Bible verse, but good soul-nourishing meat. Secondly, he was agreeably surprised to learn that the whole church was participating in a day of prayer and fasting. Now he liked that – it was Biblical and it told him these people took their Christianity seriously. Lastly, he had happened to arrive on Children's Day. As he saw the children going up, respectably dressed, well-behaved, often showing a personal spark of character as they accepted their prize and shook hands with the preacher, he felt a sadness for that which Victoria and the other children had lost. This was how they had been brought up, too, and now they had been forced to ridicule it all, to live like orphans brought up in State institutions amongst street children and everything else that went with it. What he was seeing now was how things should have been for them too.

In the evening, when he was able to meet with "the big man" himself, as most people seemed to call him, he was introduced to a Professor McLeod who spoke fluent French, whom Dr Paisley had asked in to interpret if necessary. Axel, however, had his 'speech' all ready in English, just the main events and ideas, showing how the case had been turned against the church with the kidnapping of the

[1] Isaiah 36:6

children, and the parents convicted in order to cover up and justify keeping the children in care. All he asked of Dr Paisley was to intervene in Victoria's case so that she be returned to her mother in New Zealand. Axel said clearly that he had been convicted, but he also made clear that he was asking nothing for himself, not wanting to implicate anyone else in anything that could seem suspicious to outsiders. All the same, he had no idea what kind of reaction he was going to get.

Dr Paisley listened patiently, carefully, listening for more than just facts (Dr Trumper had actually mentioned the case to him already in a letter some time ago). He was a big man, all right, he would have been taller than Axel at his age, and he had presence with it. Axel got the impression that he was being sized up just as he spoke and that Dr Paisley was someone who would tell him straight to his face what he would do and would certainly do it. His white hair told his years, but he was "wearing well", to use his own description of himself – a square forehead and large, regular features made up a face that easily broke into a hearty grin. Over his spectacles he also watched Axel patiently, and when he spoke it was with decisiveness.

What surprised Axel most was that with Dr Paisley there were none of the doubtful, suspicious or even indiscreet questions that most of the "Christians" in France had always asked. This man had obviously grasped the situation quickly, yet was very discreet about it – definitely not someone looking for an excuse to back out of helping. In fact, he was just the opposite of what Axel had seen portrayed in the paper in London just a couple of days before, on his arrival in London. All Axel could see in this man's attitude was understanding and compassion and sensitivity. The meeting only lasted around 15 minutes, then the preacher prayed with him. Yes ! thought Axel, this is a man of prayer and of action – definitely a preacher first and politics only come after !

As they stood up, Mr Paisley said just one thing, in his gruff, decisive way:

"I'm going to be seeing the French Ambassador in London about this. And I am prepared to go and see that mother in prison."

Axel didn't say a word, not even "Don't mention me," which was on the tip of his tongue. It was enough for him that Ian Paisley was going to act – at last someone who wanted to look into the case, who had the means of getting things moving, and who above all was a genuine Christian pastor ! It was an extraordinary encouragement after all the disappointments he had seen so many "Christian leaders" serve up. Axel had wanted to check this man out for himself, and he had seen all he needed to. That night he thanked God with all his heart that he had been led to meet with Dr I.R.K. Paisley.

Going home

I didn't like leaving Anutza. She had always been slim, but during the month in prison in 1993 she had lost a lot of weight and never put it back on again. I knew that sometimes she could hardly go up a flight of stairs without feeling dizzy. Unfortunately, circumstances left me no choice.

When I finally said goodbye to her – in a hurry, as usual – she was in a pensive mood.

"This is going to be a test for you," she said. "God bless you."

I hugged her and we were gone. But her dark eyes, fine features and wispy dark hair stayed with me. Easily sparkling and witty, often serious, pensive and prayerful – I would miss her.

It was only on the way to the airport that we discovered the problem. It was my fault. My New Zealand passport was out of date. I suppose I hadn't really thought seriously about going all the way to New Zealand, and now it was far too late to do the slightest thing about it. I had a French ID card which allowed me to travel through Europe, but as soon as I wanted to go any further I would need the passport. What were we to do ? The tickets were already paid for. We could only go on and see if with the two pieces of identity it would be all right. One of our friends who had accompanied us out of France took my papers to check-in. I think she had to insist a little – she didn't say exactly, just came back and said "It's all right", with a huge sigh of relief. From now on it would be up to me.

The flight to London Heathrow was a breeze. It was the connecting flight through to New Zealand that I was a little apprehensive about. First of all, would they let me on the plane? An out-of-date passport and over eight months pregnant... I had a vague feeling you weren't supposed to fly so near the end of a pregnancy, for the airline's sake ! For some reason, I wasn't really very worried about it. It was out of my hands, anyway. Axel's escape from France had taught me that if something was the Lord's will, He would look after the details. Still, I should have made sure my passport was renewed.

I had a bit of time in London Heathrow before boarding. Strange enough, the main thing on my mind was getting something to take home for the family. Six sisters and my Mum – it would have to be something small. After hunting around I took perfume – a big one for my Mum and six small ones, as well as a big box of 'Roses' for Derek and Lilian. I also grabbed a copy of "*Not without my daughter*" to read on the plane. By then it was time to board. I hadn't had time to get nervous about this. I was once again thankful for the winter coat Anutza had found for me – it fell graciously almost to my feet and just made me look rather fat instead of pregnant. Just be matter-of-fact, I told myself, and keep trusting in God.

At least I didn't have to worry about luggage – my one suitcase had been sent straight through to New Zealand. All I had to do was present my ticket and passport at the desk. The airline official happened to be a man, and he also happened to be sitting behind a tall desk. He couldn't even see my stomach (perhaps he wouldn't have noticed anyway, being a man !). He must have asked me a question, which I answered nonchalantly and he heard the New Zealand accent and I was through ! Now there was just the flight itself to get through.

Strangely, I felt no discomfort at all during the long flight, apart from having to get out of my seat and go for a walk round the plane from time to time. I think the stopover was in Singapore – at any rate I had a good walk again and that helped me through the last leg of the journey. Coming out of the plane in Auckland I suddenly realized that this was still New Zealand summer – and I had no summer clothes. I was roasting, in spite of the airport's air-conditioning.

Then, unexpectedly, came the trouble. When the officials in Auckland saw my out-of-date passport, I was taken aside and a woman came to question me.

"How did you get on the plane with that ?" she asked, as though I must have sneaked on board or something.

"I just presented it," I said. "There was no problem at all."

"The airline should never have let you on board," she said. "I'll have to go and talk to them about it. They should really take you straight back again."

"Look," I said, at last a little worried, "I only noticed at the last minute that my passport was out of date. I needed to come home quick – you can't send me back now !"

She went away to "talk to the airline". I was hot and took off the winter coat. It was quite a while before she came back so I walked around a little. Now nobody could miss the fact that I was pregnant – very pregnant – but I couldn't be bothered hiding myself any longer in the heat. Looking back on it now, taking off that coat was probably the best thing I could have done – it may have given them a very good reason not to put me back on that plane!

At last my questioner returned.

"We're just waiting for a final decision about this," she said. "The airline can be fined up to $10 000 for letting you board a plane with that passport, you know."

"I really don't want the airline to get into any trouble about it," I said, thankful that at least she wasn't talking about taking me back to London anymore.

She went away again, but when she came back the next time, I was at last allowed to go.

Having found my one suitcase – thankfully on wheels – I went to wait in the meeting point area, uncomfortable in my warm clothes. There was no sign of Derek and Lilian. Could that man over there be Derek ? I wondered. It had been one and a half years since I had seen him and I hadn't ever met his wife Lilian. Maybe they hadn't been able to make it… I was about to ask for an announcement to be made when suddenly they were there.

"Excuse me, is that you, Delwyn ?" That was definitely Derek all right. I couldn't mistake that voice, and the kindly face. And there was Lilian, a lovely dark-eyed, olive-skinned lady with long, thick, dark hair – she reminded me so much of Anutza, the same gentle gestures and sparkling eyes. I later discovered that Lilian's father had also been Greek, like Anutza's.

"We didn't recognize you with your hair cut," Derek said. "We came through here before but thought you were someone else !" I suddenly realized that sure enough I had had my hair cut in a bob since I started work in Annecy – I was the one who had changed in a year and a half, not Derek. Where was my head these days ?

"I'm sorry," I said. "I should have told you of course…" We went out to the car, and I had so much to tell…

When we stopped to get something to eat I rang my Mum to ask if she could come and get me from Derek and Lilian's home in Hamilton, halfway between Rotorua, where my Mum lived, and Auckland. She couldn't believe her ears – Delwyn, here in New Zealand, after all these years ! It had been more than ten since I had left. But my Mum wasn't at a loss.

"Yes, yes," came her voice down the phone, excitedly, "I'll be up as soon as I can – probably around mid-afternoon."

I hadn't wanted to tell her I was coming in case I didn't make it. Now she would probably be phoning the family, telling everyone the biggest surprise ever – which was saying a lot, in our family people were always springing surprises on each other. I was home…

12

Help from unexpected quarters
February - November, 1995

Positive action at last

The fact that Dr Paisley would be going to see the French Ambassador meant that Axel needed to stay in Belfast to await the outcome. True, he didn't really have anywhere else to go! Dr Paisley was quickly given an appointment with the French Ambassador in London, a certain Monsieur Guéguinou, for 2 March 1995. He was accompanied once again by the French-speaking Professor.

They were received in the study of the Ambassador himself. Dr Paisley was very clear with them on every point, most importantly that little Victoria should be immediately returned to me in New Zealand. However, the temperature of the meeting suddenly shot up when he mentioned Axel.

"Mr Schmidt has been to see me personally, and has explained the matter to me," he mentioned during the conversation.

Monsieur Guéguinou immediately took the matter up.

"You may or may not know, Mr Paisley, that the Versailles Court has issued an arrest warrant against Mr Axel Schmidt," he stated.

The Ambassador's assistant added, somewhat heatedly.

"We know Mr Schmidt is in the United Kingdom, Mr Paisley," he added. "And he should be arrested !"

"Well, if that's the case, Mr Ambassador," answered Dr Paisley, "If that, is your duty" – here he was characteristically jabbing the air in Monsieur Guéguinou's direction, effectively underlining each word he said – "go ahead, and arrest him then !"

After the ensuing short silence he took up again.

"At any rate, you have nothing against the little girl's mother. There is therefore no good reason for the child not to be returned to her mother in New Zealand."

Ah yes, that hit the nail very neatly on the head. Why indeed not return Victoria to me? The question was crucial. But it was at this very point that the French authorities simply skirted the issue and argued that if I wanted to regain custody, I should use all the legal means available, i.e. another hearing before the Judge for Children, and another (useless) appeal. Behind the scenes, though, the whispers that roamed the corridors of power in France had not gone away: how could the French Judiciary return Victoria to her Mum when her "dangerous" Dad was still on the loose ? To anybody important who started asking questions, this was apparently the French authorities' unofficial answer, while officially they said I should be using all the legal remedies open to me. And there they thought they had us. Checkmate. Game over. Victoria could not be returned to her mother unless her Dad gave himself up ! Even then, the French Judiciary would also be deciding on the "conditions" for her return, of course.

Dr Paisley's meeting ended with the French Ambassador promising to forward the judgement rendered on 9 February 1995 to Dr Paisley for his information. So Axel waited, wondering what the next day might bring forth but not able to do anything except wait. Supposing the French authorities did request his extradition, he was prepared to resist it and fight his case. The accusations were groundless, and he could argue that the Judiciary had been biased. From the moment our faith had been ridiculed and the church labelled a 'cult', the whole thing had been one elaborate set-up to "get the cult". Would the French authorities feel their case was strong enough to request his extradition?

Days, then weeks passed. He got news that our second daughter Elvira had been born, on 17 March 1995 and that we were both well. He rejoiced – and kept waiting.

Gradually it became clear that the French authorities also seemed to be waiting – apparently for proof of Axel's whereabouts. If they could prove we were together they would have an excellent reason not to return Victoria to me, but they didn't seem to want to get into extradition proceedings. After all, their case against Axel was very fragile – it had stood up in the French courts because of the 'cult' context, but it would hardly stand up to the scrutiny of courts in Britain. So Axel stayed put and lay low – he wasn't about to give them an excuse for refusing me custody of Victoria ! If the French authorities were so worried about such a "dangerous" man as him being at large, and since they knew he was in the United Kingdom, they could just come and get him. His only problem was that he was fast running out of money. He needed a job – and who would employ someone in his situation ?

A job – and understanding

Not long after arriving in Belfast, Axel had got talking with Jacqui, the "little lady" who ran the B&B. She was very understanding, and he felt confident enough to tell her exactly what his situation was and how he had ended up in Northern Ireland. When he told her how Victoria had been taken away, she had tears in her eyes, and though she didn't say anything, this spoke to Axel more than anything else could have. After the heartless "Protestants" in France who had asked endless, suspicious questions and been far more ready to accuse than to help, this compassion was unexpected. But then in Northern Ireland he was discovering that caring, compassionate Christianity was actually the norm – at least in Free Presbyterian circles, where he had been attending after his introduction to Dr Paisley.

As time went on, he was moved to see that many others took our case seriously to heart. After so many years of battling on alone except for our closest friends, amidst opposition, criticism and indifference, Axel was overwhelmed to hear that people were actually praying for us and for Victoria. Many of them had been informed about the case through Dr Trumper's magazine "1521", often in disbelief that such a thing could happen in France at the end of the 20th century. Unlike some of the people from different countries that we had come into contact with while in France, these people had no problem understanding how the French Judiciary had been able to build up a case against Axel. They understood that the case was serious, and they were really praying.

Axel had become a regular attender of the local Free Presbyterian church, and under Dr Paisley's preaching he had been strengthened in sound Biblical doctrine. We had known faith in practice in France, but this was the basis for that practice and Axel knew it was good. He was also learning things about Catholic doctrine that he had never known himself, even as a practicing Catholic.

Knowing Axel's circumstances, Cecil and Jacqui had given him a room at a special price, but with Jacqui's help he was able to find a flat to rent in East Belfast. They had recently purchased a new property which they were wanting to turn into a purpose-built B&B, with ensuites in almost every room, etc. Their new property was an old Victorian building and was going to need a lot of work – it had belonged to an old lady who had only lived in two of the downstairs rooms and the upper floor had been inhabited by pigeons for quite a while ! It would need to be stripped completely down to the structure, and built up again.

"I can give you work in the new house, Axel, if you don't mind chipping and carrying," Cecil said to him one day. Axel was only too glad to be able to work for someone he already knew and wouldn't have to explain his situation to all over again. Once again he could see the hand of God in this offer – he had just used his only remaining resources to pay for that month's rent.

So work on the house began – and it was quite an experience for Axel, or "Big Akel" as he was called on site, especially by Samuel, the head builder. Samuel wasn't a tall man, from Axel's 6-foot-something perspective. But he certainly was a great worker, both on the building site and outside of it, when he was an evangelist at children's meetings. And he always had a sparkle in his eye and a ready, encouraging grin and a good word for whoever needed it.

The work on the house involved a lot of knocking down, for a start. Then it was time to rebuild.

"Nails, Akel !" Samuel would call down to Axel from the top floor, in his broad Belfast accent. And Axel would go fetch them.

"Need more cement, Akel !" Samuel would holler again. Off went Axel again.

"Come and hold this here for me would you, Akel?"

It was good, hard work, and a big change from Axel's University work in France ! He enjoyed manual work, but the only time he had really done any had been for DIY jobs around the house during the holidays or giving others a hand with theirs. Perhaps the biggest difference was that in this job he was never his own boss – he had to run and fetch for everyone else !

The work itself was tiring and Axel often felt discouraged because of his own uncertain situation (how many times he imagined the police were bound to storm the flat sooner or later, hunting for the "fugitive"), but Samuel was a special encourage-ment to him.

"Time for a cuppa, Akel ?" During the morning tea break and lunch Samuel would often share something with him from the Bible, or some anecdote from his own experience. He always seemed to have just the word Axel needed.

"Are you eating well these days, Akel ?" Samuel asked him one day. His concern was also practical…

As he worked on in the new B&B, Axel couldn't help wistfully hoping that his parents might be able to come and stay there one day, if ever they came to see him in Ulster. He longed to be able to speak to them openly and freely. Discussion had been impossible with them in France because of all the hype against the church. Perhaps it would be possible here ?

With regular money coming in from the building job, it wasn't long before Axel was talking on the phone to me about having enough room there for all three of us …

Meanwhile, back home…

It was an emotional time meeting up with the family again after such a long time away. Some of my sisters had been told I was arriving, but it was a total surprise for my youngest sister, Jeanette.

"This can't be Delwyn, can it ?" she asked, her voice rising and tears in her eyes as she hugged me. She had been only 11 years old when I left home, and here she was at 22, in full-time work and with her own flat.

When I arrived, my Mum was actually in the midst of moving house, and had been living with my second youngest sister Heather and her husband Steve while waiting for the new house to be vacated around March 19, when I would probably be in maternity. Heather and Steve kindly offered to let me stay with them as well for a time, as did my next youngest sister Sheryl and her husband Rob, and never did I feel in the least as though this was a burden to them or to my Mum. How's that for real family ! "A friend loveth at all times and a brother is born for adversity" says the Proverb[1], and I had definitely proved that true. It was an enormous relief for me at that time.

Nevertheless, it was strange returning to a place I had known so well after going through so much. There was a huge gap between the easy-going life I had known growing up in New Zealand and the great discoveries but harsh and sombre oppression I had known in France. Coming back felt as though something didn't quite fit, and what we had known in France was incomprehensible for most New Zealanders – it just didn't make sense and they couldn't see how such a thing could happen to somebody who was innocent. Was I living in the same world, I wondered. It was so far away from Europe and events there, almost like another planet... Only occasionally did a news item from Europe filter through, with just a few sparse details.

There was also the fact that I had hardly spoken any real English while I was in France, and language and identity seem to be so closely linked that back in New Zealand I sometimes felt like the 17-year-old I had left as in 1983 ! It took an effort to bring everything I had experienced and become in France back to New Zealand with me. A good part of me seemed to have been left behind in some inexplicable way, and I'm afraid that many were the times when my mind must have seemed to be completely elsewhere.

[1] Proverbs 17:17.

What I had experienced in France went so deep that I still felt as though I were in the heat of that faraway battle. We had been harrassed by the combined attacks of our accusers, UNADFI and the French Judiciary for such a long time. I never got round to really talking to anyone about what had happened during all those years, as though I knew subconsciously that it would bring back too many painful memories – and it was so hard to explain to New Zealanders how things had happened. I of course told my Mum how the trial had gone – that was something I couldn't get out of my mind, the children accusing their own parents in a public court hearing…

For the time being I tried to relax, but there was a tension inside me that I found difficult to shake off. I think it was the result of both Victoria's removal and the danger I knew this new baby had been in in France: the fact that I was soon to be a mother again brought with it a feeling of anguish, a fear that this baby too could be taken away from me. Then too, the fact of being separated from Axel at the time made it ten times worse: I sorely missed not being able to talk things over with him. Fortunately, we were able to establish a discreet line of communication fairly quickly – but it wasn't the same as having him there beside me.

At least we had been able to decide on the baby's name together: Elvira Hannah. "Hannah" was a Biblical name, but we had found "Elvira" in a baby book along the way: it was a name of Spanish origin, meaning "defender of holiness". That was what we both felt had really been under attack in France: we weren't being allowed to live as God wanted us to, according to His Word. It was not a thing to be wondered at. "All that will live godly in Christ Jesus will suffer persecution," the apostle Paul said to Timothy. So as we named our second child this, we were asking the Lord to help us to live – and be allowed to live – in a way that pleased Him.

My Mum was a tower of strength for me at this time, especially when my anxieties rose up within me to remind me that I was entirely responsible for this little one who was about to be born. How well I remember Mother telling me firmly, as we drove out for a few days' rest to a relative's holiday "bach", as they call them in New Zealand, that "nothing bad will happen to this baby, Delwyn." I tried to relax. This beautiful, calm, restful, modern little house with its fruit-tree garden reaching down to the edge of Lake Rotoiti was definitely the perfect spot. My Mum was looking after me wonderfully.

One day in the hospital, a few days after Elvira had been born, I suddenly panicked. Looking out of my room I could just glimpse people in white blouses and navy blue skirts / trousers talking to a nurse, and I immediately thought I recognised police officers… I don't know what action I would have taken – my mind was whirling – if my Mum hadn't calmed me down.

"Delwyn, in New Zealand the police *don't* wear white shirts and navy trousers," she said firmly. Thank goodness for someone sensible ! After the upside-down world of the French Judiciary I certainly needed it.

After a few days in hospital we were able to go home – this time to my Mum's lovely new bungalow not far from the shores of Lake Rotorua. It was a charming home, airy and spacious, with an outside patio and a lovely garden. Perhaps it was possible to forget all the tragic events I had witnessed in France, after all ? I was certainly enjoying being with family again and getting to know all the nephews and nieces who hadn't been around when I left. My Mum naturally developed a special bond with Elvira, and had her laughing back at her when she was only two or three weeks old. Seeing my need (my one suitcase had consisted mainly of warm maternity clothes), my sisters dropped in with bundles of clothes, for both Elvira and myself. And when my birthday came round that year it was the perfect opportunity for a surprise family get-together. It was good to be home. Going for walks with the pushchairs, in the redwood forest, going to playgroup with other mums and babies, it was all so normal – and yet couldn't be completely.

I could talk to Axel regularly now (though not from my Mum's home – I was still very wary of the police tracking Axel somehow), and we both felt it was time to get back to writing to the judge. I also needed to be looking for support from New Zealand representatives. Surely now that I was here, home in New Zealand with my family, the authorities would be a little more enthusiastic about helping Victoria.

And what are New Zealand politicians made of ?

My first taste of New Zealand politicians (apart from meeting Mr Bradford in France in 1994) was an appointment with Mr Rob Storey, a former Cabinet Minister under Jim Bolger, and M.P. for Waikato, the constituency where my second eldest sister Marilyn and her family lived. Marilyn's husband Ross rang my Mum one day to tell her that Mr Storey would be going to France soon and might be a good person to take up Victoria's case. So a meeting was arranged. Since we had been thinking along the lines of obtaining official documents in favour of Victoria's return to me in New Zealand, Mr Storey even suggested officially asking Social Services for a report on my family situation and on my Mum's home. I was of course wary of becoming involved with Social Services after our experiences in France, but this really only concerned material living conditions – Elvira was living proof of the good care I gave my children, as the G.P. and the health visitor could testify. And if ever it was Axel anybody was interested in finding via these investigations, they could search New Zealand from coast to coast, he wasn't there to find. So the request was officially made, though the report itself didn't actually materialize until December 1995.

I went to see Mr Bradford – my Mum had been the one to get him motivated enough to take time to look into the case while he was in France. Mr Bradford had declared that the case was a "travesty of justice", but instead of asking why Victoria was being kept away from me when the French authorities had nothing against me, Mr Bradford had apparently been taken in by the French authorities' "visiting rights" line, and we knew that was useless. The judge had told us clearly in May 1994 that only a "change in our life-style" would lead to Victoria's return with us (i.e. we should turn against our friends in the church and jump on the accusers' bandwagon – totally repulsive). So visits would never bring Victoria home, and we also knew from the other families' experiences that in our cases, visiting rights were simply a way for French Social Services to find something to accuse us with – and an occasion to mess up family relations by setting the children against their parents.

I also wrote to Prime Minister Bolger again, who referred me to the Minister of External Relations and Trade, Mr McKinnon, who again said that the New Zealand Government could not intervene in French judicial procedures. By this time I had lost all hope of getting any real help from the Bolger administration. There had been a lot of talk from them, but in reality they had not done a thing, right from the beginning: they had never bothered to ask the French authorities the essential question: why are you keeping this little girl away from her New Zealand mother if you have nothing against her? They seemed to be either naïve enough to swallow the French authorities' line, or just totally unmoved by Victoria's plight.

One person I was interested in meeting was Mr Winston Peters, the leader of a relatively new party in New Zealand politics, New Zealand First (Mr Peters was later to become Deputy Prime Minister in a coalition government). He seemed a down-to-earth man, and his secretary, Amy Bardsley, whom I spoke to several times on the phone, was most helpful. Mr Peters was even said to be a Christian. When I met with him in his home constituency of Tauranga, a modernised, spreading port city on the Bay of Plenty coast, he asked a few probing questions and seemed to have a clear grasp of the situation. At any rate, he said he would be writing to Mr Bolger about the matter. When I received a copy of his letter a few days later, I was encouraged. Victoria's case was stated clearly and convincingly and Mr Bolger was being put on a spot. The New Zealand Government should be requesting that the French President recommend Victoria's return to her mother, Mr Peters was saying.

Meanwhile, a file in favour of Victoria's return to New Zealand was starting to take shape. I had been attending the Presbyterian church in Rotorua along with my sister Sheryl, and one of the elders there, who happened to be a Justice of the Peace, volunteered to write a testimony for me. I was very touched by this totally unexpected offer of help.

For the French judge's information, I of course had to state that I was separated from Axel. I even had proof of it: I was receiving benefit allowance from the New Zealand Government as a single mum. With the file coming together, I had great hopes that perhaps this was the way the Lord intended to deliver Victoria – to me in New Zealand.

Not what I thought

Out of the blue, on 31 May 1995 I received a letter from Judge Barnier summoning me to a hearing in Versailles on 1st June, just two days later. What was I supposed to do, grab a ticket, my baby and run to catch a plane to the other side of the world ? I immediately faxed and posted a letter requesting a postponement of the hearing, at least until I could get someone to represent me. Hey, I *was* Victoria's mother!

There was no reply. I waited in the hope of a summons to a new hearing, but nothing came.

Then came the blow. It seemed that the last-minute summons to the hearing had been part of the plan – just to make sure I knew it was on but so I wouldn't be able to attend. In my absence, and in spite of my letters and fax requesting a postponement, Judge Barnier had held the hearing on 1st June 1995 and had given Victoria into the care of her paternal grandparents: she was going to live with them and I had not even been consulted. By the time I received a copy of the judgement she was already with them on holiday and would then simply stay on...

For me, it was the worst possible scenario. For the first time it was stated in a judgement that Victoria's grandparents had been seeing her regularly and even taken her on holiday with them over the past two years. How could the judge possibly give Victoria to her grandparents rather than to her mother ? Once again the injustice of it "cried out to God from the ground", like Abel's blood.

And how could Axel's parents have agreed to such a thing – imagine them keeping their own granddaughter away from her mother. It seemed absolutely heartless. But I had seen the outcome of Robert and Isabelle's situation and I knew the Judiciary would use the grandparents just to keep Victoria from being returned to me. They had probably used the same argument to get the grand-parents to cooperate too: how could they leave their dear little granddaughter in State care ? They had perhaps even been told she would be put up for adoption otherwise…or face a life in institutions or foster families. But what they were planning to do in the long term, I had no idea – Axel's parents were both in their seventies.

One thing was very clear: the judge was not listening to anything I was saying from New Zealand. I could see that the French authorities were taking as much notice of voices from New Zealand as they had in 1985 after the Rainbow Warrior incident, when the papers in France had talked of "the sheep that roared".

I didn't seem to be getting anywhere fast with New Zealand MPs either. Rob Storey, the M.P. who had requested the Social Services report, felt I needed to be represented by somebody closer to France, "a European M.P. would be ideal" according to him. When I mentioned Dr Paisley's name he sounded enthusiastic and even wrote to him.

Mr Winston Peters had at least put up a fight, persistently answering Minister McKinnon's letters. Once he interestingly asked whether he could have a copy of the actual letter that Mr Beeby, the New Zealand Ambassador in Paris, had supposedly written to the French authorities, conveying "the Government's strong interest in the welfare and future of Victoria" – it was important for Mrs Jones-Schmidt to have "written evidence of Mr Beeby's efforts", wrote Mr Peters. In reply he was rather drily told that "representations were made in person, not in writing, as this was considered to be the most effective way of dealing with the French authorities on the matter". So there was no record of what had really been said…

By his third letter, Mr Peters was becoming incisive. After refuting the Minister's evasive answers and facing him with the facts, Mr Peters ended his letter strongly.

"The time will come when the New Zealand Government will be publicly asked what action they took to help Mrs Schmidt and to save a five-year-old Kiwi trapped in proceedings which have been described as a 'travesty of justice' by Max Bradford, after he looked into the case in 1994. Please bear in mind that the life of a five-year-old girl is at stake… The French authorities have acted wrongly in this affair and deserve to be sharply confronted."

It would have been difficult to put the matter any plainer !

Minister McKinnon must have felt the pressure, because he now showed his true colours. Slander came first: our church was matter-of-factly called "the cult", and Axel had been convicted for "assault and mistreatment of minors", which could falsely imply anything and everything… and then he brought out entirely false information (that we had been given visiting rights from the beginning; that a "panel of medical experts" had found that Victoria had "suffered mental trauma as a result of the treatment she had been receiving", and that this was "one of the determining factors in the Court's decision to issue a removal order". The truth was that there had been absolutely no investigation before Victoria was removed, and I had the documentation to prove it). The French authorities were not only expert at the slander game in this case – they could also lie brazenly and get New Zealand Government Ministers to lie for them too ! So much for hoping for help from the New Zealand Government under Jim Bolger.

In February 1995 it had seemed as though I had returned to New Zealand for good and that our family might be able to get back together there. Now I wasn't so sure. Apparently God was leading us down a different path.

Back to Europe – and Ulster

After talking to Axel on the phone, we both agreed that in the present situation it would be best for me to go to Northern Ireland, even if it was just for a while. Dr Paisley was intervening more positively for Victoria than anybody else ever had, and if I could be there as well it would give his intervention added weight and perhaps get things moving in the right direction. Perhaps he would even be able to bring Victoria out of France to me in Northern Ireland…

Of course, everybody in New Zealand thought I was mad. What was I wanting to go to Northern Ireland for ? That place where "Christians" fought each other. I could see the family thinking "Here she goes again". I hadn't even been home for a full year. But I would still be asking for Victoria to be returned to me in New Zealand, and my Mum's home was still the one we wanted her to come to. I wasn't thinking of settling down in Northern Ireland permanently. All I knew was that it was the right thing to go to Ulster at that moment.

Once again, I so much appreciated my family pulling together when I really needed them – in spite of the questions and doubts. We had to arrange for tickets in a slight hurry to avoid high-season prices. This meant a lot of running around town (this time I had at least made sure our passports were in order !). Thankfully, my eldest sister Tricia lent me her trendy little car for a few days and even a considerable amount of money for tickets, which I paid back as soon as I got to Northern Ireland.

My sister Christine had been looking into the possible psychological effects that Victoria's separation from me could be having on her, and she dug up a library book on maternal deprivation by the well-known British child psychologist John Bowlby. This gave me a lot more insight into how this separation had probably affected Victoria, and the different stages she must have gone through or could still be going through. It also warned me that Victoria's return to me would not be the end of the road – it would take a lot of patience and understanding to help her to read-just and overcome the consequences of that separation, even once she was back home. Above all, it warned of the consequences such a separation can have, especially if unresolved before adolescence: depression, difficulty forming relationships, anti-social behaviour, etc. I had been warned; and it certainly gave me extra ammunition against the French judge for keeping Victoria away from her family. I was more determined than ever to fight on for custody.

Waving goodbye again to my Mum was an emotional moment – after all the trouble I had put her to these last months. I appreciated Sheryl and Heather both coming to say goodbye too, at some unearthly hour of the morning. My time in New Zealand all felt like a dream as I stepped into the little plane that was to take us from Rotorua up to the main airport in Auckland.

Derek Pearce had made a special effort to come to the airport in Auckland to say goodbye too. These dear people, who had been such a lifeline for me spiritually in New Zealand – there were precious few people like them left. He wasn't able to stay long because he had to get to work, but Christine arrived before he left. Then finally, after last-minute reminders and hugs, we were waving goodbye to Christine too, and off we went, just Elvira and I.

Elvira was a good little baby, though unlike Victoria she had given me the wake-you-up-at-night treatment from the start, which was an eye-opener for me. What fond memories I had of the restful nights I had had as a first-time mother when Victoria slept all night through. When we got onto the long flight, Elvira actually seemed to enjoy herself, especially as we had a little fold-down bed just in front of my seat where she could kick around or go to sleep if she wanted. Thankfully, we were flying Japan Airlines and would be getting a night stopover in Tokyo at no extra cost. It gave me a rest as well as the chance to get better organised. When we arrived in London they even transported us round in one of those little airport jeeps. It would have been a nightmare trying to push Elvira in the pushchair *and* carry our luggage as well. The Lord was looking after me so well – somebody must have been praying.

At last here was Belfast International Airport. It didn't look so bad. In fact, it seemed quite as civilised as London. And suddenly there was Axel, with a grin all over his face. We went straight to him, feeling a little emotional with the relief of it. It had been hard by myself – we were so much stronger together. It was strange to be introducing Elvira to her Daddy, but she topped it all off by going straight into his arms, to his delight – there was no fooling her, she knew *him* all right ! As for me, it seemed like only yesterday that I had said goodbye to him. I hardly noticed that people were staring at us as I hugged him; it was quite a reunion.

Then I realized there was someone with Axel, and was introduced to Jacqui (until then I had only heard her voice on the phone a couple of times) – a lovely, warm, homely person, delighted to see us all together. She soon had us packed into her car and whisked us off to her home first of all to meet Cecil, her "hubby". I remember the beautiful view of Belfast Lough by night as we came sweeping over the top of the hill into the city. We must have talked for hours at Jacqui's – and Elvira was soon going to her as though she'd known her for years. What a time that was. I had left home for home. Strange, that...

But the question still remained – would we be able to get Victoria "home" as well ? Our final run-in with the French Judiciary about Victoria was only just beginning...

13

Together to fight again
November 1995 – September 1997

Life in Ulster

Our arrival in Northern Ireland was marked by Elvira having a very bad case of jet-lag. It took her at least two weeks to get out of the habit of sleeping by day and playing by night. Just when I was ready to fall asleep, she would be sitting up in her cot (freshly repainted by Axel before we arrived), giggling and just waiting for someone to play with her. Axel also remembers her sitting there at night, with her big brown eyes looking up at him in some amazement, as if to say, "I realize you're someone special, but are you really going to live with us now?" She had only known life with her Nan and I until then.

Right from Elvira's youngest days I had spoken some French to her, and now her Daddy spoke it to her regularly too. Even before she started talking, she was also aware that she had a big sister. In New Zealand I had often shown her photos of Axel and Victoria and she had an uncanny understanding and acceptance of this, often giving her big sister's photo a kiss (more like an affectionate sniff, at the time) before she went to bed.

Straight away, it was the hospitality of the people in Northern Ireland that struck me. My family had been supportive of me in New Zealand – but here I was a total stranger; and yet the very first day a friend of Jacqui's had thoughtfully prepared a whole basket full of shopping so that there was something in the house to eat – Axel seemed to have been living on bread and butter.

Jacqui herself invited us all to dinner on Sunday, even though she was teaching Sunday School in the afternoon. There, we met up with our thoughtful provider as well as Cecil's Mum, who were both to become great pray-ers for both Victoria and ourselves. That morning we had been to the service at Martyrs' Memorial Free Presbyterian Church, and been much encouraged once again by the friendly welcome we received and Dr Paisley's compassionate ministry. That evening we went to meet him, along with Professor McLeod, the fluent French speaker.

Like Axel, I was most impressed by this man's empathy and understanding. He really took Victoria's situation to heart. As a father and grandfather himself, he was obviously concerned and therefore determined to get things moving – that was clear in the letters he wrote. Since his visit to the French Ambassador, Dr Paisley had written to several people, including Judge Barnier in Versailles, to ask that Victoria be immediately returned to me. He had even offered to go over with his wife Eileen to pick Victoria up in France and give her over to me in person. I was amazed and very appreciative of the time and effort both he and his wife were putting into helping us. With all their commitments, it wasn't as though they had any spare time on their hands !

Madame Barnier's only reply to Dr Paisley had been that it was impossible for her to just hand Victoria over to him and his wife so they could bring her home to me, even though I had given them a power of attorney specifically for that purpose. So all we could do for the moment was continue to prepare the file in favour of Victoria's return to me in New Zealand and wait for the next hearing, which would be coming up in June or July 1996. I was going to have to stay in Northern Ireland for longer than I had planned.

The Christian people of Ulster continued to help us in many different ways. It wasn't long before a big bag of baby clothes from

Samuel's wife arrived with Axel one evening – very much appreciated, as Elvira was quickly growing out of those I had brought with us. One of Jacqui's nieces very kindly loaned us her sturdy pushchair, which was extremely useful, not only for transporting Elvira, but also for the shopping ! I was learning to appreciate what a luxury it is to own a car – and what it meant to be without one. Then there were young Christian families that it was great to be with too, and encouraging to find that there were young Christians our age who were seeking to please the Lord in their lives. Elvira wasted no time in making friends with their children.

Not long before Christmas, Jacqui suggested we attend the local Free Presbyterian church's annual Christmas dinner, while she looked after Elvira. There we made several new friends, especially one couple who invited us to spend the evening with them on Boxing Day. This friendliness was a tonic after our forced isolation in France under the no-contact rules imposed on our church and the wariness of other churches, and also the relative solitude Axel in particular had known over the last ten months. It takes time to readjust to a different country and culture, but it seemed these people were going out of their way to make things easier for us. It was a little unfortunate that at the time, our thoughts were still so taken up by the fight for Victoria, that I doubt we were much fun.

We were delighted to discover that Belfast was not the "concrete and grime" slum that it was and still is so often portrayed as. Our flat was small and simple, but we weren't expecting anything more – it was great to have a place to call home. There was a handy shopping street not far from the flat, and Elvira enjoyed our walks to the shops. If ever we ran out of anything, there was even a little corner shop just across the road, too. The Ormeau Park was only 300 metres away, and that was to become Elvira's real favourite, whether it was for a short walk to the swings on the near side or a long walk to the playground on the other side of the park, and the Ormeau Road shopping street just beyond it. The amazing thing about these shopping streets was that people would leave their babies in buggies on the footpath outside the shop door. That was one custom I found very difficult to get used to – I couldn't bear to leave Elvira on her own even for a minute…

Since I had been on benefits in New Zealand, we decided I should apply for it again, and much was our relief when, with the help of friends, that was granted to us. Axel had always thought that if he found himself in exile, he should use his time wisely, and was able to enroll for a PhD course in law at the University, although he knew this would put his name on an official list. Our budget was tight, but with God's help we got by. It would have been very difficult without help from different people in the church. So many times we found ourselves faced with some big bill, or simply without money to put in the electricity box (in those days we bought cards to put in a pay-as-you-go box) and just at the right moment our need was provided by some attentive soul or souls in the form of an envelope under the front door. May God grant us one day to do the same for others.

So our life in Northern Ireland took shape. Whenever we could we took whatever jobs we could find to earn a little extra money – cleaning, painting, decorating, typing etc. – we preferred not to live out of other people's pockets if at all possible, even if we were living like refugees.

We had survived the last attack of the French authorities when they had sentenced Axel, we had escaped from France, and we were now back together as a family. The road ahead was not going to be easy, but we would press on and trust God to lead us.

One step at a time

After a few months in Northern Ireland our landlord told us that another house he owned had just become vacant, and that we were welcome to move in there if we preferred. We did ! This was a furnished terrace house in the same area – a two-up, two-down, as I heard them called – and it was a real home. We considered ourselves extremely fortunate to be able to live there. I was already forgetting how quaint I had found all these rows of identical houses at first. A small front garden with a lilac tree (a real tree!) at the front gate, a warm, welcoming front room with an open coal fire which fired the heaters throughout the house; the original wall between the front room and the kitchen had been knocked down to create a through living / dining-room / stairs, with a new kitchen added on – recently papered in cheerful blues – plus two bedrooms and a bathroom upstairs: it was all we needed.

Meanwhile, the report from New Zealand Social Services had come through from my Mum. Along with the reference letter from the Justice of the Peace in Rotorua, a letter from my Mum and photos of her home, where we were hoping Victoria could be returned to, we now had a presentable New Zealand file for the Judge for Children, as well as all the evidence that I had looked after Victoria perfectly well before she was taken.

We were expecting a hearing in June or July 1996 about Victoria's case, but because we were hoping to have Victoria returned to New Zealand we preferred not to inform them that I was in the UK. The obvious solution, and one that all the French authorities were pushing for, was to have a French lawyer represent me at the hearing, and continue to ask for Victoria's return to me in New Zealand.

We found that Maître Eveline Devillecourt, who had defended Axel in February 1995, was available to take up Victoria's case before the Judge for Children. The only problem was the enormous amount of money she was asking for: £ 3300 for just one hearing before the Judge for Children, and that was without her having to prepare any written submissions – we provided them for her. Unfortunately, we didn't have much choice –and she *was* supposed to be an expert in children's cases. We could only hope that Maître Devillecourt would treat us decently and defend us properly in court. We were very much at her mercy.

Our friend Professor McLeod went to meet with her assistant (in a meeting room in a hotel in Paris – at our expense) to make sure everything was in order. He took with him the submissions Axel had prepared and the full file in favour of Victoria's return to me in New Zealand. The assistant told him that our case was well prepared and strong, that Maître Devillecourt would be present at the hearing in person and that she would be firmly putting forward a case for Victoria's return to me in New Zealand.

June 18 came. The day dragged. Towards the evening I phoned Maître Devillecourt. It was then that I learned that she had "not been able to be present" at the hearing in person as she had promised, but that her assistant had gone instead. She didn't mention anything about the case being strong or the arguments her assistant had presented. She had only one thing to tell me: that Judge Barnier had stated very clearly that there would be absolutely no progress in the case unless I went to see her personally. So much for investing all that money in a French lawyer. As usual, the strategy of the French authorities was obviously to sap us of all resources in an attempt to prevent us from being able to defend ourselves.

Assuming I was in New Zealand, I suppose the judge may have felt fairly safe in making this ultimatum, doubting that I would come all the way from New Zealand to see her. We were familiar with this strategy too: trying to put me in an impossible situation. What's more, the judge had kept the pressure on me by saying that she would be available until mid-August 1996 to receive me in her office.

Axel and I were extremely wary of the French authorities. I didn't even feel safe to enter France, after what we had been through up to February 1995. Who knew what accusations they might level against me in order to get their hands on me and then on Elvira? I knew how merciless the French authorities could be with us. Once I was on French soil not only could they fabricate accusations against me, they could arrest me, question me, place me in *garde à vue* (police custody) for at least 24 hours without the right to consult a lawyer.

We felt the dangers were too great. I couldn't go to France without clear guarantees that I would not be hassled or falsely accused. This Judge Barnier had already been playing around with us – the last-minute summons in 1995 was an indication of the way she played – and now she had put us to all the trouble of paying for a lawyer, only to say that there would be no progress unless I came to France. Why had she not simply written to tell me that ? Not only had this lawyer been useless and costly, she had also been used as an excuse for the judge to refuse to receive Dr Paisley as my representative, since I was "already represented by Maître Eveline Devillecourt".

A few years later we did something we had never done before: engage proceedings against Maître Devillecourt to request that two-thirds of the sum she had demanded be reimbursed, since it was excessive and she had not done anything to justify such a bill. At least another lawyer was not necessary for these proceedings, but they could unfortunately take several years before reaching a conclusion, unless the lawyer paid up straight away. Somehow we got the feeling Maître Devillecourt wouldn't – and she didn't, but she eventually lost the case before the Court of Appeal in Aix-en-Provence and was condemned to reimburse us exactly what we had asked for.

1996 was the year we took a step in another direction: an application to the European Court of Human Rights. This was quite an arduous task, as it involved going through the facts of the case and pointing out how the different articles of the European Convention on Human Rights had been violated. We knew that one of the requirements for applying to the European Court was that all the legal remedies in the home country be exhausted – and we had not appealed to the French *Cour de Cassation* (Supreme Court of Appeal) because we knew they would cover for the Court of Appeal in our case. It wasn't even any good going to the Court of Appeal themselves, as we had found out in 1994, since they would also cover for the Judge for Children. However, in "particular circumstances" this requirement could be overlooked, and we argued that the remedies in France were neither adequate nor effective, and especially in our case, they were void of all chance of success. However, because of this matter of exhausting all legal remedies in France, our request was eventually turned down – before it was even properly looked into. So we would have to start all over again: appeal the Judge for Children's decision, appeal the Court of Appeal's decision, and only once we had a negative decision from the *Cour de Cassation* would we be able to apply to the European Court. It would take years.

1996 was also a year when the French authorities were taking more draconian measures against "cults" – and there was still no distinction between truly dangerous groups and Christian churches. On 10 January the French *Assemblée Nationale* published a parliamentary report on "cults", mentioning us as a prime example. Also on their list were Baptist churches, the Assemblies of God, even breakaway Roman Catholic groups etc. However, the authors had been obliged to admit openly that they could not give a legal definition of what the French word "secte" ("cult") actually meant. They even said they had been about to bring their report to a complete halt because of this problem, but had finally decided that they would simply accept the "common understanding" of the word. How's that for an example of the clear, rational *"esprit cartésien"* (the "spirit of Descartes", the famous French philosopher) ! It was also hypocritical, to say the least, from a government which just a couple of years before had been so fussy about using proper French that they had attempted to forbid the use of the English word "hot dog" (and most other commonly used English words), which would have obliged shopkeepers to change it in their menus and signs to *"chiens chauds"* – and prompted tourists to wonder whether the French really ate dogs, as well as just frogs and snails. We thanked God that we were out of France, and comforted ourselves with the fact that at least this parliamentary report was now concrete evidence of what we had been saying all along was happening in France.

As for Dr Paisley, he wasn't taking steps, he was striding along at full pace – writing to the Judge for Children, the French Ambassador, the French Prime Minister, the French President, the President of the European Parliament. Amongst the letters which Dr Paisley received in reply was one from the French Ambassador in London, and another from the French President's advisor. They contained the following statements:

"Mrs Schmidt's fears concerning her freedom of movement in France are unfounded…"

"Mrs Schmidt is not the object of any proceedings in France…"

If I wanted to go to France, I could use these letters as guarantees – surely people so highly placed could be held accountable if ever anything was done against me while I was in France. I knew Dr Paisley thought I should go, but I was still beset by fears of what the French authorities could do. This was truly a matter of taking our courage in both hands.

Rising above fear

It was a nightmare going back to France. Thankfully Jacqui was able to come with me (though she would never be allowed into the judge's office), and Professor McLeod also – as my interpreter. I didn't want to find myself alone with this judge, and vulnerable to any misinterpretation she liked to make of my words – I wanted a witness there with me. And I also wanted to make sure I understood everything perfectly. Although I had requested several times that the judge confirm that she would be willing to receive me with an interpreter, I had received no answer. So we had to go without knowing – causing us more and perhaps unnecessary expense, thanks to the French Judiciary.

It was strange returning to the country I had fled in 1995. I was still very apprehensive about how this visit would go, both in terms of my own security and of the hearing with the judge. My stomach was in knots as we got off the plane in Paris Charles de Gaulle airport. It was only as we mounted the *navette* into inner Paris that I realised that there was something different about me this time. I felt like a foreigner in France. I was no longer just the wife of a French-man, completely under the thumb of the French Judiciary; I was a New Zealander, with my own rights, and the French authorities couldn't be allowed to treat me however they liked.

We had booked into a hotel in inner Paris for two nights so that we would be rested for the hearing in Versailles the next day – September 12. Jacqui and I were lugging travel bags around, while Professor McLeod had only a thin little briefcase, in which he had packed away everything he needed, each item perfectly in place. He was a very efficient person and we could only admire him as he strode blithely round the French *métro* stations. We arrived at the hotel in the evening and I tried to rest, but it was impossible to sleep well, with everything going round in my mind – and forget breakfast for me next morning. I felt ill and our *croissants au beurre* and *café au lait* just would not go down.

We left early, but took the wrong train and had to get a bus to the right part of Versailles. It ended up a bit of a rush – poor Jacqui was getting to know France the fast way. At least we still got there, just on time.

Then we were kept waiting outside the judge's office. After a while the door finally opened and an Asian-looking family came out. Then the court clerk came out to check who we were. I let her know that I wished my interpreter to be present with me in the judge's office. She returned inside, and shortly afterwards the judge herself came out – a small, slim, smartly-dressed young woman, probably about my own age: short, blond, tightly-curled hair, pert features, cool, dominating blue eyes.

I explained once again that I wished to be accompanied by my interpreter and that he had come all the way from the United Kingdom...

"You only have the right to be accompanied by a lawyer," Mrs Barnier informed me, with tight-lipped authority.

When I insisted that he had come so far, and asked why she hadn't told me in writing not to bring an interpreter, she only became more snappy.

"He is not coming into my office," she said flatly – then bitingly: "You either come in with *my* interpreter or too bad for you, Madame Jones-Schmidt." And she disappeared back into her office.

What a dragon ! This was a totally different character to Madame Degrelle-Croissant. I rolled my eyes at Jacqui, who looked as though she didn't want me to even enter the dragon's lair. We discussed briefly whether I should go in or not, but I didn't really have much choice. The judge was forcing my hand: I couldn't leave without a hearing, and she knew it. As I went in I remember thinking, "Lord, you're the only one with me now." And there, as I went in, between the chair pulled up for me and the judge's court-appointed interpreter, was an empty chair. I knew the Lord was with me in there in a very real way and the confidence that gave me was vital.

The judge's almost vulgar "or too bad for you" had told me she was probably on edge herself – thanks to Dr Paisley, the case had been brought to the attention of a lot of highly-placed people and it mustn't have left the judge feeling very comfortable. She was putting on a haughty front though, looking very sure of herself, with that blank, questioning blue-eyed look that was intended to throw me. The whole room had been changed around since Madame Durand's days. Madame Barnier's desk was on the left of the room as soon as I came in, slightly on a slant which gave her listeners a little more room, but still fairly much in a line down half the length of the office, with her back to the huge window. I just took two steps in and there was my chair.

Madame Barnier was sitting at her desk studying me, her elbows on the desk and her hands flat against each other, the tips of her fingers propping her chin, in a "great thinker" attitude. I nodded a *"Bonjour, Madame"* to her and to the court clerk, whose much smaller desk was perpendicular to Madame Barnier's, on the right of it.

I was introduced to the interpreter, a decent-looking, open-faced, youngish man, a little heavy-built, well-dressed – probably from a mixed French-English home, I thought to myself. He had apparently never met Madame Barnier before, as they had obviously just finished introductions. I quickly sensed that Madame Barnier was being careful of what she was saying in front of him – not wanting to appear too inhumane ! So he was an outsider, then. He sat on my right, opposite the judge, like me – almost 'on my side'. Madame Barnier must have felt obliged to bring him in because of my letters asking for the right to have an interpreter with me.

Down to battle

After observing me for a few minutes – something made me keep quiet for once and just wait – Madame Barnier started firing questions at me. Where was I living, where had I come from, how long was I staying, when was I leaving, where would I be returning to, did I have friends in Northern Ireland, what about my husband ? I answered calmly, simply.

As for Axel, or *Monsieur Axel Schmidt*, as I called him, what had he got to do with it, I asked her. He had disappeared in 1995. I was (officially) separated, and had been since 1995 when I had gone to New Zealand (the court clerk noted that). My heart was settled on this point: I wouldn't give them any excuse for not letting me see my daughter. The whole business called for the "wisdom of serpents".

We had prayed about this, and come to the conclusion that this was the only way of dealing with it. It was not done lightly. David's wife Michal had deceived King Saul's soldiers when they came to take David from his house to kill him. Even the apostle Paul had been hidden by Christians to protect him from the Jews. The French authorities weren't out to kill us physically, but they were certainly bent on destroying our family every other way, and especially our little daughter. I had to fight as separated from my husband in order to protect and reunite our family. What else could I do, before God? Thank goodness I had remembered to take off my rings before we landed in Paris: I *was* officially separated.

The judge left the matter there, and got onto questions about Victoria.

"How long has it been since you have seen Victoria?" she fired at me.

"Four and a half years," I answered steadily.

"Yes, at least that," she murmured. "And why have you not been to see me before this? I have been waiting to see you for three years!"

"Madame Barnier, first of all, my husband and I asked to see you in 1994, but you refused –" (here Madame Barnier looked all innocence) "in December 1994, you refused to see us. In 1995 I received your summons in New Zealand two days before the hearing was due to take place here in Versailles" ("How was I to know the mail would take so long?" murmured Madame Barnier) "and then you must remember that I lost everything in France – my child, my husband, my friends, my job – I have seen so many travesties of justice in France that I was not prepared to risk coming to France with my second child."

Madame Barnier didn't like hearing all that, especially in front of the interpreter, who was starting to look uncomfortable.

"And why have you come to see me now, then?" she asked, leaning forward on her elbows.

"I have received written guarantees from the highest French authorities, Madame," I began. My French was stumbling a little.

"Really? From who exactly?" She gave me such a blank, questioning look that I turned to the interpreter and, speaking in my fastest English (for Mrs Barnier's benefit), explained that I had been concerned for my safety but that Dr Paisley (who as Madame Barnier knew, was very concerned about the case) had received letters from the French President's office and the French Ambassador in London, assuring him that there were no proceedings against me in France and that I was guaranteed freedom of movement while on French soil.

When the judge got all that interpreted back to her in lovely, clear, precise French (the interpreter even got the tone of voice), I could see Madame Barnier kicking herself for ever having called him in.

She jumped back at me, though, with: "And why the French Ambassador in *London*?"

So I explained to the interpreter that MPs in New Zealand had recommended that I contact a European MP (Dr Paisley), who had himself contacted the French Ambassador in London. The interpreter seemed to be starting to enjoy his work – in fact he was doing a better job than most French lawyers (with the exception of our Court of Appeal lawyer, Maître Lamont) – at least an interpreter only said what you wanted him to say, and had no reason to side with the judge !

"At any rate," went on Madame Barnier, "I can tell you honestly that I have no file open under the name of Elvira Schmidt" (the mere suggestion of it sent a shiver down my spine) "so you can travel round France with Elvira in absolute freedom."

"You could open a case in a minute," I objected.

"But I have no reason to do so," smiled the judge. "Unless she is in danger in France…"

"There is no way I'm bringing Elvira to France to visit," I told her bluntly. She shrugged her shoulders.

What of Victoria's future ?

Then she started talking about Victoria. That she was doing well, she was first in her class at school, she was learning to play the piano… and that she didn't talk much. I immediately suggested that was not normal.

"Well, she doesn't talk very much in front of *me*," added Madame Barnier. It sounded very much like she was trying to cover up the fact that Victoria didn't actually speak much *at all*.

I asked if Victoria was learning English, and was informed that she was learning it at school, like everybody else. They were not taking any special consideration of the fact that my mother tongue was English and that therefore Victoria should be able to speak it fluently.

Madame Barnier continued on to talk of the grandparents.

"Are you aware that Victoria's grandfather intends to travel to New Zealand ?"

I certainly did not, however much she made it sound as though I should. Why ? I asked. Mrs Barnier took up her explanation in a matter-of-fact tone of voice.

"The grandparents are concerned about living conditions for Victoria in New Zealand, and also want to be able to tell her about the place she will be going to."

I was silent, taking it in. She was watching me carefully to see my reaction. I shrugged my shoulders.

"Victoria will probably stay with the grandparents for another year, as I see things. So Victoria's grandfather will go to New Zealand – you don't have to receive him if you don't want to. He will do as he likes, your mother will do as she likes, and after that you will be able to come and see Victoria…"

"But Madame Barnier," I was trying to get my head round this, "Why are the grandparents, my adversaries, being sent to New Zealand to do a job for *you* ? Do you not trust the report I have given you by New Zealand Social Services ?"

She shrugged her shoulders in turn, dismissing the report with a gesture.

"I can hardly go myself, can I ?"

I gave up. The judge was working hand in hand with my legal opponents and I could do nothing about it for the moment.

One thing I had to do was get things straight about visits. Now that Victoria was older, we felt visits had become an option, but were still wary of French social services and of Axel's parents' attitude towards us.

"You're talking about visits, Madame Barnier," I began. "But what good can I possibly hope to come of meeting with Victoria if she is going to be returning each time into an environment that is hostile to me ? Anything positive I build with Victoria will be undermined by the grandparents and Victoria will be torn between us. I want to avoid that at all costs," I explained.

"I believe Victoria's grandparents are taking steps in the right direction in that respect, Madame Jones-Schmidt. Now that you have also made the effort to come and see me, we should be able to make progress," replied Madame Barnier, patronizingly.

"Madame Barnier, if I start visits with Victoria, I want to know where they will lead to and how long it will take," I said firmly.

"But even I don't know that," retorted the judge. "It could take a year, 2 years, six months…"

"Well, I am very concerned about the effects of visits on Victoria – she is going to have to be separated from me after each visit, which can only remind her of the separation in 1993," I added.

Perhaps it was all getting too much for Madame Barnier. I don't think she expected I would actually stand up to her. She had probably expected a "zombie", such as are supposed to be produced by "cults". I had also repeated several times during the conversation that she had nothing to reproach me with, and it was getting to her.

"You'll have to prepare her for visits yourself then, Madame Jones-Schmidt," she retorted, with exasperation in her voice. "And the first meeting will be in my office, in the presence of the grandparents."

I ignored her last remark and went for the bit that interested me. It had rather surprised me.

"Oh, right," I replied. "So I'll just write to her to tell her I'm coming to see her…"

"And ask her how she is, as well – don't write a stereotyped letter," retorted the judge sarcastically (treating me like a "zombie" from a "cult" again).

"Sorry, what do you mean by that ?" I asked, a little sharply.

"I'm not going to dictate what you should write to your daughter, Madame," prickled the judge.

"I am only making sure our arrangements are clear," I answered.

"And I hope they are," she replied. She seemed to be the one who had been 'programmed' to "fight the cult", and it hadn't worked.

So that was that. I would be able to visit with Victoria – I just needed to prepare her for it and perhaps after six months or a year she would be able to come home ! That was what the judge had said. As I sat talking to Jacqui and Professor McLeod in the waiting area outside the judge's office, we noticed that she kept the interpreter in to speak with him for quite a while. At last he emerged, avoided looking at us and was off, apparently anxious not to engage in conversation. We could only suppose that Madame Barnier had said something very discouraging to him…

My first ice-breaking visit to France was almost over – without any hassle. Only one incident gave me that sinking feeling in my stomach once again: as we changed trains to catch the *RER* for the airport, we suddenly found ourselves faced with a barricade of French soldiers, guns at the ready. Professor McLeod just looked at them in some surprise and wended his blithe way through, and Jacqui and I followed suit. They were obviously searching for someone. It was only when we were through and a wave of relief had washed over me that I remembered Madame Barnier's question: "When are you leaving?" Surely they couldn't have been looking for Axel, I thought…

At any rate, we returned home full of hope. Surely now there would be a way forward, even if we were going to have to be careful with visiting rights. At least there was the hope of actually seeing Victoria in the near future… We would have done better to wait for the written judgement issued by Madame Barnier on 30 September 1997. She was about to show us her true colours.

14

Double dealings
September 1997 – July 1998

Not what she said

Madame Barnier may have said she wanted things to be clear, but her judgement dated September 30 was anything but what we had agreed orally. She made no mention whatsoever of our final agreement that I would write to Victoria to prepare her for a meeting and that we would then arrange a suitable appointment to meet in her office. No, Madame Barnier was setting down conditions which *must* be fulfilled before I could even start to think of seeing Victoria.

By the time we received the judgement in December 1997, Axel's Dad had completed his visit to New Zealand. Now *my Mum* was to come over to France to visit Victoria in the grandparents' home. Only after that would it be possible to envisage visits between Victoria and I, according to Madame Barnier, and even then she indicated that I still needed to change my 'version of events' to fit in with the grandparents' and the judiciary's explanations to Victoria.

It was extremely frustrating. The judge had told me to write to Victoria and I had done so. Now she was refusing to keep her side of the bargain, and Victoria was left wondering why her mother had been talking about a meeting. I wrote to Madame Barnier in protest. She had no right to undermine my child's faith in me. Nor did she have any right to treat trips by Axel's Dad or even by my Mum as more of a priority than me seeing my daughter! It was outrageous. And all a matter of delaying tactics, of course.

Make Victoria a Catholic

In April 1998, another letter brought another disclosure: Victoria's grandmother wrote to tell me that Victoria was going to be baptized into the Roman Catholic Church at Easter time. That was barely a month away. She said that Victoria herself had asked for it, of course. I doubted that, but had no way of knowing for sure. It looked like I was going to have to impose my wishes as her mother and explain to Victoria afterwards, because the implications of such a baptism were extremely worrying. I could almost see the head-lines: "Protestant mother attempts to wrest Catholic girl from her Catholic grandparents" etc.

I immediately wrote to Madame Barnier to voice my concerns that this baptism was completely contrary to international law – and to ask why she had hidden this from me when I saw her in September. The preparation for baptism had been going on for a year, since April 1997, and the judge must have known about it… but she did not reply.

When Dr Paisley was informed of this development, he immediately contacted the French Ambassador in London. He let it be clearly understood that doing this to a child from a Protestant family was not acceptable, and also wrote to the judge and other French authorities to tell them so.

By April 6 we had still received no answer, and the baptism was due to take place on April 11. I phoned the local French bishopric responsible for the area where the grandparents lived. It was against the law to baptize a child without the parents' consent, but the priest in charge at the bishopric refused to provide written confirmation that the baptism would not take place.

"We won't write you a paper," he said. "We'll inform the priest, and that will be all… how old is Victoria ?"

"She's only young – eight years of age," I answered.

"Yes, well if she had been twelve it would have been a different story," he stated coldly, implying that my parental responsibility would have been useless if she had been a little older.

Finally, I phoned the parish priest myself and informed him that as Victoria's mother I was opposed to her being baptized into the Roman Catholic church.

"If you really have parental responsibility over the child, she will not be baptized," he assured me. "But she's going to be very disappointed, after being prepared for it for a year…"

Cross with the grandparents for creating this difficult situation – it would never have arisen if they had respected my beliefs as Victoria's mother – but concerned about Victoria's reaction to the cancellation, I sent her a miniature garden tray and a note via Interflora to try to help her understand that I wouldn't have done this unless I really had to. My emotions were torn between what I knew I had to do to protect Victoria, and the possible effect it might have on her, without me being there to explain and comfort. Once again, it was a situation only God could deal with.

In the end Victoria was not baptized. Nevertheless, the whole business had been aimed at driving a wedge between us and dividing us even further, in spite of our already difficult physical separation. But it also proved that there *was* a strong link there, or it wouldn't have been under such attack. We had certainly been very close before she was taken. Perhaps it was my letters to Victoria that had helped keep that link alive. I believe it was prayer as well. And there were so many people praying.

The follow-up to this was that in May 1998, my Mum received a letter in New Zealand summoning me to a hearing in Versailles on May 14. Not knowing what was going on and having experienced this kind of thing in June 1995 (I received the summons too late, I was unable to attend the hearing, and the judge did exactly what she wanted), I phoned that day to see what was happening.

It was a nice surprise for once to hear that the judge was doing something positive: she wished to remove Social Services from the case, although until then she had always insisted that they should remain involved. The move came so close after the episode of

Victoria's attempted baptism into the Catholic church that we could only assume that Social Services (a secular, State funded organisation) had not appreciated being associated with it. In any case, I was certainly not contesting such a development, though I appealed the fact that at the same time Mme Barnier had once again confirmed Victoria's placement with the paternal grandparents in spite of the attempt to baptize her against my wishes.

For the first time, the French Judiciary had been forced to backpedal and remove Social Services from the case. The attempt to make Victoria a Roman Catholic had turned in our favour. There was an unpleasant backlash to it all, though.

On 2 June 1998, after my letters to Victoria's school principal had remained unanswered, I telephoned Madame Blanco personally to ask for copies of Victoria's school reports which I was perfectly entitled to. I didn't realise what I was getting myself into. The woman absolutely tore into me.

"You are damaging your child, destroying her future, wrecking her chances... (What exactly had they had planned for her, I wondered). Your parental responsibility is worth nothing... it means nothing... it's useless – you don't have any rights over your child !"

She refused to give me any information about when Victoria was free – I wished to enroll her for English lessons at the British Council, I explained, and needed to know. Madame Blanco told me Victoria was already learning English at school... No, she didn't want to hear that I had been falsely accused, that my daughter had been withdrawn without reason. And she couldn't stop praising the grandparents.

"You couldn't find better people than them to look after your daughter, whereas you...! I do not wish to receive any more letters from you, Madame."

Well, frankly, there hardly seemed any point. But I would be informing the judge that I had been refused access to my daughter's school reports...

Pressure on my Mum

Right from the judge's decision in June 1996, in which she "called upon the maternal family to work with social services" in order to "help Victoria be reunited with her family", the pressure had been on my Mum to take on the *beau rôle* of 'grandmother to the rescue'. That judge certainly knew how to use people's emotions. My question was, why bring the rest of my family into things, when *I* was the one that Victoria needed to be seeing so that we could eventually be reunited. The answer was simple: the judge was using delaying tactics once again. If she could get my Mum to feel responsible for the situation and get her involved in visiting etc. before and instead of letting *me* visit, she could easily buy a couple of years' time before being obliged to allow me visiting rights – two years before getting anywhere near a family reunion, two years which would make Victoria almost old enough to speak her own mind – and the judge would be only too ready to help her do that...

So she made things easy for my Mum. In her 1996 judgement, she said that Victoria's maternal grandmother would only need to write to the judge to ask permission before going to see Victoria. I would not be allowed to do so before going to see the judge personally – the so-called visiting right we had been granted in July 1993, which had turned out to be unworkable and damaging for Victoria, had been withdrawn in 1995.

My Mum didn't really have much choice but to receive the grandfather and his brother into her home during their visit to New Zealand, and Axel's Dad was then able to convince her to 'do her duty' and take part in visits. He also told her that he and his wife would not be able to care for Victoria much longer and that my Mum should take over and ask for Victoria to be given into her care in New Zealand. She was a lot younger than them, after all...

The only way out would have been for my Mum to say, "This has nothing to do with me – see my daughter about it." But she had no-one she felt she could turn to in New Zealand to back her in taking that stand. She was alone and without support because of being so far away from me. So Madame Barnier won that battle: my Mum agreed that she would visit Victoria in the grandparents' home in July 1998. This was going to help the judge to delay giving me visiting rights until July 1999 – two years later.

Mother was due to visit Europe at the end of June, when she was coming to see Elvira and I first, before going on to London. There she would meet up with my youngest sister, Jeanette, who was working in London at the time, and they would both be going on to France where they would be staying with the grandparents. Jeanette had majored in French at University and would be able to help my Mum with the language – she obviously needed to be able to communicate with Victoria somehow.

I didn't agree with her visit to the grandparents. I was concerned that it would only reassure them in their opposition to me – make them feel as though they now had my Mum 'on their side'. The grandparents were hoping to persuade my Mum to come round to their point of view, of course – and ultimately bring me around, too. I hardly dared voice my fear that she would find herself in such a position that she would be obliged to take a stand against me, her own daughter, in order to have custody of Victoria. I knew there was no way that judge would let Victoria go out of France with someone who was favourable to me and not 'against the cult'. If she let my Mum think any different, she was just leading her on.

As far as I was concerned, the grandparents were still my accusers, and their custody of Victoria was wrong. I was prepared to be civil to them for Victoria's sake – but I was convinced of my position and I refused to yield to their demand: "agree with what we say and you'll be able to have your daughter". They considered that I had been involved in a "cult" and that Victoria had been "at risk"; that I must be made to admit that, if I wanted to regain custody of Victoria.

It was with mixed feelings, then, that I welcomed my Mum to Northern Ireland in June 1998. She felt that I didn't understand where she was coming from, that she was trying to break through the stalemate of this situation somehow and bring the 'two sides' together. I felt she was giving in under pressure, that she was putting us in danger and didn't realize how merciless the French Judiciary were in our case.

Elvira was delighted to see her Nan again – she couldn't really remember her of course, except from photos, but there was still a lovely closeness between them. We did a bit of sight-seeing and Mother also had a meeting with Dr Paisley. I remember her coming out and saying "He's a real pastor at heart." The visit had relaxed her, too – Dr Paisley had had the right words for her. She was also pleased to meet Jacqui and Cecil... And she remained convinced that she should visit Victoria in France.

Knowing that Mother would be staying with the grandparents and that she also had a hearing with the judge coming up on July 8, it was a tense time. I kept wondering what questions they were going to ask her about us and how much my Mum would be forced to say. No way could I even mention Axel, and I was forever watching over Elvira to try and make sure she didn't mention "Daddy". The controversy seemed to have poisoned my own family and made me distrust even those closest to me.

It was a difficult moment when my Mum finally left to go to France. She was going to see my daughter when I couldn't. She was convinced that she was doing the right thing, but I was equally convinced of my position: I couldn't give in to this pressure, it was my duty to fight right. I was persuaded that Victoria herself would thank me in years to come for not giving in to this blackmail, not lying to her because it was the easy way out. The first simple step would be for Elvira and I to go and stay with the grandparents, just like my Mum... But that would only be the beginning of a process aimed at making me say I had belonged to a "cult", that my belief in God was just a façade. I knew I would never have peace of mind if I gave in.

Madame Barnier moves at last

When my Mum went to see the judge, it was as Axel and I had expected: she was very closely questioned about my circumstances in Northern Ireland. I was glad I had been careful. Mother made it plain that she wanted to see Victoria back with me, especially as, according to what Axel's Dad had told her during his visit to New Zealand, they would not be able to continue caring for Victoria very much longer (they were both 73). The judge did not deny this, but said she would need to know more about my situation in Northern

Ireland before going any further. Holidays for Victoria in New Zealand would be possible, she said, as long as it was clear that no-one would try to keep her there contrary to a French ruling. My Mum insisted that there needed to be a meeting between Victoria and I, and eventually Madame Barnier suggested 13 July – just 5 days away.

When the summons for the hearing arrived by fax, I learned with some emotion that this time it was to be in the judge's office, with both Victoria and the grandparents, as well as my Mum. At last the judge was organising what she had promised me back in September 1997 – my first meeting with Victoria since she had been taken in 1993, over five years ago ! That was really something to look forward to, and I took time out over the next hectic few days to prepare presents for her: clothes, hair ties, books, chocolate… and I sent her a telegram straight away so that she would know from me that we were at last going to be seeing each other. In the rush I didn't realize that the summons was actually thanks to my Mum's insistence with the judge.

Over the school year 1997-1998 I had been teaching French to beginner adults. We had been able to purchase a car also – just in time for the job interview, for which I had to travel the 30 miles from Belfast to Ballymena. During the year I also attempted to help a teacher who wanted to brush up on her French pronunciation: Jane was a Christian lady who had heard about our story and rung Jacqui to find us. We came to know her quite well – and Elvira adored her. She was the kind of person children found fascinating.

I decided to ask Jane if she would be at all able to accompany me to France for the hearing and was very relieved when she accepted (Jacqui at that time was spending a lot of her time looking after her Mum, who had a serious illness). I still felt it was important to have somebody with me when I went to France – I didn't want to just disappear without anyone knowing anything about it ! It was equally important to have the moral support of a friend with me. I didn't have the faintest idea which way things could go in Madame Barnier's office…

In 1997 the judge herself had kept me waiting for news of a meeting with Victoria, so it was perfectly normal for me to have stayed on in Northern Ireland – and since then I had found friends, and a job, a nice, comfortable house and a car... I could now tell the judge that everything was ready for Victoria to be returned to me, this time in Northern Ireland.

Tickets had to be bought in a hurry – it was the peak season of course. We were flying from Dublin this time, and that meant leaving home at 3:30 a.m. to make the two-and-a-half-hour drive down to catch the early plane in order to be in Versailles for the afternoon. It was quite a marathon – in July weather, too. Thankfully I was able to sleep a little on the coach on the way in to inner Paris, but I doubt whether Jane did. We only had a little time in the hotel room in Versailles to freshen up before heading off to the *Tribunal*. At least we had found a not-too-expensive hotel not far from it.

We were both very conscious that we were desperately in need of God's help in this: we didn't know what kind of reception we would be getting, whether Victoria would be open towards me or bitter, whether the judge would be seeing us all together or separately first... Jane asked me how I could be so calm. I had to think about it for a minute.

"I'm afraid I'm pretending to myself that meeting Victoria like this is something I do everyday," I answered. Strange the way the human mind works and protects itself. Once again, it was a purely instinctive reaction – simply the only way I could cope with all the overwhelming emotion and strain of the situation.

Bonjour, Victoria – for the first time in five years

It was a beautiful, sunny summer day, that 13 July. As we came out of our hotel, on the main avenue in Versailles, the *Avenue de Paris*, we could gaze down to our left at the famous *Château de Versailles* itself, with it's big, black, wrought-iron gates and fence, and cobble-stone court-yard, fronting the imposing, typically King Louis XIV-style building. All we needed to do was cross that main avenue and take one of the smaller streets opposite to arrive in front of the same huge *Tribunal de Grande Instance* where we had first been to see Judge Degrelle-Croissant, where Anutza and I had fled from, and which Axel had left so casually on the evening he was to be sentenced.

This was it. I took a deep breath and tried to remind myself that this was just another step along the way. It was all in God's hands anyway. I had to let go. Finding my way through the maze of that *Tribunal* shouldn't have been too difficult, but that day I had to ask someone. I stopped at an open door marked "*Renseignements*" to ask, and when I said my name and asked where Madame Barnier's office was, the two women who had been chatting inside both turned to stare at me. Somehow I got the feeling that they knew my name, and that I didn't quite look like the person they were expecting – the "zombie".

"Through the double doors, Madame, and it's the second door on your left."

As we followed their instructions – through the double doors – I looked at my watch: 2:00 p.m. exactly. Then suddenly there was everybody, sitting there in the waiting area in an end-of-smile quiet – as though someone had just made a joke and the smiles had just died away. There seemed to be quite a crowd, but I was only interested in finding Victoria. Surely that couldn't be her, that big girl sitting there with her back to me, that must be a cousin or someone...

My Mum was the first to get up.

"Oh, here's Delwyn," she said with her bright, cheery smile, covering me with hugs and kisses.

"Hello, Mother," I murmured, but I wanted to get to Victoria... I said a general "Bonjour" to everyone just to be correct, and then they all made room and there she was, sitting waiting for me, her brown eyes seeking out mine, a little shy – she had a chair for me next to her. My Mum was looking after Jane.

"*Bonjour, Victoria*," I said gently.

"*Bonjour, Maman*," she answered. It was wonderful. There was no sign of the judge for the moment.

"I've brought you a few things," I said. "Would you like to see them ?"

She nodded.

It was all a little stilted, what with everybody listening to us and watching, but I didn't care. I was with Victoria, and she was just drinking it all in. She opened her presents – I could see she loved the shorts and top set from Next, but didn't care that much for the hair things. Actually, she didn't look like a little girl who cared very much about her appearance – though amazingly enough she was actually wearing a summer dress ! We had always been told that since she had been in State care she <u>hated</u> wearing dresses. When I told her she looked nice in it, she said she had put it on for me. She also had a Maori hairband stuck nonchalantly into her hair – my Mum must have brought it over for her... We started talking about that, then about other things, school, etc. I half noticed that the judge had arrived and was talking to somebody in front of her office door. The grandmother, seated on the other side of Victoria, was starting to join in our conversation...

Then the judge was there, greeting everybody. I gave her a fairly guarded *"Bonjour, Madame,"* and everybody got up to move into her office. After about five minutes the judge came out and invited us in – except Suzanne (Axel's sister) and Jane, who had to wait outside. Normally Jeanette wouldn't have been allowed in either, but Madame Barnier was letting her in as my Mum's interpreter – to save the French Judiciary the cost of paying for one themselves, of course.

Thinking back, I realise how that first meeting with Victoria was very badly organised by the judge. We had no time to ourselves, no space for our emotions, just five minutes together in front of everybody and then straight into the judge's office – straight into a highly-charged conflict. It was almost doomed to disaster. The seating had already been arranged so that we were all in a semi-circle in front of the judge's desk, the grandparents on the far right-hand side, with Victoria next to them, a chair for me, then my Mum on my left and finally Jeanette.

The judge started positively enough.

"Well, Victoria, are you happy to see your *Maman* ?" she asked. At Victoria's rather shy nod, she went on.

"Yes, I can see that, because I've seen you smiling – even laughing, Victoria – for the first time. That's a good thing..."

Down to business

Then she turned on me.

"You have lodged an appeal, Madame Jones-Schmidt ?"

Obviously it didn't matter to her whether we talked about legal matters in front of Victoria or not, but it mattered to me.

"I would prefer not to speak about this in front of Victoria," I said. "I don't want her being upset."

Victoria made a move as though to go out, but Madame Barnier waved her back.

"*Non, non*," she said authoritatively. "Victoria can stay here."

I couldn't understand her reasoning. Did she think she would silence me by having Victoria there? Well, I certainly had nothing to hide from Victoria.

"Very well, Madame Barnier. Why did I appeal your decision to continue Victoria's placement with her grandparents ? Because Victoria's grandparents will not be able to care for her much longer." My Mum had said that Axel's Dad had told her that very clearly when he came to New Zealand. But to my surprise, both grandparents erupted.

"*Ah, non* ! We never said that !" The protests continued on for a few minutes. I turned to my Mum for confirmation of what I had said, but she rolled her eyes and shrugged her shoulders a little as though to say, "I know, but you weren't supposed to say it in public."

Who were they trying to hide it from, then – the judge or Victoria ? She would have to face up to it one day, wouldn't she – her grandparents might be long-lifers, but they wouldn't live forever…

When she saw and heard her grandparents' reaction, Victoria had gone very quiet and begun edging towards her grandmother, as though seeking refuge. She could obviously feel the division between us. I was aching to hug her, but I dared not make a move, even to comfort her, in case she rejected me completely – I could feel that at this stage that could be disastrous. Going to her grandmother had now become a habit for her, I realised, with an inner wince. I mustn't take things too fast – she *had* been totally separated from me for five years.

But then, as her grandfather raised his voice, explaining his position, Victoria started crying. It was too much for me.

"Madame Barnier, I protest," I said, my frustration spilling over. "I specifically asked that Victoria be spared any distress, and you didn't listen to me… You are entirely responsible for this !"

Victoria was heading for the door, still crying, and Jeanette was going with her, herself in tears. I had to just let them go, still helpless to comfort my own daughter.

The hearing went on, with Axel's Dad bringing out the accusations I had heard so many times before, and me defending myself. Sometimes the accusations seemed so ludicrous to me that I turned to my Mum to let her know what they were saying. Axel's parents were obviously still convinced that the "cult" story was for real. UNADFI and co. had done an expert job in getting them onto the bandwagon. It was a relief to have Mother there supporting me – yes, she was definitely supporting me, in spite of all my fears to the contrary. I owed her an apology.

The accusations were all hear-say, of course. Except that, as the judge said, they had the children's statements.

"Yes, children who were removed from their home from one day to the next, forbidden to see their parents, and pressured until they 'confessed'," I said. "There is absolutely no proof of any of these accusations. And by the way, why didn't you carry out investigations into the children's situation while they were still with their parents ?" I remarked drily. "Imagine – you might have found them with marks on their bottoms !"

The judge could say nothing to this, of course, just raised her eyebrows. Everybody knew that no evidence of ill-treatment had ever been found, and that on the contrary, all the proof was there to show that the children were all very healthy and well-developed.

She changed the subject by saying that *she* wouldn't like to have some of the other parents (i.e. parents of the other children who had been removed in 1993) as her friends.

"You choose yours, I'll choose mine, Madame Barnier," I told her, quick as a flash. Who did she think she was – she was about to tell me, just like Madame Degrelle-Croissant, who I was allowed to be friends with ! Madame Barnier looked a little taken aback. She was definitely not used to people talking to her in that way – I had better be careful, I thought. No need to get her nastier than she already is.

The judge changed tack.

"You must acknowledge that Victoria's grandmother, in particular, has been very kind in taking your daughter in and caring for her so as to avoid seeing her sent back to State care, Madame Jones-Schmidt."

Axel's Mum now spoke up.

"I have been a mum for Victoria – but all the while I've told her clearly that she still has her own Mum, and that no-one else can replace her…"

The judge was very pleased.

"You see, Madame Jones-Schmidt, you two could get along very well – have a really close, woman-to-woman relationship …"

I looked at her for a minute, wondering who was using who here.

"What I don't understand, Madame Barnier, is why Victoria's grandmother doesn't ask that my daughter be returned to me, her real mother – that's what she needs above all," I answered steadily. "And what's more, I don't see how there can be any sort of understanding between the grandparents and I when they are always endlessly accusing me, as you have seen today in your own office."

"No, no, it's not you that we're accusing," both grandparents protested. "It's the cult we accuse !"

"Oh, thanks," I said. "So you're just accusing me of being a zombie then, and an irresponsible mother ?"

They looked at me as though they had never quite thought of it that way before. And the picture didn't fit…

Arrangements, arrangements

The judge saved them from answering by changing the subject again.

"I cannot allow Victoria to come and visit you until I have more information about your situation in Northern Ireland," she declared.

"Madame, giving my address in the past has only led to harrassment," I replied. "I can only give you information if it is kept officially confidential."

"Everything that is in the file is confidential," she answered. "But I will need verifiable evidence of your details."

I asked her what exactly, to which she didn't answer, so I went on to describe the house to her, the school where Victoria would be able to attend ("well, it won't be this September, anyway," the judge murmured) and where I was to be teaching, that I even had a piano teacher for her…

"What about the conditions in which you could see Victoria ?" asked the judge. "We could organise something from September onwards…"

"Madame Barnier, I am free now, but I will be working in September," I said. "Actually, I am here until the day after tomorrow. Can we not organise visits now ?"

"No, no, we shall let Victoria enjoy her holidays," said the judge – as though my presence would prevent Victoria from enjoying herself – "and then you will be able to come with Elvira…"

"That is out of the question, Madame," I said quickly.

"Oh, yes, we *would* like to see our other little granddaughter," exclaimed the grandparents.

"Grandparents do have the right … they can claim their rights legally…" brought in the judge.

"Elvira will not be coming to France, not after what I've been through with Victoria," I said firmly. "Everybody, even the Public Prosecutor, said Victoria was a little darling, and then they kept her from me… how can you expect me to have any confidence in the French Judiciary ?"

"Madame Jones-Schmidt," spoke up the judge, trying to calm me, "I have promised not to do anything against Elvira – it's not as though as soon as you cross the border I will immediately say to the *gendarmes* 'Do what you have to'…"

My heart almost stopped beating. The way she said that made me all the more determined never to come with Elvira. Anyway, I knew that another judge could be appointed at any time by the Public Prosecutor in a new case concerning Elvira – Madame Barnier wouldn't need to know anything about it. I shook my head resolutely.

The judge sighed and went on to sum up her arrangements.

"Right, so you will come – without Elvira, if you like – then Victoria will perhaps go for a holiday to New Zealand so she can meet the family over there, and after that she will be able to go to Ireland... My only problem is that I have no guarantee that she will return safely to France – will you even be able to wander around France without attempting to take her out of the country ? I'm not sure."

I could put her mind at rest on that point.

"Madame Barnier, I would never do that, I would never perturb my child in any way. I think that everything I have said and done to this day has shown that that is exactly what I want to avoid at all cost – distressing Victoria."

The judge appeared satisfied. After Victoria going out in tears because she, the judge, had refused to listen to me when I pleaded for her not to distress my daughter, she could hardly contradict that.

While I was being so open and affirmative, she quickly popped in a prickly question.

"And about your husband, Madame Jones-Schmidt, have you any news of him ?"

"My husband's situation hardly concerns me, Madame Barnier, and anyway, I can't have anything to do with Mr Schmidt, he's a criminal," I ventured.

"No, no, that's not true...It wasn't his fault..!" The grandparents were defending their son. I went a little further.

"He was convicted as a criminal, you must admit."

"Yes, but he wasn't the real criminal, he shouldn't have been convicted, it was the cult's fault, not Axel's..."

"So you would say there was a miscarriage of justice concerning your son ?" I asked, as logical and matter-of-fact as possible.

"Oh, yes, there's no doubt about it..." They were both adamant. I glanced at the judge, to find her looking furious but unable to keep the grandparents quiet. Their position was not as hard against us as I had imagined.

"So you admit there was a miscarriage of justice for your son – why would that not be the case concerning Victoria, then ?"

But they could hardly say anything against that in front of the Judge for Children. Still, I had made my point: in reality, there was no difference – no proof against us, all the proof in our favour, just as there had been no proof against Axel and all the proof in his favour. The problem was that the Judiciary had taken a decision about Victoria before investigating anything; then they had refused to back down and admit there had been a mistake, when that became obvious; and finally they had tried to cover it all up by convicting Axel.

The judge had brought the hearing to an end although I had many things I still wanted to say… At least visits should now be getting underway, I thought, as we all filed out of the judge's office.

Outside, Victoria was sitting on her aunt's knees and refused to look up. Oh, no, I thought, she's blamed everything on me. Then before I knew it the judge had beckoned to Victoria and whisked her away into her office – completely alone, not even the court clerk was present – and the door was shut. When it finally opened again Victoria came out, nodding to the judge – they had obviously come to some sort of an understanding. Madame Barnier even gave her a kiss on each cheek as they said goodbye, and Victoria nodded again, shyly. It surprised me – such a gesture seemed strange and out of place for a judge, especially when I was desperately trying to build a relationship with Victoria myelf.

As Victoria looked round, her attitude towards me seemed rather cold and a little resentful … I went straight to her, concerned, and little by little I felt she was once again warming to me. It would just take time – and today we had time ! The judge had allowed us to spend the afternoon together. In the presence of her guardian grand-parents, of course, but it would still be my first, real visit with Victoria.

15

Clarifications
July 1998 – July 1999

One beautiful July afternoon in Versailles

It seemed to have been more or less arranged with the judge that we would go to the gardens of the *Château de Versailles* for the afternoon. At any rate, I had no doubt that the judge had taken all the necessary measures of security, and knew exactly where we were. I understood her fears – if ever Victoria was taken out of France and French jurisdiction, any fair judicial system abroad would give her into her mother's care almost immediately. We were very probably under surveillance, but who cared – it wouldn't stop me from savouring this time with Victoria.

The gardens are perhaps the most famous feature of Versailles, spreading down from behind the *château* in large tiers with statued fountains to the canal below with its rowing boats, and the surrounding forest with its many wide avenues and hidden historic sites.

For the short trip to the gardens the grandparents kindly took me in the back of their car with Victoria and Mother, so we had a chance to relax and talk together. In fact, we hardly stopped talking !

Victoria was a little shy, but very content to be with me. She showed me some of her school workbooks and school and music reports (which I had been requesting for a long time) and I showed her some Paul White "Jungle Doctor" books in French that I had brought with me.

Once in the gardens we strolled over to the canal. Victoria was obviously excited. First she sat down and dangled her feet over the concrete walkway, prompting her grandfather to tell her to be careful not to fall in. Then she was up and running alongside the canal with her sandals off, showing us her cartwheels, which she certainly did very well – poised and precise. I could only admire her coordination, and she smiled with pleasure.

We met up with people the grandparents knew – a little girl Victoria's age who had been in her class at school at one stage, with her little brother and Mum and Dad, whom the grandmother introduced me to (they must have known about the situation to some degree). The little brother was on his bike and rode straight over my shoe, leaving a dirty big tyre mark on the black patent leather. I just raised my eyebrows... I was more interested in seeing how Victoria got on with the other little girl, and there was definitely a reserve there – not much chumminess. It reminded me of what John Bowlby, the British child psychologist, had noted about children separated from their mothers early in life: that they often had difficulty making friends...

My Mum and Jane were chatting away, as were my sister Jeanette and Axel's sister Suzanne, while the grandparents strolled along between them. Victoria and I had time to be by ourselves or to wander in and out among the others as we liked. It was almost idyllic – the sunny summer afternoon, the relative quiet of the gardens, the tranquillity of the canal, we were able to relax and be ourselves... it was like a dream, and I refused to dwell on the underlying discordance with the grandparents. I was savouring every moment and Victoria was obviously delighted.

Soon she started running along the concrete walkway beside the canal, and her grandfather felt he had to call to her again to be careful. I was starting to understand why they felt they couldn't go on like this. It was a constant stress for them to keep an eye on her.

As for persuading her to put her sandals back on before we went for a cup of tea, that was another story ! She refused to listen to either of her grandparents and just kept running along the walkway, even jumping over the laps of people sitting there. The grandparents seemed to give up and walked over to the *café* for afternoon tea.

I was left gazing after Victoria, with my Mum and Jane nearby, all three of us caught between the need for somebody to keep an eye on Victoria and the grandparents' walk-away-and-leave-her attitude. So I took matters in hand and wandered after Victoria to explain to her that she *did* need to get her sandals on to come for something to eat. Was this a test, I wondered. To see how I would cope with Victoria being disobedient, perhaps. In fact, I felt she was just being mischievous and wanted attention more than anything else, though I did have to tell her not to jump over people – that could be really dangerous. I gave her time and she gradually came away from the water towards the *café*, with her sandals in her hands. I just kept talking and joking with her, keeping everything low-key.

Jane appeared with a camera (I had asked her to take some shots if she could, especially of Victoria and I) and with Victoria in a mischievous mood we got some brilliant ones: her standing in front of me with her sandals in her hands; the sandals in mid-air above my head, me ducking, and Victoria with her hands innocently by her sides and a big, mischievous grin on her face; then both of us laughing to the camera, with the sandals where they landed on the grass behind us; and finally Victoria sitting on the grass, with me doing up her sandals. She was enjoying letting herself be looked after and I was just loving being able to do such a normal, mother's job. In so many other ways I felt I couldn't yet be anything other than a 'stranger', but there was definitely that belonging. We were family. We were together for the moment and we were enjoying it. We were content.

We walked back to the *café* together and Jane managed to get there in front to get a photo of us arriving hand in hand, both of us smiling. She really did an excellent job taking photos, capturing the affection and fun and pure enjoyment – they were photos Axel and I were to treasure over the next year. I had been dismayed at first to see that when I had kissed Victoria hello and tried to hug her, she had stayed as stiff as a plank – even a casual arm around her shoulders was shrugged off. This was in such stark contrast to her responsiveness to the judge's kisses on both cheeks, and so unnatural that I began to wonder whether she hadn't been instructed to do it. On our way to the *café* she didn't seem to mind holding my hand, but when I took her by the hand again later on – somebody must have got a chance to say something to her in the meantime – she suddenly didn't want to ! I asked her why not, and her only answer was to grab my hand and attempt to run off with me...

Misplaced distrust

We all sat down around a big table in the *café* for real English Earl Grey and *du cake*. I couldn't finish my two slices, and offered one to Axel's Dad, who looked at me in surprise before accepting. It was bizarre to be sitting there getting along perfectly well with people who had just been my adversaries in the judge's office. Of course there were undercurrents – that could hardly be avoided. And now that we were all talking, I discovered there was a certain distance between the grandparents and my Mum – even between my Mum and Victoria – that I was surprised at.

Mother had already spent a few days with the grandparents, but Victoria hardly seemed to be attached to her or interested in her, in spite of all my Mum's obvious and persevering efforts. The fact that the grandparents had been appointed by the judge to supervise my mother with Victoria naturally put a barrier between my daughter and my mother. In spite of my apprehension about my Mum's visit in the first place, I couldn't help feeling disappointed for her – she had come all the way from New Zealand to get to know Victoria and try to help in some way, only to find that because she remained supportive of me she was given the cold shoulder. She wasn't fitting into what the Judiciary had planned.

Actually, I was to discover later that at an early stage of her visit the grandparents had brought out all the accusations about the church in France. I was so glad that Mother had been to the church and knew the truth for herself – if she hadn't seen it with her own eyes, the accusations could well have festered. As it was, she refused to become an accuser – and the grandparents therefore retreated, along with Victoria, to a safe distance. From their point of view, they couldn't possibly trust someone who didn't wholly condemn the "cult". It was heart-rending for my Mum.

First I had distrusted my Mum because I thought she had been turned against me, but she had proved me wrong by refusing to jump on the 'cult' accusers' bandwagon. Now the grandparents appeared to distrust her because she was supportive of her own daughter and refused to say our church was a 'cult'. And finally, the grandparents and I mutually distrusted each other because we were also at logger-heads over the 'cult' issue and therefore legal opponents. Yet here we all were getting on surprisingly well, for Victoria's sake. In fact, if the 'cult' accusations could only have been taken out of the equation, there would have been no grounds for any discordance in the family, no reason for Axel's exile, and Victoria would have the chance to have a real, normal family life once again. For the first time I glimpsed the chaos UNADFI and the Judiciary had wrought in the family – they certainly had a lot to answer for.

Suddenly Axel's Dad brought up the subject of Victoria's New Zealand passport, which we had got for her in 1992 and which had expired recently. I explained that in the current situation I couldn't apply for a new passport for her – there was some requirement I couldn't meet because she wasn't living with me and he suggested that they could perhaps help me. I said I would think about it.

"For the moment she can't go anywhere, you know," he said. It was a remark I was to brood over later on, and one that Axel's Mum was to bring up again in a later letter. Where could they be wanting to take her? I certainly didn't want to do anything that would enable anyone to make Victoria disappear somewhere.

After a while Victoria became restless – she had finished her lemonade and finished reading the Paul White cartoons I gave her – and started throwing stones up into the trees nearby: attention-seeking again, I thought. It was time to move. When we left the *café* and she suddenly grabbed my hand and started to run, she took me completely off-guard and with me wearing a tight skirt, she didn't get very far.

"I'd love to run with you, Victoria," I said, "But look at the shoes and skirt I have on !" It was as though she was wanting us to run away together. The visit was drawing inevitably to an end, and she could feel it. I timed her running to the gates and back instead.

"I still have a little present for Victoria back at the hotel," I explained to Axel's Mum. "Could we go and get it ?"

"I don't see why not," she said, looking questioningly at her husband, who agreed.

In the end I was even 'allowed' to take Victoria up to our hotel room – with my Mum accompanying us, to make sure we didn't run away...

There, I gave her a 3-colour gold bracelet that I had found for her in a shop in Belfast before I left. I couldn't mention anything about Axel, but I could talk about Elvira.

"Look, there's three strands, one for you, one for me and one for Elvira," I explained to her. "And we're all united together, like I hope we will be one day." She just looked at me and nodded, but she kept the bracelet on and fingered the delicate, plaited gold. I showed her a few photos of Elvira too, and talked to her about how I hoped I would be able to see her more often and that she would eventually be able to come home... It was our goodbye talk, though we avoided saying the word goodbye just yet. It was so special just having that little time to ourselves – my Mum was very discreet. Why wouldn't people let us keep on being together like this ?

Downstairs, the grandparents were becoming restless. Jane had to come up and tell us so.

"Shall we just have a little pray together ?" I asked Victoria. She nodded...

Once we came downstairs, Victoria seemed happy enough to go off 'home' with her grandparents. Our goodbye talk and that last present had settled things, avoided a difficult parting and got her looking towards the future. As I gave her a last kiss (in front of her grandparents again) she was still as stiff as ever, but giggling with it this time. We understood each other. I just ignored it completely and waved goodbye to her with a smile. She was under certain obligations and restraints, and I was too in a way, since I couldn't tell her about her Daddy. We just passed over what we couldn't change. She walked slowly away, jumping over bollards, fingering her bracelet, and I was the one who was left feeling bereft of her bright, mischievous presence, yet I much preferred it to be me rather than her. My Mum was the last one to leave us, lingering as though she would have liked to talk, but she also had to go. The grand-parents were waiting for her. Victoria would have ten days with her aunt and three weeks with her grandmother, but she was only allowed three hours with her *Maman*.

Reactions

Because I hadn't known whether the judge was going to let me visit with Victoria straight away or not, I had booked Jane and I into the hotel for two nights, just in case. So we were stuck in Versailles for the next day with nothing to do – ironically July 14th, the day of the Bastille liberation. It would have been nice if the French authorities could have retrieved a little of that spirit of freedom and freed my daughter!

What with being without Victoria again and seeing my Mum go away with her and the grandparents, I felt depressed. Poor Jane must have been totally bored. My mind was so taken up with it all that the fact that it was 14 July completely escaped me until the fireworks started going off that night and stopped us from sleeping. At least I could comfort myself with the fact that I had good news to take home for Axel. This first visit had gone really well, and I had also been able to score a few points in the judge's office. But would it really make a difference, and how long was this process going to take ?

Now the judge was saying that no progress could be made before she had my address and all the details about my life in Ulster in her file. Yet she had had all that information when I had applied for Victoria to return to New Zealand and it hadn't made a scrap of difference. No, she was simply wanting any pretext to prolong the process, as she had always done. If it wasn't my personal and professional details, it would be something else. Anyway, since I had appealed her last decision, the case had been sent to the Court of Appeal – again – so she could now sit back and consider it as being out of her hands. We were waiting for another summons to appear before the Court of Appeal. Things seemed to be going round in circles.

Back in Ulster other people were beginning to feel the drag too. It is difficult to pray on and on for years for someone when no progress seems to be happening.

"Do you never feel like just giving up and leaving Victoria in France ?" we were asked once. It cut to the quick and left me feeling weak, almost out of breath, though I realised they were only trying to be realistic. Humanly speaking there wasn't much I could say – there wasn't much we could do except wait for the next hearing – but we just couldn't bring ourselves to give up on our daughter.

As time went on and it seemed that Victoria was not going to be given back to us in the near future, I could also see some people, especially young mothers, backing away. I understood: it was too close to home to see two ordinary parents – especially with Elvira there with us, now a normal, bubbly child of three – and know that they had been deprived of their child simply because of their faith. It was too much because they inevitably looked at their own lovely children and wondered "How would *I* ever bear such a thing?" They perhaps didn't realise that we had never had to contemplate such a situation – we were placed before the *fait accompli* before we had time to think about it.

I knew only too well the anguish our situation could raise in a mother's heart – actually, the most difficult thing about the trip to France in 1998 was that I had had to leave Elvira behind: a little girl who was just the same age Victoria had been when she was taken. It brought all the emotions back and the fears of it happening again. Even while I was still in France with Jane I was constantly phoning home to check that everything was all right, and when I came out of the plane in Dublin and saw Axel and Elvira waiting there along with Jane's husband, my relief was overwhelming. I had always been that way with Elvira, but it seemed to be worse right then.

As time went on I realised too that I was entering new territory for me as a mother. I had not known Victoria after the age of three, so this was all new to me. Elvira was now going regularly to play group to prepare her for school in September 1999. Life went on.

Axel was still working away at his thesis, working at the odd job when he found one, advising a couple of friends about legal situations, etc. I was working part-time teaching French to secondary-school children.

I got some feed-back on the July 1998 visit from my sister Jeanette when she came to Portrush on holiday. She remarked to me that she now understood that they had "thrown themselves into something they should never have set foot in". The following year, when my Mum happened to return to Europe on a visit to Israel with one of my aunts, she decided not to visit Victoria – it wasn't worth it given the circumstances. I thought it wise of her. We had received Victoria's reaction to her first meeting with me by way of a short note, brief and to the point: she wanted to stay with her grand-parents, she wrote, "for a very long time yet" ! I was very glad that I had been with her, and knew that there were things Victoria had to do and say, although the truth lay elsewhere.

Meanwhile, Dr Paisley had been asking the President of the European Parliament to take action. In October 1998 he learnt that a European M.P. (M.E.P.) had been specifically designated by the President of the European Parliament to look into the case. Now the French authorities were being questioned by the European Parliament.

Over the last year we had come to know a man who was to open many doors of progress over the next few years: Mr Stephen Wilson. This man was a jewel. Fairly tall, in his fifties, with sparse grey hair, a ready grin, a mean sense of humour – and a laughter-wrinkled face – he started off by talking to us, listening mostly, joking us, and discreetly observing us. Elvira absolutely loved him and was always poking fun at him – and was always teased back of course.

Stephen was the one who advised us to be on the offensive, rather than defensive, in our approach to the French authorities. He also treated us to a B&B holiday near Portrush in August 1998, which really was a treat – though we had travelled, we hadn't truly been on holiday since Victoria had been taken. Stephen brought normality much closer to home than it had ever been since 1993.

In fact, he booked us in at the same place for an unexpected holiday in the summer of 1999 – and told us he was expecting to see us there with Victoria, perhaps next year…I remembered Professor McLeod saying something similar after taking us to the beach at Crawfordsburn, not far from where he lived on the east side of Belfast Lough. Victoria's separation seemed so utterly wrong, and these people were not only praying for justice to be done – they believed God would answer.

The first of Stephen's door-opening exploits was to introduce us to Mr William Wright, a councillor in Ballymena and a very successful Christian businessman. As he said himself, he had decided early in business to set apart 10 % of his profit for Christian ventures, and anyone could see how much God had blessed him in return. A respected member of the community, Councillor Wright was also someone who wanted to be sure about what he was doing, and met with us himself a couple of times, even taking us out for lunch; and by January 1999, with a hearing in the Versailles Court of Appeal coming up for 28 January, the Wright Evangelical Trust had offered to help us with our increasing legal and travelling expenses. To say we were grateful would have been a gross under-statement. We were just scraping by as it was, and each trip had meant a lot of calculating and juggling of our meagre financial resources. That didn't mean we were going to take advantage of Councillor Wright's generosity – we would still be flying economy class all the way – but this was truly sharing our burden. And this man and his wife would also be faithfully praying for us too!

Preparing the proof for Victoria's return

Others were moving – we knew we too needed to do everything we possibly could. We were beginning to feel that time was running out: Victoria was now almost nine years old. We needed to get things moving.

Back in 1998, before I had even seen Victoria for the first time, I had sent her booklets which were the translation of a fun book for children which helped them understand the Bible – by Rhonda Paisley. I translated it myself and sent Victoria a chapter at a time, and she had already sent me back a few that she had finished (there were games and drawings for her to do). What else could I do to give her some sort of Biblical instruction ? I didn't feel I could send her to a Protestant church in France without eventually drawing them into the legal wrangle, which I wouldn't have wished on anybody, and anyway, I didn't know any church I could really rely on in France.

I had also sent her an English story book, along with story, song and pronunciation tapes and a few written exercises. Although she completed some of these and sent them back, she never got round to doing the speaking part – the most interesting. I could see that whatever I did and however I presented it, it was not going to be received with enthusiasm. It all depended on the grandparents' attitude to these things, of course. Nevertheless, it was a start. I was doing what I could.

When this approach to Victoria's English did not seem to be having much success, I inquired about the possibility of her taking up lessons with the British Council in Paris. Everything was worked out, and Victoria was enrolled for the year – one lesson every Wednesday morning (a day she had off school, as in many schools in France). Then I had to insist that the grandparents take her in for it, and that proved difficult, although they had said at the hearing in July that they were all in favour of her learning English. I had to write to the judge about it (without a reply, as usual) before she was finally taken to the second lesson of the year, on 7 October 1998.

Victoria did very well at the British Council, and her teacher said she found her a delight to teach, and very meticulous in her work. Everything was looking fine until March 1999, when suddenly, just at the time the teacher was about to prepare the class for the end-of-year Cambridge exam, the grandparents stopped taking her. I could not understand it. Just when Victoria had been doing so well, she was being deprived of the fruit of all her conscientious, hard work. I had spoken to both the secretary and Victoria's teacher over the phone, and had explained to them that I hoped Victoria would soon be able to come and live with me in the UK.

Whatever the reason, Victoria's English lessons were abruptly halted, and when at my insistence she sat the exam anyway, she obviously didn't do nearly as well as she would have after proper preparation. We had been paying for the lessons ourselves, and it was frustrating to see something so positive for Victoria being thrown away, seemingly at a whim.

It was Stephen who thought of another way of preparing Victoria's return: why not get the opinion of an expert British child psychologist, someone who could assess Elvira and reassure the judge as to our living conditions and the care Victoria would receive? And while we were at it, a medical report from an independent paediatrician wouldn't do any harm. And he knew just the people we needed, too…

So in January 1999, the expert psychologist visited us in our home in Belfast and talked with Elvira and I; then he visited Elvira again to observe her at play group and got independent feedback from the play group organiser, who knew nothing of the situation with Victoria; and finally returned a third time to our home to carry out a few simple tests with Elvira.

The report was excellent and the psychologist had done what I hadn't expected – given a very positive assessment of me as a mother. I had also asked him for advice about how Victoria should be returned to my care in the least stressful way, and he actually outlined in his report some very clear recommendations. The process should take about three to four weeks, to allow Victoria the time to adapt to the idea, but no longer than a month so as to avoid her feeling any distressing uncertainty about her future. It was plain good sense, as anyone could see, and it was going to be an essential part of the Court of Appeal file for Victoria.

Elvira's medical assessment was also duly carried out, by a consultant from an independent clinic in Northern Ireland, and it was also very positive.

We also needed to renew Victoria's New Zealand passport so that the judge would not be able to say that she couldn't visit Northern Ireland because she didn't have the necessary identity documents. So we sent off for a new application form – and found to our amazement that the rules had changed ! Because Jane had seen Victoria in July 1998, she was able to help us and we posted the application off with two photos that Victoria had sent me at Christmas – why she had sent two, I don't know, unless one was perhaps implicitly destined for her Daddy. Ultimately, God had known we needed two.

Finally, a young Christian couple whom Axel had known in Belfast even before Elvira and I came over from New Zealand, had recently gone abroad for two years. Their lovely, newly-decorated semi-detached house was sitting empty, and they would have preferred to have someone in it during their absence. Our home in Belfast was very comfortable, but we could not give that address to the French Judiciary because Axel had been far too 'visible' there over the years – all the neighbours knew him, etc. So we decided to rent their house from them for a while, so that we could give that address to the judge.

Everything seemed to be falling into place...

The Court of Appeal, the second time round

Jacqui made the effort to travel over with me for the hearing on 28 January 1999, and I was extremely grateful once again for her presence.

This time I got the chance to meet up in Versailles with a legal adviser named Gabriella, who had come especially from Brussels (from the office of the M.E.P. who had been designated by the European President to look into Victoria's case, following Dr Paisley's representations). She had some experience of dealing with the French Judiciary as well as French lawyers and could appreciate the difficulties I was facing. She seemed disgusted at the way the French authorities were treating us.

Her presence caused quite a stir in the comfortable Court of Appeal routine. She had to repeat her name and position several times before the court clerk at last understood that this was someone sent by the European Parliament to check up on them. It was quite novel for me to see them so uncomfortable, but the hearing was eventually postponed until May (was Gabriella's presence their real incentive for postponement ?). The Court was very probably aware that with European elections coming up in June that year, May was a good safe time to be able to have a hearing without any 'interfering busybodies' from Strasbourg !

Gabriella's advice was to get a good lawyer, and get one quick – although she understood my qualms about this, after the Deville-court fiasco in 1996 and the huge sum of money we had had to fork out. I followed this up after the hearing by contacting our former Court of Appeal lawyer, Maître Lamont – the only French lawyer who had done a good job for us. He eventually took the case on again and was there to defend me in May 1999 when the appeal hearing finally took place.

The official reason for the postponement was because I had lodged a formal complaint against the President of the Court, Mr Bauer, for implying in his 1994 Court of Appeal decision that Victoria was not even our child. Such a complaint had to go through the Supreme Court, *la Cour de Cassation*, and we had received a copy of the ruling in December 1998 – they covered for Mr Bauer, as we had expected. However, when I went to the hearing on 28 January 1999, more than one month later, the Court of Appeal claimed that they had not yet received a copy of that judgement and so could not proceed with the hearing – therefore postponing it until May. Mr Bauer had been covered for, but the complaint had still had an effect: this time he would no longer be the President of the Court of Appeal, but only one of the counsellors – no small demotion for a Court of Appeal magistrate.

The memory of our visit to Versailles in January 1999 was dominated by the terribly cold weather we had. Poor Jacqui froze, though at least she had thought of bringing a warm hat – and you really needed it that winter. Once again, since I was making the trip from Northern Ireland to France anyway, I had requested to be able to see Victoria – it was her birthday on January 27, and I had all her birthday presents with me to give her. Although I had asked to see her at least a month before the hearing and several times since then, I had received no reply at all. So once again, I was obliged to book in to the hotel for several days, just in case there was going to be any possibility of spending time with her at some stage. The French Judiciary seemed to be doing this to me regularly, on purpose, wasting other people's time and money.

I did ask the President of the Court (who was soon to become a member of the National Observatory on Cults – the *Observatoire*

Interministériel sur les Sectes – which had been set up in France in 1997) for permission to see Victoria over the next few days, since I was in France, but he replied curtly that only the Judge for Children could decide on that. In other words, there was no hope – I had already written to Madame Barnier and received, as usual, no reply.

Biding our time – and a last try before the Court of Appeal

Since I wasn't going to be able to see Victoria, I tried to lay aside my deep mistrust of the grandparents and phoned them on the Saturday to ask if I could come and give Victoria her presents. Although they had encouraged me to do so in the past, they now refused to do anything without the judge's permission. In the end we went to the grandparents' home on the Sunday to hand over the big bag of presents. We fortunately arrived at the same time as another resident and so were able to get through the coded-entry outside door, but there was no answer to my ring at the doorbell. I decided to try the neighbours, and was greeted by a lady who was all smiles until she learned who I was… still, she took the presents and told me she would make sure Victoria got them.

At least we didn't waste our time in France. During the couple of days we had left, we managed to go to the *Cour de Cassation* (the Supreme Court) in Paris – quite a scary experience, I think Jacqui was wondering if we were actually going to make it out of the place – and withdraw the 9 December 1998 decision concerning Monsieur Bauer that the Court of Appeal had claimed they hadn't yet received. Now we had the proof, at least, that it had been rendered and that they should have had it.

We also fitted in a quick visit to the British Council, to meet Victoria's teacher and see around the place – very modern and well-equipped, and they obviously employed teachers of a very high standard. In her letters Victoria had been saying things like she "didn't like the way the teacher taught" and that she "didn't have any friends there". However, her teacher said the opposite: that she was cheerful, a good worker and got on well with the other children. Unfortunately, she did often arrive late…I had suggested Victoria attend a Saturday morning class, because the traffic was so much lighter going into Paris on a Saturday, but the grandparents had decided on the Wednesday lesson so they could go to their country house at the weekend.

By the time the postponed Court of Appeal hearing finally took place on May 25, Victoria had sat her Cambridge exam and still got a fairly good result in spite of having left off half-way through the year – but I was feeling more and more frustrated with the grandparents. However, all this came out in the Court of Appeal hearing. This time it was held in the big, wood-panelled courtroom and the judges were really listening – well, two of them were: Monsieur Bauer just sat and watched, without saying a word. Maître Lamont pleaded the case so well it was almost like living through it all over again – I almost walked out, it was so painful to hear.

As the Court had foreseen, nobody from the European Parliament was able to attend the hearing in May because of elections, but the Court did receive a very supportive and sympathetic letter expressing concern in particular at my "lack of access" to Victoria.

The President of the Court made a surprise statement: the only thing preventing Victoria from being returned to me, he said, was the Judge for Children's *Commission Rogatoire*, a kind of investigation order, that had been sent to the Belfast Royal Courts of Justice and apparently not yet returned. It was the first I had heard about it.

The President and the woman counsellor, were particularly sensitive to the fact that the grandparents were influencing Victoria against me, and this came out in their judgement. The Court ordered that Social Services be called back into the case, but only to monitor the grandparents' custody of Victoria. Nevertheless, they did not overturn the Judge for Children's ruling, and returned Victoria once again to the grandparents' care! Madame Barnier had won again – so we appealed to the Supreme Court in France, the *Cour de Cassation*.

Eventually I did receive the investigation order and a clerk from the Belfast Royal Courts of Justice delivered the writ to me in the new home we had started renting just a few months before. I provided all the necessary evidence of my circumstances, and the

Courts sent the investigation report back to France in July 1999. I got a distinct feeling that they had never done such a thing before, i.e. carried out an investigation into someone's circumstances on behalf of another country. It wasn't even as though there were extradition proceedings against me or anything.

The atmosphere in Madame Barnier's office on June 29 that year was rather tense. The judge had been covered for by the Court of Appeal, but there had been so many troubling incidents during the last couple of years – the attempt to baptize Victoria in 1998, the battle about English lessons over the past year, and now the Court of Appeal partially criticizing her judgement... I also informed her that all the information she had asked the Belfast Courts for had been sent to her, and even provided her with a copy of it. She was obliged to give in somewhere. Perhaps the fact that she was expecting a baby herself made her feel vulnerable and a little more sympathetic than usual – even French judges have human feelings... don't they ?

Best of all, at that hearing Victoria said in front of everyone that she wanted to come and live with me, and the judge even added that the grand-parents would just have to get used to this idea, and show all due respect for my parental responsibility. The judge openly acknowledged that Victoria should eventually be returned to my care, gave me an unconditional visiting right in neutral surroundings and said that I could see Victoria whenever I liked. At last things seemed to be moving !

16

The heat is on
July 1999 – July 2000

A crucial year

The visiting right was undoubtedly a major breakthrough. I was also able to have another visit with Victoria after the hearing – this time we all went to the hotel where Jacqui and I were staying, and had a little wander round the shops in Versailles. It was such a natural thing for a mother and daughter to do, and I certainly savoured it, once again – taking Victoria's hand to cross the road, calling her "my daughter" to other people... We were able to go on ahead and Jacqui cheerfully brought up the rear with the grand-parents, though how she managed to communicate with them, I cannot imagine. Like many French people, they could read and write English far better then they spoke it, and like many English-speaking people, Jacqui – er – didn't really speak a second language either, though not for lack of trying.

For the first time we had brought a video camera with us, and Jacqui had the unenviable task of trying to be unobtrusive with it. Although the grandparents did not seem to appreciate being filmed – who does – I found them much more relaxed this time, as though they were starting to accept me as Victoria's mother at last. I was also able to have a little time with Victoria by myself again.

Now that we had the visiting right, though, it was going to be another matter to exercise it in good conditions. Once again, Madame Barnier had not given any specifications as to time, place, frequency, etc., just like Madame Degrelle-Croissant before her (and contrary to French law, as was the fact that as usual she sent us the judgement much later than the legal limit of eight days). She certainly wasn't being any help in getting visiting rights organised in a hurry. So it was up to us to negotiate with social work "assistants" as they call them in France, and we had reasonable doubts about the sincerity of their "assistance". In our case anyway, and in the cases of the other families, they had been anything but. I remained apprehensive about them, knowing by experience what French Social Services were capable of in the way of family destruction – but in Maître Lamont's opinion we wouldn't be able to make any further progress if we didn't use the right to visit. What it boiled down to for me was: was I entirely trusting in God ? If I was He would "pluck my feet out of the net"[1].

Both Axel and I felt very anxious to get things moving – this was going to be a crucial year for Victoria, who would be turning ten in January 2000, and we felt we had to give it everything we had so that she could return home as soon as possible. That meant I had to give up the secondary-school teaching I had been doing the previous year so that we could get these visits going. Elvira was now in school, and enjoying it, and that did make it easier for me to get away, though as time went on I was to feel more and more torn between Victoria in France and Elvira in Northern Ireland – an emotional rack.

From the beginning, we got the distinct feeling that the Versailles Social Services were not too keen on being back on the case. Their handling of the case in November 1993 had ended with us writing to them to say there was no point in continuing to try and work with them, since they refused to give us a programme of visits or anything more than a half-hour visit with Victoria, although they had nothing to reproach us with. It had already been a 'hot potato' case, and nobody seemed willing to pick it up again. Then there was

[1] Psalm 25:15

the fact that Social Services had been speedily dropped from the case after the grandparents attempted to have Victoria baptized into the Roman Catholic church in 1998... Social Services were definitely in a delicate position.

Throughout August and September we continued to ask for appointments just to get things started. Could I ring back... somebody else was looking after the case... they didn't have a copy of the judgement... If it wasn't one thing it was another. I had been given an unconditional visiting right, so it should have been up to me to decide when I wanted to visit and for how long – I was Victoria's mother and I was the one coming all the way from Northern Ireland. The judge had clearly said I could see Victoria when I wanted. Social Services disagreed. Maître Lamont wrote to them to protest that they were setting themselves above the judge by adding conditions to what she had ruled. They refused to budge an inch.

They unreasonably insisted that I should come for an initial meeting with them only, refusing to let me see Victoria at the same time: first they had to have a meeting with me, then one with Victoria and the grandparents, and only then would they be able to agree on a meeting between Victoria and I. This was of course a total waste of time and money for me – if I was coming to France anyway, I wanted to be able to see Victoria. More importantly, the grandparents surely shouldn't have any say in the matter – if it had been a case between husband and wife, it would have been understandable, but in the circumstances the grandparents were only custodians, legally speaking. There was no need to consult them, except for travel arrangements, which could be done by phone – and they were both retired and did not live far away. What was the problem ? In the end, Maître Lamont advised me to fix a date for a meeting with Social Services and to tell them that I wished to visit Victoria afterwards – put them on the spot. I followed his advice and went to see them on 26 October 1999.

Into the "lions' den" of French Social Services

As was to be expected, it was a prickly affair. The ARPE premises

– *Service d'Aide à la Rencontre Parent-Enfant* or Assistance for Parent-Child Contact – struck me as rather attractive. It was behind a huge wooden door on one of the main avenues in Versailles – rather grand-looking from the outside. Inside, the grounds were well-looked after, with low buildings arranged in a triangle, and the twenty-something girl at reception was very polite, even welcoming. When she heard my name she gave me a second look, though. Perhaps I should carry an ID badge around France, I wondered – everybody seems to doubt who I am. She showed Jacqui (who was my faithful moral support once again) and I into a bright little room obviously designed for young children, with little chairs, toys and big windows – the perfect showroom.

I was then invited – "alone, please" – up into the office area, where I was received by a long-brown-haired girl about my own age whom I had spoken to on the phone several times: Mme Fabre. She watched me closely, and appeared not to relish what she was doing. She attempted to take a very logical, reasonable attitude towards the whole thing, but of course she had a big problem – the whole case was totally illogical ! I had to wait a while in the office too... At last another woman appeared – "Madame Bachelet", very made-up, with long, dyed hair up in a bun – who apologised for being late. She was not any more at ease than her colleague.

When we at last settled down to business, Madame Bachelet started by saying that she knew I would prefer to see my daughter every day, but that that was not possible in the circumstances, i.e. with me living in Northern Ireland. Very observant of her – but it told me one important thing: she must have known all about the case from the very beginning, because those had been my very words to Social Services way back in November 1993: if we were going to be having visits, I wanted to be able to see my daughter every day.

I laid down my arguments about seeing Victoria in the coming days, after my visit with them – and got nowhere. They were refusing to do what the judge had ordered, it was that simple – and now I had proof that they were preventing me from exercising my legal visiting right.

Their excuse was that that was not how they worked, they had to see Victoria and the grandparents first, separately – no, they couldn't group the meetings over a couple of days, or do things the other way round, the grandparents first and me afterwards, followed by a visit between Victoria and I. And it was out of the question that they make any exceptions, even though I was coming from abroad. They were, after all, part of French Social Services, and it was well-known in France that they were a "state within the State" – used to laying down the rules and seeing everyone else jump.

They took note of my suggested programme of visits (increasingly frequent visits over a period of four weeks, based on the British psychologist's recommendations), and they had already arranged a meeting with Victoria and the grandparents to see if the arrangements made with me "suited them" – so basically the grandparents would decide, in the end. I pointed out that this should not be the case, especially after the Court of Appeal had criticized the grandparents for being biased against me, but they didn't want to hear. As the conversation drew to a close, I said I hoped everything would go well when they saw Victoria. Unfortunately, they took it badly.

"But it is *us* who hope *you* will get on well with your daughter, Madame Jones-Schmidt," answered Madame Bachelet, visibly annoyed, then almost bit her tongue. She had shown her true colours in that moment, in spite of her previously honeyed words. So the problem was me and how I got on with Victoria, was it ? Typical social work fault-finding. Nobody else had dared even suggest such a thing, not even the judge. It was clear to me from that moment that these people would be no help in preparing Victoria's return home. In the short silence that followed I made a mental note of it, but said nothing.

One thing was for sure: we had been right not to start those visiting rights when Victoria had been small – it would have been certain disaster for us all.

What's best for Victoria

That day, after Social Services had refused to arrange a visit with Victoria, I spoke to Maître Lamont about it and decided to try the grandparents again. The ARPE people were refusing to arrange a visit with Victoria while I was in France, and how could I leave without seeing her, I asked. How about we got together just as we had already done in 1998 and 1999 after the hearings with the judge? I did have an unconditional visiting right, after all.

Well, not only did they agree, to my surprise, but I was able to speak to Victoria on the phone for the first time ! So we met with Victoria after school and the five of us (Jacqui was with me again) went out for a very enjoyable meal – we even had a friendly row over who would pay the bill. It was brilliant being with Victoria in such natural circumstances, no strings attached – I wasn't seeing Victoria on the condition that I call the church a "cult" or give information about Axel, I was seeing her simply because I was her mother. Victoria was relaxed and happy – on the way back to the hotel she laid her head on my shoulder. In spite of the separation, we were becoming closer every time we met. It was a great consolation amidst our battles with Social Services – though only a second-hand consolation for Axel of course, who had to keep quietly in the background.

Social Services were soon going to try to attack my growing closeness with Victoria, though. They met twice with the grandparents after meeting with me and strictly warned them never to agree to any visits except at the ARPE, also persuading them that visits every week were far too much, although the grandparents themselves had been to see Victoria *every week* as soon as she was taken in February 1993. To me, their excuse was that my programme didn't suit the grandparents – which I knew wasn't true. I had in fact telephoned Axel's Mum a few days before travelling to France for that first meeting with the ARPE to make sure that the programme of visits I was submitting was all right with the grandparents. She had told me clearly that they would be able to bring Victoria to meet me on Monday and/or Tuesday evenings in Versailles, from 5-8 p.m., and that this fitted in with Victoria's time-table. What's more, I knew Mondays and Tuesdays were better for the ARPE, because they had said they were very busy on Saturdays.

So after me arranging everything happily to suit Victoria and the grandparents, Social Services were now destroying it all with their double-dealings, lying to me that my programme didn't suit the grandparents.

To top it all off, Social Services also decided that after the first three visits they would be drawing up a report on how the visits were going, although the judge hadn't asked for that and it was totally unnecessary since visits were only to allow Victoria and I to get to know each other better in view of her return with me. Having seen the contemptuous, judgmental attitude shown by Madame Bachelet and knowing how Social Services had treated the other families back in 1993 – 1994, I could already see what way the report would be likely to go.

But Social Services had done far worse than just making the grandparents withdraw their agreement to my visiting programme: they had made not only the grandparents suspicious of me – tense and distrusting again – but Victoria too. They now actually had her echoing her grandparents and telling me that it was better to have visits less often – imagine a daughter telling her mother that after almost seven years of separation ! I was heart-broken to see her caught up in this tangled judicial mess and suffering from it. They were very obviously manipulating my child against me – and I was not going to put up with it.

No wonder Victoria was ill-at-ease when I saw her again, ten days after our enjoyable meal together. The visits with Social Services had clearly upset her and she no longer felt free to talk to me spontaneously.

"Why can't you come and see me at the ARPE ?" she asked me, almost resentfully, as though I was just being difficult. It was like a stab to my heart. Her attitude was totally out of character and I could only conclude that she was under a lot of pressure. And she had only been to see Social Services once – what would the result be after a year, I wondered. It was high time for an ultimatum.

I informed Social Services that in Victoria's best interests I needed guarantees that they would not try to use visits as a means to prevent the end (i.e. Victoria's return home), and that I wished the visits to be unsupervised, since my visiting right was unconditional and there had never been any charges against me. They refused both. Given the circumstances, Axel and I decided to write immediately to cancel all arrangements with them and ask them to stop all contact with Victoria and the grandparents. They seemed more bent on promoting conflict than contact.

When I discussed the situation on the phone with Madame Fabre, she simply said:

"Well, Madame Jones-Schmidt, go and find another organisation to arrange your visits!" Her tone implied there weren't any others. So where could we turn now ?

First, we attempted to arrange visits in the most simple way – through the grandparents. After all, this had worked well until now on four different occasions, and Maître Lamont wasn't against it. But the ARPE people had seemed to have put them irretrievably on their guard against me and anything I might suggest, and they were definitely not willing to cooperate as they had done in October: they seemed to have regressed back to the uncooperative attitude they had had towards me in the past. Instead of encouraging the grandparents and I to get on better together, in Victoria's best interests, Social Services had reinstated distrust and division between us. We were back to square one.

So Axel and I decided to look into the "another organisation" idea that Madame Fabre had unwittingly put into our heads. In fact, we found two organisations which weren't linked to Social Services as such – called Mediation Centres. One wasn't too far from Versailles, and the other was in inner Paris. I tried the one near Versailles first, but they did not accommodate people coming from abroad, only from the area, as they depended on the municipality for funding. The one in Paris was the only possibility left and… yes, they accepted parents from abroad ! However, we would need to have the judge's permission to be able to use their facilities…

One important change had come about during our negotiations with Versailles Social Services: I had started talking to Victoria on the phone. We hadn't wanted to do this until contact really started up regularly, but at this stage we felt it was absolutely vital. Victoria needed it, especially as the failure of the ARPE Social Services had plunged us both once again into the uncertainty which the expert psychologist had already warned us was so unhealthy for Victoria.

Visits start – but Victoria disappears

To be able to start visits at the Mediation Centre, or more exactly, the "House of Mediation" – and it was so much more like a family home atmosphere – I needed the judge's consent. How could I possibly hope for that from Madame Barnier ? I knew she was as thick as thieves with the ARPE people. But I was in for a surprise – and it wasn't a change of heart by Madame Barnier.

When I had written to the judge to state my reasons for putting an end to negotiations with the ARPE people, I had stumbled on the fact that Madame Barnier had just left on maternity leave (yes, of course – she had been pregnant at the hearing back in June…). First I was told that there was no-one to replace her, which I protested. Then, a few days later, a judge replacing her wrote back to me – refusing to allow me to arrange visits through the grandparents. So we decided to ask this judge for a change of venue for the visits – the House of Mediation instead of the ARPE – and on 10 December 1999, she sent us a letter agreeing to this. We were over the moon. We really hoped that this would be a whole different story to the ARPE experience.

The grandparents were *not* happy – they would have to take Victoria all the way in to inner Paris to see her mother – much worse than just taking her to Versailles, which was practically next door to their home town. Now that I was phoning Victoria, I also spoke to them a few times, and they were obviously very reticent about the House of Mediation – another one of my "wild ideas", they seemed to be thinking, like the British Council lessons... But the interim judge had given her consent, and there was nothing they could do but comply. Besides, the new venue was so much better for Victoria.

The House of Mediation was almost a complete contrast to the ARPE. They had only just moved into new premises, so they weren't as nice yet – but atmosphere and the rooms were homey and relaxed. The difference was overwhelming. Here, the objective was clearly to mediate between parents so that their children could know and appreciate both of them in the best possible conditions. It was an invaluable find – and came at just the right moment.

Almost the first question they asked me was whether I held parental responsibility. Once they knew that I did, and that there were no charges against me, they appeared rather puzzled as to why the grandparents had custody. It didn't make sense to any logical mind. As for the grandparents making use of visits to ask me whether there was any news of Axel, it simply sounded completely out of place. I dismissed any discussion about Axel and tried to bring the discussion back to Victoria and me again.

Understandably, with Victoria having lived with them for the past five years, the grandparents were very attached to her: Victoria had almost become their last little daughter and it was extremely difficult for them to come round to the idea of letting her go... and Victoria, being a sensitive child, felt an obligation of loyalty towards these elderly grandparents who had "rescued" her from State care. However, in the Mediation Centre, the grandparents were brought little by little to recognize and accept my place as Victoria's mother.

To be fair to them, they had been encouraged not to accept it in the past – by the judge herself. Madame Barnier had told them that the Court of Appeal decision had changed nothing; and that they should not allow me to see Victoria without them being present. With that being put into their heads by the judge, it wasn't surprising that I still had problems trying to arrange visits with them, even at the Mediation Centre. For example, five minutes before the end of our third visit the grandmother suddenly appeared in the room unannounced, and Victoria immediately shut the book she was writing in – a diary of what we did during our visits together – and stood up with a look of guilt on her face. She couldn't really be at ease, and my heart ached for her.

What really got to me, though, was when I saw that Victoria was still being influenced against me. For example, when I suggested to Victoria that she complete the course she had started the year before at the British Council, she was quite positive about it, and said yes, she would like to. The next time I saw her and mentioned it again, she became quite upset and said she really did *not* want to return. When I asked her why, she said she didn't know – she only knew that she didn't want to go ! It was exactly the same story with the holiday in Northern Ireland over Easter – she was enthusiastic to start with, but the next time I saw her she definitely did *not* "want" to come. When I asked her why that was, she said that "the Easter holidays are the best". I had to just let these things go, not wanting to bring Victoria under further pressure.

I suppose things were bound to come to a head sooner or later, and it eventually happened in Easter, 2000. Both the grandparents and Victoria had told me that they were going to their country house for the Easter holidays, and Victoria confirmed that to me when I rang her just before they left. These were the holidays I had hoped Victoria would be spending with me, and here they were "going away" once again.

However, when I rang them at their country house a couple of days later, they weren't there. So where were they ? I rang back the next day, and they still weren't there. I was starting to become seriously worried. I rang the judge, but she wouldn't answer, so I sent her a fax: where was my daughter, I wanted to know. The days passed, and still no news of Victoria. I wrote to the judge again. Finally, one week after they had disappeared, they reappeared out of nowhere.

"Actually, we've been for a short holiday to Crete," the grandmother had to confess when I finally got them on the phone. "It was a birthday present for me from my husband."

"Crete !" I exclaimed aloud. "But you can't just disappear to another country with my daughter without asking me or at least informing me – and how did Victoria get to Crete without any papers…"

"Oh, she has a French identity card," she told me serenely. I couldn't believe my ears. In France the only way a child can be issued with an identity card or any other identity document is at the specific request of one of her parent(s) – one of those with *parental responsibility*…

"Where did you get the identity card from ?" I asked, a little breathlessly.

"Oh, er… through the Town Hall at home," answered Axel's Mum. "They were very good about it."

It was another *fait accompli*. But we would be looking into it – the French authorities had made a big mistake on this one.

Good times at the House of Mediation

In spite of outside pressure, Victoria and I were still able to spend some excellent moments together thanks to the House of Mediation. Just being able to relax with each other was a treat. I brought enough things to keep us busy, and Victoria sometimes brought games she liked as well. After the first two visits, lasting two then three hours respectively, we were able to spend more time with each other and have a meal together too – two visits for four and a half hours, and two that lasted for six.

But we couldn't stay cooped up inside all that time, it was off-putting for Victoria and there was no reason for it – especially with things going so well that Victoria had said to me during our visit on 29 March that "what she really wanted was to be with me" (I later learned that she had said this to her grandmother as well, and told school friends that she would be going to school in Northern Ireland the following year). It was of course very encouraging, but I was wary of saying this too loud or too publicly in case the judge or anyone else decided to make Victoria say the opposite the next time she saw me. It was galling to think that the judge could and would use anything Victoria said, but that I couldn't for fear of bringing Victoria under further pressure. So I just kept the knowledge of it preciously to Axel, myself and people we could trust: I knew what Victoria really wanted and that was what mattered most.

Judge Barnier was back on the scene, and despite Maître Lamont's insistence, she was still not answering our letters asking for freer visits. The House of Mediation people took pity on us and organised themselves so that one of the members of staff could accompany us for about an hour's walk outside – usually very enjoyable because they were mostly very nice people, often voluntary workers interested in mediation work as a way of getting families back together.

I was impressed with their devotion to people and the way they let the families just get on and enjoy being with each other without making them feel under pressure of being "watched". They offered mediation sessions for the adults involved, but if the parents made no progress in getting on with each other for the sake of the children, mediation usually stopped after a year. I had quite a few sessions of discussions with the grandparents – well, mostly with Axel's Mum, actually. And the mediation people were there to offer advice if people asked for it – an offer which I took up myself, but the only solution to my situation was a judgement in my favour, they told me, however unjust that seemed. Once a case was in the courts, they were limited in what they could do to help.

It was my lawyer I had to get onto then – and he had promised that after the first few visits he would ask the judge that I be able to exercise a real, free visiting right. True to his word, Maître Lamont sent in a request on 21 February 2000, asking the judge for weekend-long visits in France for Victoria and I, followed by a holiday over Easter in Ireland, and finally Victoria's definitive return by July 1st at the latest. I had done everything the judge had required and the information she had requested from the Belfast Royal Courts of Justice had been provided. Surely there was no reason for her to delay now.

Knowing Judge Barnier fairly well by now, we should have expected her to come up with something twisted, I suppose. Finally, after many letters from both myself and Maître Lamont, she rendered a judgement on 31 March, 2000, without a hearing or the possibility for us to debate what she intended to do – but then we probably couldn't have stopped her anyway. In France a Judge for Children could basically do what she wanted, and there were very few rules to restrict her.

At least the judge was now allowing Victoria and I to go outside unaccompanied, as long as I left my passport and plane ticket at the House of Mediation – a ridiculous measure, according to Maître Lamont, since it wouldn't stop anyone from leaving the country if they really wanted to. It was humiliating, I suppose, if that was what the judge had wanted – making me hand over my ID like a naughty schoolgirl under supervision. In fact, this measure was more a grudging surrender to pressure from above – none less than Mrs Nicole Fontaine, President of the European Parliament, had written to the Ministry of Justice to ensure that visiting rights were being effectually put into practice.

Madame Barnier seemed incapable of doing anything in a clearcut, open way. In the same judgement dated March 31, she also designated an expert psychologist (court-appointed) to carry out a report on Victoria – to be handed in by the end of June, i.e. before the next hearing in her office. That definitely did not sound good – far too easy for the judge to control and manipulate. Besides, there was no reason for a psychological report, since Victoria was not showing any psychological imbalance or difficulty. But as usual, we couldn't do anything about it – we were totally at the mercy of the judge. So much for the Court of Appeal saying the only thing lacking was the return of the investigation report from Belfast Royal Courts of Justice – that hadn't seemed to make the slightest difference. Madame Barnier just put up another barrier, in this case a psychological report.

However, we were now free to go outside, and it marked a new stage in our visits. What a difference it made getting out and about, and doing whatever we felt like – our six or seven hours passed in a flash. Actually, our very first 'free' day happened to be during Elvira's Easter holidays, and Axel and I decided it was time to take her to meet her big sister– extremely exciting for Elvira: the plane trip, then the bus and the train and the *métro*… Ruth Purdy, a Christian girl about to sit her degree in French, had been coming to us for a bit of French conversation over the past few months, and was able to make the journey with us so she could be with Elvira if I needed to be alone with Victoria. Elvira loved that too.

I didn't tell Victoria until the last minute, after Axel's Mum had brought her in to the House of Mediation and left. So it was a total surprise for Victoria… and right from the start the two girls sat side by side to colour in, walked hand in hand to the park, played in the playground together, with Victoria leading the way; then they agreed to go to McDonalds for lunch, and after a short rest back at the hotel we were off to the swimming pool – with Victoria even offering to carry Elvira on her back on the way ! I was very surprised to see how good Victoria was with Elvira – I knew she had younger cousins, but still… It was a great day.

So visits went on for Victoria and I – memorable outings to see the sights of Paris, though we didn't get up the Eiffel Tower because Victoria said she had already been there; we rented bikes and biked round Ile-St-Louis, a small island in the middle of the Seine; went to the swimming pool again with my youngest sister Jeanette, who was on holiday in Paris during one of my visits; visited the *Jardin des Plantes* – the big Paris museum of natural science; took in the 'Museum of African and Oceanic Art' (Victoria especially liked the aquarium) and finally went rowing on the lake of the *Bois de Vincennes*, on the east side of Paris.

Our outings were interspersed with time spent in the House of Mediation, if there weren't too many people there, or at the hotel: time we enjoyed reading together, writing cards for Elvira or my Mum in New Zealand or playing games etc., or sometimes just talking. Although Victoria was usually spontaneous with me and always affectionate, I could tell she wasn't free to say everything she wanted to. During Jeanette's visit, for example, she suddenly took to talking like a squirrel – little chirping noises that of course couldn't be understood, but she pretended to be speaking to us and was much more expressive that way than in real speech ! Jeanette and I both felt that she seemed to be telling us how she would love to be able to talk openly…

I didn't want to say anything to Victoria – she had things hard enough already – but sometimes after visits I returned to my empty hotel room to cry my heart out. It was painfully clear to me that Victoria was being pulled and tugged in different directions, but the Judiciary certianly didn't seem to care. This visiting phase could *not* go on...

A short visit to Axel's home town

Halfway through June, following the advice of the Mediation people, I was able to make an appointment to see the new head-mistress of Victoria's school, Madame Evin. The difference between her and Madame Blanco was like day and night – she was warm, charming, and had that obvious sympathy for children while still remaining professional.

My visit had got off to a 'flying' start – after pressing the buzzer outside, giving my name through the intercom and waiting for the click of the lock, I was just pushing the heavy iron door open when Victoria came flying round the corner of the nearest school building and almost knocked me over. Her expression showed surprise to see me – as I was to see her – and pleasure as she kissed me hello and took me round to the principal's office. It was a treat to bump into my daughter in such an everyday way.

I was able to talk very naturally with the principal about Victoria. She understood my wish for Victoria's return home to take place as naturally and serenely as possible, and I was able to point out that during the coming summer holidays would be by far the best time – Victoria would have time to adapt to her surroundings during the holidays, and have one vital year in an English-speaking primary school to prepare her for secondary education in Ulster, which, I informed her, had an excellent reputation. The primary school where Elvira had been attending had kindly said they had a place for Victoria for the coming year – another element in our favour to put before the judge.

The principal was careful not to take sides – perhaps her predecessor's experience had forewarned her. Unfortunately, my meeting with Victoria's teacher wasn't so satisfactory – she had obviously been fed the 'cult' story, and her attitude was rather piqued and aggressive, but when I defended myself she seemed to calm down, and invited me afterwards to see Victoria's classroom. At any rate, it was good to see Victoria's school and get an idea of her everyday life surroundings – and I would be able to inform the judge that I had met with her teacher and headmistress so that the change of school could take place in the best possible conditions.

The village was a picturesque one, full of tree-lined streets and flowers everywhere of course, at that time of year. I enjoyed a short walk under the huge old trees in the grounds of the music academy, where I stopped to have my lunch. I had come straight from the plane that morning and was still trailing my little overnight suitcase – I had not had time to get to the hotel before coming out for the appointment at the school. It was a warm June day and I had to take my grey suit jacket off – something more to carry, unfortunately.

I decided I might as well visit the music academy where Victoria went for her piano lessons, and see if her teacher was in – she wasn't, but the receptionist very helpfully gave me her telephone number and told me when was best to ring. As it happened, when I rang a couple of days later, Victoria was actually there with her having her piano lesson. Another surprise contact with her and a good contact with her teacher – it was as though everything was falling into place and my hopes were rising that soon I might be arranging for piano lessons for her in Northern Ireland… and I could feel how vital it was for Victoria to have seen me concretely present in everyday life situations. I felt we were a step nearer to her return home.

As I made my way back to the train station that day, I passed the grandparents' apartment building – and happened to meet Axel's Mum, going in. She looked very surprised – and a little unnerved – to see me. We just said hello, and in answer to her question I told her I had just been to see the principal of the school. She asked if she could give me a lift down to the station, but I said no, thanks. See you tomorrow – end of conversation.

How sad, I thought, as I walked on: here I am, walking past my parents-in-law's doorstep and because of this ridiculous situation, because the Judiciary had destroyed all mutual trust between us and set us against each other, I couldn't even go and enjoy a cup of tea with them – and I would really have welcomed it that day ! Not that I minded – I was seeing Victoria the next day, anyway. Besides, I was really hoping that we were reaching the end of this marathon of visits and I was quite at peace within myself because I felt we had done everything possible. All the same, it did seem ludicrous – I could go and see Victoria's school principal but not her grandparents!

Perhaps after the progress I had made in their own home town that day, Axel's Mum felt more inclined to let me take my place as Victoria's mother – at any rate, the following day, when she brought Victoria to the Mediation Centre, she agreed to ask the judge, in accordance with the Mediation people and myself, that Victoria be allowed to spend three days with me, from July 12 to 15, 2000. It was an encouraging surprise, and I hoped it meant she would be looking favourably on Victoria's return with me during the summer holidays. The Mediation people had been an enormous help in clarifying the situation between the grandparents and myself, by simply upholding my parental responsibility. Now, thanks to their mediation efforts, we had been able to come to this agreement. Those three days, at least, were something to look forward to – providing the judge approved...

Illegal actions from French bureaucracy

I also briefly visited the Town Hall in the grandparents' village that day, to hand in a letter for the Mayor. It was time they put their cards down: who was it who had illegally issued an identity card for my daughter, Victoria Schmidt ? I had checked with the appropriate French authorities and had been assured that not even a Judge for Children could have an identity card issued without the consent of the person holding parental responsibility, in this case me. It seemed nobody wanted to own up to it, but we were not about to let such a gross administrative mistake be overlooked.

What made it worse was the grandparents' sudden holiday in Crete at Easter time. Not knowing what could happen in the future, I requested that the identity card be returned to the authorities.

The Mayor replied in writing that the 'State services' possessed a judgement dated May 1998 entrusting Victoria to her grandparents. I wrote back to him that this simply went to prove that the grandparents only had custody of my daughter, *not* parental reponsibility. In his next letter, the Mayor referred me to the Head of Police (*Monsieur le Sous-Préfet*) of the area, who had actually issued the card.

So I wrote to *Monsieur le Sous-Préfet*, and then decided to ring, as we were nearing the end of June 2000 and I wanted this matter resolved before Victoria's summer holidays started. They tried to get around the problem and put me off by telling me that at any rate all the information on the identity card was correct. I also learned that the card had been issued on the basis of information provided and backed by the grandparents' local Town Hall and presented in such a way as to facilitate the delivery of the card. This had ensured that there had been no questions raised at any stage. To get round the "no parental consent" problem, they had stated that there was no way of contacting me, although my address was on the very judgement they had in their possession.

I wrote back to the Town Mayor again, asking him what he had to say to all this and would he kindly request that the grandparents return the identity card to the authorities, as I did not wish to have to lodge a complaint about this matter – but nothing further was done. Since we had been accused of belonging to a "cult", it seemed we were considered second-class citizens – they could deal out any injustice to us, however illegal, and it was just brushed under the carpet and everybody covered it up. We later learned that the French Government had set up information and coordination cells within regional administration centres to fight against "cults", so in such a context we could do nothing – our complaint would not even be considered because all the administrative bodies were working together against us.

However, by this time Madame Nicole Fontaine, President of the European Parliament, had been informed of the matter. Formerly a lawyer, Madame Fontaine knew what she was talking about and on 6 July, 2000, she wrote a two-page letter to the French Minister of Justice, Madame Elisabeth Guigou, expressing her concerns about this illegally-issued identity card. The French authorities were in an increasingly embarrassing position.

But with the identity card issue still in the balance, it was already time for the final showdown. After all our efforts during the year to arrange visits in good conditions and really get things moving, we were about to see some results. Surely this time Madame Barnier would have to fix a date for Victoria's return…

17

Big decisions
July 11–27, 2000

The end of the road ?

On 11 July 2000, Mrs Barnier divided us all up so that the hearing began in slithers. First, she interviewed Victoria alone.

An M.E.P. designated by Madame Fontaine, the French President of the European Parliament, had asked to be present at the hearing because of how the hearings in 1998 and 1999 had gone, and to ensure that the case was being conducted with impartiality. My lawyer, Maître Courtray-Lamont (Maître Lamont's daughter and colleague, as the Maître himself was not available) was doubtful as to whether the judge would allow an M.E.P. into her office, and in fact by receiving us all separately, the judge had somewhat allayed our fears of a repetition of Victoria's tears and distress. Why she hadn't done the same thing in previous years remained a mystery (to deliberately set the grandparents and I against each other, or to show us as ridiculous, arguing grown-ups in front of Victoria?), but I believe she was forced to conduct things more humanely this time because of the European Parliament's intervention.

After Victoria, it was time for the grandparents to go in. Victoria was waiting round the corner with her aunt, Suzanne, so I left the M.E.P. to go and be with her. It was a little hard to wean her away from Suzanne for some reason, but in the end she came and sat beside me to look at some photos. When the judge came to call me, she was furious to see Victoria and I sitting comfortably together – that was what the problem was, I thought, she must have left strict instructions for Victoria to stay with Suzanne. Her tone, as she called "Madame Jones-Schmidt !" was ominous. She had a lot of reasons to take revenge on me that day, and I could feel it coming.

Once in the judge's office I first of all asked that the M.E.P., who had made a special effort to be there that day, be allowed to attend the hearing.

"You will bring nobody else into my office other than your lawyer," Madame Barnier answered bitingly.

She then launched into a long monologue about the history of the case from her point of view – 'cult' story included, of course – and when I attempted to interrupt, she glared at me coldly and disdainfully asked me to keep my questions and comments until she had finished. Maître Courtray-Lamont signalled to me to let it go, that there was no use insisting, but in fact Madame Barnier never quite got round to 'finishing'. As soon as she had brought us up to date with the case as she saw it (the court clerk had been busy writing all this time), she passed quickly over the visits I had had with Victoria and then asked if I had received a copy of the psychological report.

"Yes, Madame Barnier, and I would like to point out the numerous contradictions and omissions in this very subjective report…" I started to say.

"Madame Jones-Schmidt," interrupted the judge, with that cold stare again, "We will first see exactly what Madame Andropov has to say…" And she went on to quote the psychological report practically from beginning to end (which mainly claimed that it would be "premature" and psychologically "risky" to return Victoria to me at that time, and "not what she wanted" anyway), after which she left me no time to respond, but went directly on to saying what would happen next.

"You have complained about not seeing Victoria during her school holidays, Madame Jones Schmidt," she stated. "So we are now going to allow you to see Victoria during her holidays – for two days only, as Victoria herself has said that she does not wish to see you for longer than that."

"When did Victoria say that ?" I burst out. "She told me that all she wanted was to be with me, that she would like to come for a holiday to Northern Ireland – for a week at least…"

"Victoria has told me today that she does not wish to spend longer than two days at a time with you, Madame," the judge replied. "We must respect her wishes…" I could just imagine how she had got Victoria to say that – a series of those cold, hard, questioning looks until she said exactly what the judge wanted.

"… and I'm sure you welcome the decision to allow you to see her during her holidays for two successive days – it will be less tiring for you and more economical."

I couldn't believe what I was hearing – my mind felt numb. I couldn't take in the fact that after everything we had done, Madame Barnier was prolonging visits for *another* year.

Then she really got her knife in.

"I have also requested that Victoria have regular sessions with Madame Andropov, the psychological expert, and I have told her that she may come to see me in my office, any Wednesday afternoon, so that I can answer any questions she may have and explain the file to her."

It was unbelievable. All my efforts had just been kicked back in my face…

"And next year, Madame Barnier, can you tell me that Victoria will be returning home?" I asked, breathlessly.

"I can promise you nothing, Madame," said Madame Barnier, with a cold little smile. "That will depend on Victoria."

So Madame Barnier had finally produced her trump card: a biased psychological report used to further her own ends, i.e. to turn Victoria away from me, and eventually turn her against me. It was as though the last round had been played, the fight was over and I was beaten. Madame Barnier had conquered, and I could only hold on desperately to the thought that at least I would be seeing Victoria during her holidays, for longer...

I hardly heard Maître Courtray-Lamont bring up the subject of the three-day visit that had already been agreed between the Mediation Centre, Axel's Mum and myself.

"It will go ahead, won't it, *Madame le Juge* ? It has already been agreed by all the concerned parties," she was saying.

The judge allowed it – reluctantly, because it was for three days, not two...

After we were shown out, I appealed to Maître Courtray-Lamont.

"Is there nothing we can do, Maître? That judge is walking all over me with just a little piece of psychological paper – what about the President of the Tribunal – the Court of Appeal – the Ministry of Justice – the President of France ?"

She shook her head at each suggestion.

"So there's no way out."

"I'm afraid not," she agreed. "We'll just have to do the best we can with what we've got..."

The M.E.P. decided to leave at this point as she had other engagements and felt she couldn't do anything further. I thanked her for her help – her presence there that day must surely have helped somehow, if only in sparing Victoria the distress she had been through at the last two hearings.

The judge now wanted us all in for the final stage of the hearing. When we were all seated, Madame Barnier made a point of saying, while looking intently at the grandparents, who nodded their agreement, that my parental authority, my place with Victoria and her place with me in Northern Ireland were all "understood and recognised and respected". That sounded good, but... turning to me, she said that I would be able to visit Victoria during her school holidays, for longer, but no longer than two days at a time; and that the grandparents were even prepared to have Elvira and I stay with them or near them in their country home sometime during August, if I wished... She was waiting for an answer. I said I would think about it: the grandmother would still be "mother", I was thinking to myself; and I would be the stranger; and there would be pressure on me to give in to the 'cult' story just as there had been pressure on my Mum...

She also repeated what she had already said to me about psychological follow-up and Victoria visiting her in her office any Wednesday afternoon. Then, with her attention still on me, Madame Barnier gave me a surprisingly charming smile.

"Now, Madame Jones-Schmidt, I do appreciate being in communication with the parents of the children I look after, but getting almost a letter per week is a bit much – could you write to me a little less, this year, do you think ?"

Her smile had so surprised me that I caught myself half smiling back. It was true that I had written 24 letters to the judge between November 1999 and July 2000, but I had had good reason to ! With Victoria there now and the tone of the meeting quiet, I didn't want to make any waves, though. Madame Barnier had got me where she wanted me. I acquiesced with a slight nod.

"And you will look after the little misunderstanding at the *Chancellerie*[1], won't you ?" she continued. She was referring to the illegally-issued identity card – she had mentioned it rapidly during her monologue to me earlier on, saying with contempt that the matter had "even reached the *Chancellerie* !"

"Mmhm..." I answered, noncommittantly. I would see about that...

So the hearing ended as Madame Barnier had undoubtedly intended it to – in a general consensus. Uneasy though I was at the way Madame Barnier had still refused to set a date for Victoria's return, the humiliating way she had shut me up and the chilling prospect of psychological follow-up for Victoria, I was still clinging to the idea that there had been progress made, since I would be seeing Victoria for longer, and during her school holidays... I said goodbye to Victoria, and to the grandparents, telling Victoria I would probably be ringing her in the evening anyway, to see about what she should bring with her for the next day. As Jacqui and I headed back to the hotel I was just getting over the shock of having no end in sight to all these visits, no end to all this constant effort and expense and strain... I had made 15 visits to France since the beginning of the year.

---

[1] Another name for the French Ministry of Justice

Reflecting

The whole hearing was still going round in my head as we went to get something to eat. Jacqui and I were both relieved it was over and that there hadn't been any scenes or distress for Victoria. But as I told her how the judge had refused to let me talk, I couldn't get rid of that gut feeling of unease.

The mere thought of continuing on with visits to France was impalatable. I had had enough of the continual to-and-froing, being pulled and tugged between my two girls, between France and Northern Ireland. In such a situation neither Axel nor I could work, and we were spending all our time writing letters to the authorities in France, phoning the lawyer, complaining to the judge. Then there was the financial aspect: Councillor Wright had been very generous in paying for travelling expenses until now, but just how long could we expect him to go on ? The judge had given me absolutely no idea of how long the whole thing could last. This was exactly why I had been so wary about starting visits in the first place, and had specifically asked for a time-table and a date for Victoria's return. The Mediation Centre wouldn't be able keep the case after January 2001 anyway, and then where would I be – begging the mercy of the Versailles Social Services?

As I thought about it – her letting me see Victoria for longer, during the school holidays… I realised that that actually meant I would be seeing her much less often than fortnightly, as I had been over the past six months. School holidays – why, that could mean only twice a term, six times in the year, with a few long weekends thrown in if the grandparents weren't "going away" ! And in-between, the judge would have plenty of time to distance Victoria from me, turn her against me, find all sorts of reasons to make her resentful and rebellious – after all, she was coming into her teenage years, and the judge especially would know just how to take advantage of that…That day I had once again seen the judge embracing my daughter, and as I thought of it, I could see her gaining Victoria's confidence, befriending her, taking away my child's natural attachment to me by ruse and manipulation, after having taken her away physically.

Then there was the "psychological follow-up". I had seen what the psychologist was capable of doing after just two short visits from Victoria. Her report was stunningly lacking in rigour and objectivity.

The number of contradictions in it was astounding, to start with. She talked about Victoria suffering from the "initial trauma" i.e. her removal in 1993, but then stated that Victoria "did not feel that she missed her mother *or that she could miss her*". What could the trauma have been about then, and why did Victoria have to "organise herself psychologically in order to cope" if she didn't miss her parents? Of course Victoria had been taken at an age when a child's memory is only just beginning to develop, and it would be under-standable that she had repressed any memories of home just to be able to cope with the situation that had been forced upon her – and no-one in Social Services had ever talked to her about her parents. So the psychologist should not have quoted her as saying she "didn't miss her mother" – she was implying that Victoria had never been attached to her mother at all, which was entirely false.

What I found totally abhorrent was that it appeared from the psychological report that the judge and the psychologist were trying to use the pain of separation from her parents that Victoria had known in 1993 to discourage her from even imagining a return with me, because she would then be 'separated' from her grandparents, cousins, etc. "It would mean being uprooted, which would undoubt-edly reactivate what happened when she was three years old…" It had all been twisted to suit the Judiciary. Plain common sense would tell anybody that the best way to heal a child of the pain of separation from her mother would be to restore that child to her mother, especially as there had never been any charges against me or any doubt as to my competence as a mother.

Actually, the "initial trauma" was never described (at least not in the report's conclusions, which was all we were allowed access to) – I suppose because of the inevitable fact that it had been caused by the Judiciary when they had taken her away from her home and family so unexpectedly and unreasonably.

Only one very telling line in the psychological report made any mention of the pressure exercised on Victoria: "One could think that

Victoria has been influenced". It also mentioned further on that Victoria "knew her grandparents' position". Her grandfather referred to Northern Ireland as a "foreign country torn by political battles", so it wasn't surprising that Victoria thought she might be "scared" to go there. What was that if it wasn't psychological pressure ? All this was never presented in an unfavourable light, but as though these were Victoria's authentic feelings.

Finally, there were all the accusations against myself: especially that there was no real affection between Victoria and I. I was supposedly only interested in Victoria's return because I had "a lot at stake" in it. That kicked a mother's love out the door hard and fast. As for Victoria, she was supposedly simply "curious" about me, though "distrusting" at the same time (there were the grandparents again – with the whole 'cult' story that had been put into their heads). Victoria "did not feel any psychological pressure from her grandmother" (why the need to say so then ?) but the psychologist stated that she did feel psychologically pressured by *me* ! That was a good one, after all the times I had seen the effect of the pressure put on Victoria by the judge through the grandparents and all the times I had just let matters drop to save her from coming under further pressure.

Amazingly, according to the psychologist Victoria "perfectly understood" the 'cult' story explanations she had been continually given (she "understood" that her mother had "a lot at stake" in her return home, as the report claimed), but when I answered her questions about her father by explaining that he had fled the country after being wrongly convicted, she "did not want to listen because she did not understand", reported the psychologist. The fact was, poor Victoria was *not allowed* to "understand" the plain truth.

Professionally-speaking, the report was a disgrace to any self-respecting psychologist. There were no objective references to research and no objective criteria applied, nor did she make the effort to visit Victoria in her everyday environment. We didn't even know what questions had been asked, or in what order the comments produced had been made. We had written to the psychologist twice, on 11 and 29 April 2000, to ask her in the interests of objectivity to record the interviews and supply us with a list of the background information given her by the judge, but we never had any reply. She knew the judge would cover for her anyway, I suppose.

Maître Lamont, who was after all a French lawyer and therefore stuck uncomfortably between the judge and his client, had advised me to actually go and see the psychologist, although the judge had never asked for this. However, it was clear to us that the judge's sole intention, in ordering the report, was to obtain a document which would allow her to stall if not stop progress towards Victoria's return. And the psychologist knew what the judge expected of her – no "independence" here, the sytem didn't allow it – she was the judge's mighty right arm, just as the psychiatrist Moreno had been Mrs Degrelle-Croissant's no-argument weapon against us back in 1993. Finally, Maître Lamont had told me himself that judges invariably follow psychologists' recommendations. Whatever I said it was useless and would just be used against me. So there they had me – catch-22 yet again.

It was solely on this rag report that the judge had based her decision to prolong Victoria's separation for a further year, after seven and a half years of legal proceedings and my constant requests for her return home, and in spite of all my efforts to meet the French Judiciary's requirements. In spite of the fact that I was entirely innocent. It was too much.

And if that was what the psychologist had done after two short visits, what would she do over a whole year ? They would never give her back… and it was useless to appeal. Hey – they would *never* give her back !

A make-or-break decision to take

It was on the phone with Axel that night that all this suddenly hit me. Axel was very concerned – no date for Victoria's return, visits to continue for a year with follow-up by the psychologist and the judge, me not allowed to defend myself in the judge's office – it was all working against Victoria's return home.

"Listen, you're the only one who can really judge," he said. "You're the one on the ground, you'll have to decide in the end, but

I wonder if we shouldn't just bring her home now, before they turn her completely against us."

It hit me like a ton of bricks, as they say. One went right to the bottom of my stomach and made me feel sick. But as I turned the day's events over in my mind – the moment the lawyer said there was nothing we could do flashed across my mind, the moment I realised we could do nothing to stop this judge – I knew it was right, it was the right thing to do. God help me, I had to do what was right. Axel said to go away and think about it and ring back later.

Seeing me walking away from the phone, Jacqui got worried too.

"Your face," she said. "We were so relieved that it was all over and now you've got that tense look back again. What on earth is the matter ?"

"It's OK," I told her. "I know what we've got to do."

"What ?" she asked. "How can it be the right thing if it's getting you into such a state ?"

It was a strange sensation. I was becoming more and more convinced that we had to get Victoria out of France now – we had three days, and we'd never have such a chance again, Madame Barnier would make sure of that. The conviction that this was the right thing for Victoria gave me peace. My conscience, my affection, my concern for my child all dictated it, suddenly and forcefully. Not that that stopped the adrenalin flowing, or the butterflies in my stomach. I explained everything to Jacqui, but she remained unsure about taking on such a responsibility. She was worried and concerned for us all. What about Elvira, how was she going to be affected by all this, even if I did make it back to Northern Ireland with Victoria ? It seemed such a huge "if"... In the end though, she had to leave it up to us. If ever anything went wrong… it was a risk we were going to have to take.

After a short spell at the hotel, we went out to phone again (I never phoned from the hotel, just in case the calls were traced) and Jacqui had a talk to Axel. He and I were both agreed now, and in the meantime Axel had been making inquiries… It was going to be a long journey home, and we had no guarantee we would make it – but both Axel and I believed it was our duty before God as responsible parents to protect Victoria from further abuse and distress, and ultimately a regrettable future. The same concern for my daughter that had made me tell Madame Barnier I would never cause Victoria distress, now dictated that I take her out of France to protect her, once again, from distress.

It so happened that for the first time I had taken Victoria's New Zealand passport to France with me (we had unexpectedly been able to renew it in April 1999). The reason I had it with me was that we had met some Swiss people in Ulster just a few months before and they had invited us to visit them in Switzerland; and when I had asked Victoria one day where she would like to go for a holiday, she had said Switzerland or Austria. So I was hoping we could spend some part of our three days with them – if it was possible to go out of France. If it wasn't, I was planning on spending our holiday in the Normandy area, and had bought a book and organised an itinerary so that we could enjoy a few different activities like horse-riding, boat rides, canoeing, biking etc. as well as seeing the country. Personally, I would have preferred to go to Switzerland, of course, since I knew people there.

As for myself, way back in 1992 I had obtained a French identity card, which I had used regularly when travelling to France. The French authorities would easily have been able to find out about that if they had wanted to, but apparently they hadn't. The thought did cross my mind that perhaps Madame Barnier had been pushing me to try to flee... I would probably never know. We certainly had everything we needed to make our escape. One thing was certain: if we didn't get Victoria out of France now, we probably never would.

That evening, since we had rented a little Renault Twingo at the airport, I took Jacqui on a whirlwind 'farewell' trip, north out of Versailles and past our old apartment block, which looked just the same. It was already dark by then and becoming difficult to find my way around, but it did help me in some unknown way. It was as though I had to get France out of my system. My driving must have been a bit erratic, since I hadn't driven on that side of the road for a while – poor Jacqui didn't say much, just hung on. Eventually I started getting lost down side streets, so we went back to the hotel: we were going to have an early start the next morning and needed all the sleep we could get.

Everyone under pressure

Needless to say, we didn't get much sleep that night. My whole perspective had changed in one short evening – just a few hours. I knew little about what lay ahead of me, except that Axel had said I should take the train to Annecy. It was a journey I had often made while I was working there, and that would make it a logical place to go – a place I knew, that I could show Victoria round, take her for a walk through the old town and along the canal… Annecy was my destination, but everybody else – including Victoria – thought we were going to Normandy, because that was what I had told them all the day before. Axel's Mum had even said she would bring me some maps of the area.

So that morning we were up early. I was going to drive to the train station in Beauvais – Jacqui was flying out of Beauvais that day – and then she would have to drive the rest of the way to the airport while I attempted to make it to the Mediation Centre for 11 o'clock. I had originally thought I would keep the car for the three days I was in France, but that was now impossible, and it was out of the question that I leave Jacqui to negotiate the French roads and motorways all the way to the airport on her own.

By the time we got to Beauvais we were already running a little behind schedule.

"Look, Jacqui," I pointed out to her, "to the right takes you to the airport, and to the left takes you into the centre of Beauvais. If you can get back to here you'll be all right."

Unfortunately, it wasn't quite as simple as that. It was complicated getting to the station, there was a one-way system and an underground tunnel to avoid. I was running late as it was and couldn't really help her to get her bearings. When we arrived at the station I hurriedly asked about train times and phoned Axel's Mum to tell her that I would be late and not to hurry. She thanked me – it meant she could let Victoria sleep on a little.

Jacqui and I were both under strain and feeling very emotional. It was difficult parting, and I was trying to reassure her that it would all be all right and tell her she should go, but I'm afraid I was rather half-hearted about it – I would have loved to have Jacqui with me. After rather heavy-hearted goodbyes and last-minute reminders, she was away at last – driving on the right-hand side of the road at least. It was yet another of those situations where we were totally helpless to do anything, humanly speaking. For the moment, I had that train to catch…

Jacqui's journey to the airport was supposed to have been short, but unfortunately it lay across several fairly new, almost unsignposted roundabouts that seemed to have been built in the middle of nowhere, surrounded only by bare, unplanted fields. She seemed to take one wrong road after another, and though she could get herself understood fairly well by imitating planes when she asked for directions, the answers she got were harder to follow. She was getting more and more desperate as time ticked by and praying hard when suddenly, at last, she saw a sign for the airport pointing in the way she was already going – she was on the right road at last. By the time she arrived at the airport she was hot and flustered. Parking the car outside the airport was a trial of patience, but when she finally got in to return the car keys and papers to the car rental company, the man at the desk was impervious to the rush.

"Please leave the car in the car park over there, Madam," he told her, pointing into the distance. Jacqui just stared at him. After her desperate race to the airport – and she was still very close to missing her plane – that was all she needed…

Arriving late at the Mediation Centre, I tried to appear only 'normally ruffled'. Smiling, I explained that I had had to return the car to the airport that morning, since it was better (as one of the staff from the Mediation Centre had advised me) to take the train most of the way to Normandy and then rent a car once we were in the area.

Axel's Mum had brought the maps, which I thanked her for. She seemed a little apologetic, as though she understood how disappointed I must be after all the efforts I had made had produced such meagre results. She asked whether I would be visiting them with Elvira during August – I said I would be in touch about that. She said she could arrange for me to see Victoria during a long week-end in September – I thanked her and said that would be good.

The head of the Mediation Centre was there in person to take in my plane ticket and passport – the guarantees that I would not flee the country. He had to remind me about the passport – it was hard relinquishing it, and I thought he might forget, just this once... but he didn't. He was a responsible man and I respected it and appreciated all the good times we had had thanks to the Mediation Centre. Anything in my manner could easily have been put down to that morning's rush and the excitement of the three days' holiday. Axel's Mum was the only one who seemed a little clingy – then at last we were out the door.

Just Victoria and I – or not ?

I took Victoria down the road to the park where we had come together so often (memorably with Elvira on the day she came to see her big sister) and we sat down on a park bench there, in the quiet. I knew I would have to take this very gently with Victoria. It was out of the question to tell her we were leaving the country – she had been conditioned against it for too long. I knew what she truly wanted and desperately needed, anyway: her home and family back again.

"Well, Victoria," I announced cheerfully, "I've actually got two possibilities for our holiday – we can either go to Normandy, as I had planned, or if you want we could go the other direction – to Annecy. Which would you prefer ?"

Victoria shrugged her shoulders. What I would have done if she had said she wanted to go to Normandy, I don't know. I knew she had already been there – well, to Britanny anyway, which was in the same direction.

"What say we go somewhere new for you – you've never been to Annecy, have you?"

That was all right with Victoria. I told her a little about Annecy and how pretty the train journey was, especially up in the mountains. And we set off for the Gare de Lyons, me trundling my roller-suitcase and Victoria with her travel bag slung over her shoulder. The change of plan was making this much more exciting for her, I could see that.

After waiting quite a long time in a queue to get our tickets we bought freshly-made French bread sandwiches and some ice tea (Victoria's favourite drink) at a kiosk in the station and wandered leisurely over to find our train. The station was bustling, it was that time of year, which was why we had had to wait so long to get tickets – and why they had cost so much. Everybody and his family seemed to be leaving for the July 14 holiday break, which that year happened to fall on a Friday, so they had the weekend as well. Many people left for their annual summer holidays at that time anyway – it was one of the busiest times of the year in France. Even the judges would be on holiday and the Mediation Centre was closing after the weekend… Months of planning wouldn't have given us a better time to flee France.

We enjoyed ourselves in the train on the way down to Annecy, and I could see Victoria starting to really relax at last. She was off on holiday with her Mum – and I would be looking after her 24 / 24. When we finally got there I went straight to a phone to "arrange for the night" – i.e. ring Axel to see what we were supposed to do next!

Suddenly I froze. I was at a set of four public phones grouped around a pillar – and there at the next phone was Victoria. I had seen her tinkering about there as I talked but had thought she was just playing with it. Now there was absolutely no doubt about it – she was talking to someone.

"Axel, you won't believe it – she's phoning someone, probably your parents !" I hissed down the phone. Thankfully we had already been able to fix a meeting place and a time for a friend of our Swiss friends to come and pick us up. My heart was starting to thump. It had seemed for a second as though Victoria had been turned into a spy who would report our every movement to "headquarters", whoever that was. Could my own daughter be that far set against me ? On second thoughts, I decided she was simply following instructions. After all, she knew she would get into trouble if she didn't keep to what she had been told to do – she had no idea yet of my plans to free her from all that.

I tried to remain as natural as possible.

"You were phoning, too, then ?" I asked her casually. "Your grand-parents ?"

She nodded yes, with a little smile that was part unease, part "you understand, don't you?"

Yes, Victoria, I understood. So now they knew we were in Annecy. Suddenly I had visions of police descending on that telephone box. Axel had told me to make sure we weren't being followed.

"Let's go and get a taxi," I said, feeling an urgent need to get as far away from the station as we could – fast. We still had to wait five minutes or so for the taxi, but at last we were on our way, and no time now to have even a quick look round Annecy: we were getting into the rush hour traffic and the taxi-driver said that if we went round by the lake it would take us twice as long – and would cost twice as much, obviously, I thought to myself. So long, Annecy. I would have so much liked to show Victoria round, show her where I had worked, etc., but my priorities were unfortunately elsewhere.

We got to the meeting place almost one-and-a-half hours in advance. There was a little restaurant, but we were told the chef wouldn't be there until 7 o'clock that evening (this is France, I reminded myself – people never eat as early as half past five), so we finished our sandwiches from lunchtime, had a drink, and went out for a walk in the countryside. It was beautiful and the fresh air did us good – we realised we were quite high up. When we got back to the restaurant, I phoned but was thankful Victoria couldn't, since she only had a card and the phone was a coin one. She decided to kill time by playing solitaire on a games machine. I went out from time to time to check that there was no-one waiting for us. It seemed to take ages.

At last he was there – I recognised Raphael from his distinctively Northern colouring: short, blond hair going bald and reserved blue eyes. He apologised at once and profusely for being so late, and even got a smile from Victoria – he was forgiven. Raphael didn't know much about our situation, but I knew he played the organ sometimes and was a keen musician. When I told him that Victoria had been learning the piano for the past five years, he was delighted. What pieces had she played this year, he wanted to know

– oh, yes, Debussy's Little Shepherd, he knew that, and he hummed away at it. Victoria was quite charmed. While they chatted on about music I had a little time to unwind. We were on the way…

Swiss charm

We arrived late that evening at the Rivière's simple but tastefully-furnished home, and were warmly greeted by Geneviève and Jacques. They had never met Victoria, of course, but they looked after us as if we had been family. We had two camp beds in our own little room, and Victoria and I were delighted. Victoria went to bed peacefully and I was able to ring Axel and reassure him that everything had gone all right. We were both relieved that at least we were out of France at last…

The next day we woke late and breakfasted light – Geneviève had arranged for us to have lunch that day with "the workers" at the neighbouring farm. That was quite an experience in itself. Honorée, the farmer's wife, provided the workers with their midday meal every day. People were in and out, her daughter came in to say hello, then was off to look after her horses, and the workers didn't seem to mind us strangers as jokes were bandied round the long table, interspersed with the different subjects that preoccupied each one. The wet summer was proving a big problem for the farming people. We weren't hungry after our late rising, but it was good wholesome country food and we enjoyed the company. I realised how good it was for Victoria to be with me in other people's home – it made us belong to each other more…

After a short walk round the farm with the family dog – Victoria loved dogs, I discovered – Geneviève and Jacques took us off up the mountains for a drive. The scenery was brilliant. This was what Victoria had wanted on holiday, the vast view of mountains stretching away to the horizon, country houses and country people. But the biggest surprise awaited her back at the house.

The afternoon was a little wet towards evening (what the farmers really *didn't* want at that time of year), and Victoria chose to sit in Geneviève and Jacques's comfortable *salon* and watch "Asterix and Obelix" starring Gérard Depardieu.

I was free to phone Axel, and we decided it was time to bring Victoria one step closer to home. I put my head round the *salon* door – her Daddy wanted to speak to her on the phone, I said casually. Would she like to ? Would she ! I had to say it with a certain reserve – until then I had always had to tell her I was separated from him. Hence my take-it-or-leave-it attitude. But she jumped at the chance and I could see her mind working overtime once the conversation was over and she had put the receiver down again and gone back to watch the rest of the video. I just left her to it – she needed time to get used to such a development, and I was going to give her just that. Axel had told her he loved her, of course.

"I would love to see you," he had said.

"Me too," Victoria had answered simply.

"Just stay close to Mummy and we'll be able to, all right ?" Axel told her. Victoria had no problem with that. Now she had a fair idea that somehow her Mum and Dad had stayed together, in spite of everything I had had to tell her to the contrary. For the moment I just let it all sink in… It was great to have Axel sharing 'parental responsibility' again at last, and Victoria's contact with him and her eagerness to see him was essential.

But there was still more in store for us that day. Since the wet weather had set in, the farmer was going up the mountain with a few of the workers – and they were going to be making cheese in a little chalet he owned there. It was a memory that would stay with me – the cheese bubbling away in a huge cauldron over an open fire, our meal of pizza and homemade *kugelhopf* (a light cake typical of the area), and then the cheese-making itself: the men lifted it out in big lumps into a cheesecloth to let the liquid drain away, then stuffed it all into the big cheese-molds so it would take a real cheese form. We even had a taste of last year's cheese – a delicious, compact but flexible, mid-yellow cheese with a special homemade taste to it. What an end to our day. The expert cheese-maker's little boy François was there – he must have been a little younger than Victoria – and he was a real character. They ended up calling him *le Roi François Premier* (King Francis I) and then of course Victoria had to be called *la Reine Victoria* (Queen Victoria) !

Switzerland left us with an impression of warmth and country goodness, both in the people and their way of life. That memorable day of holiday would have to last us for a while – we were to leave early next morning to catch a plane from Zürich to Amsterdam as we continued on our long journey home. There were going to be crucial moments ahead.

Unexpected difficulties

First of all we arrived in Zürich late, and missed the plane we had been supposed to take. Then we had problems with the tickets – although Axel had reserved them and they had been paid for, we were told that in fact they couldn't be paid for from Britain by credit card unless a copy of the card and the owner's signature were sent by fax to the office in the Zürich airport. When Axel finally did manage to get a photocopy of the credit card done, for some reason the fax wouldn't come through. I didn't have enough cash on me, and my British bank chequebook was no use to me either. What could we do ?

Raphael had been kind enough to drive us to Zürich from Geneviève and Jacques's home, and he had stayed to make sure we got on the plane – thank goodness. When he saw the straits we were in, he very kindly offered to pay himself – I could pay him back later. It was very embarrassing – I was glad Victoria was sitting on the bags away from the counter ! I said I would try one last time to see if the fax would get through, but it didn't, so I had to accept Raphael's generosity and assured him we would pay him back as soon as possible. We were having to travel first-class, too, as those were the only places left.

Victoria meanwhile was becoming understandably bored, as plane after plane was announced and left, and we had still not boarded. Then, after finally paying for the tickets with Raphael's loaned money, we had to run for the plane – until we got to the queue at customs. It was time for the ID checks.

I had papers for us both, but it may have seemed a little strange for me to have French ID and my daughter a brand new New

Zealand passport. Perhaps it was also that Victoria and I didn't really look very similar, as she had Axel's colouring (light brown hair, brown eyes) and I had very dark brown hair with blue eyes. Whatever the reason, we were taken aside a minute and told to wait. After a few minutes, an airport official came and spoke in French to Victoria.

"So, tell me, Valerie… "

"I'm not called Valerie, I'm Victoria," Victoria protested, with a surprised smile.

"And you're running away to New Zealand, are you, Victoria ?" asked the official.

Victoria puckered her lips and shook her head.

"I'm on holiday with my Mum," she said, tucking her arm through mine. That was all they needed to know. Good for you, Victoria, I thought. And we were through, onto the plane and on, to Amsterdam.

Amsterdam had a very different feel to eastern France and Switzerland – very metropolitan, modern and, of course, flat. We had a little time to shop around before catching a train out to Rotterdam, where we were to board a boat for Harwick that evening. We bought a pair of nice brown leather shoes for Axel, as a hello present from Victoria. She kept asking when she would see him, of course, and I told her we had to take a boat first. She accepted that. It was actually all I knew at the time, anyway. At least we weren't stuck in an airport anymore. The train was a quaint old one and the ride was so different to the one from Paris to Annecy, through this seemingly never-ending flatness, criss-crossed with canals and small towns. The novelty of it fascinated us both.

At last we arrived in Rotterdam, only to find that there was no boat to England that evening – only a boat coming *from* England, which was hardly any good to us ! We would have to wait until the next morning to catch the next one out. It was a mystery how that mistake could have been made – some overworked ferry employee had booked us on a boat that would take us from where we wanted to go to where we already were… We were going to have to spend the night in Rotterdam, then. There was only one hotel there, so we booked in and had a meal in the rather impressive old wood-panelled dining-room which had been done up to look like the inside of a ship. After a walk and a phone call – Victoria of course could not use her phone card here any more than in Switzerland, so I had no worries and she asked no questions – we had a fairly good night's sleep in our modest twin room. This was Victoria's second night with me and we were both enjoying the freedom of just being together as family.

All these problems – payment difficulties, being questioned at the airport, arriving to take a boat that wasn't there – confronted me time after time with the reality of what I was doing. If I'd not learnt during our time in France something of how to keep persistently on trusting God, I suppose I would have had every reason to give up. But I honestly don't remember the thought even crossing my mind. With each problem I was sure there was a way – I just had to find it.

When we thought about it later, the problems actually had one significant advantage: they made it very difficult for anybody to track us. Our day's holiday in Switzerland wouldn't have been the usual thing to do for people who were fleeing a country, to start with. Though the constant chopping and changing of plan had been wearying at times, especially in the airport in Zürich, we were concealing our tracks without knowing it.

The crucial last leg

We were up early again the next morning to catch the first boat across the Channel – and thankfully had no problem with tickets, payment or boat departure times... We were delighted to find that we had seats in the luxurious "Panorama" cabin, and the view of the harbour as we left it truly was panoramic, and it was a beautiful day for it, too. Victoria soon wanted to have a look around the boat. It was the first time either of us had been on a big ferry, so we both enjoyed exploring, though at one stage Victoria felt quite sick and we went and watched a film until she felt better.

Victoria knew this was the day she would be meeting her Daddy for the first time in more than seven years, and this added to the excitement she naturally felt at so many new places and experiences. It perhaps made her a little nervous too. After all, she didn't really know what to expect. Those few days we had together were the perfect time to build on the trust and confidence she had already come to have in me over the past year. I knew she was going to be needing a lot of trust to fall back on in order to get past the obstacles which had been put into her mind in France about coming to live with me in Northern Ireland. I was also waiting to find the right moment to tell her that we wouldn't be going back to France – not for the moment, anyway.

It was with some relief that I saw the shores of England approaching. I could understand how Axel had felt when he had arrived in England in February 1995. All I needed to do now was find Graham and Irene, friends we had met back in 1997, who were to be there waiting for us. Graham had always said, as so many others had, "Just say the word, and I'll be over to France to get Victoria." We had always known that if we did want to make a move like this, there would be people to help us. Except that he apparently wasn't there yet !

This was none of Graham's fault, however, as I learnt when I rang Axel. When he had learnt that the evening boat to Harwick had been the sad figment of someone's imagination, Graham had phoned the ferry company and been told we were due in on a boat that was to arrive in Harwick around 10:00 a.m. He and Irene, who had only come with him at the last minute on this 'dangerous mission', had therefore decided to stay overnight somewhere in England and continue their journey early the next morning. However, the ferry people had apparently made yet another blunder – it was the busiest time of year, after all – and our boat in fact got in around 9:00 a.m. Which was why Victoria and I were there waiting.

To be fair, we hadn't really been waiting very long. In fact, I had just left Victoria by herself for a minute, next to our luggage. When I came back, there were Graham and Irene walking down the waiting hall towards us – they had obviously already recognised Victoria and were bearing down on her with frightening speed, while Victoria looked at them a little sideways, trying to make out whether that could possibly be her Daddy…

Now I felt truly relieved, knowing we were in good hands. Graham and Irene were going to look after all the practicalities. There remained only a telephone call to make to the Mediation Centre from somewhere in the middle of England so that they weren't kept waiting indefinitely for our return.

As I prepared the message I was going to give them by phone, Victoria's curiosity got the better of her. She wanted to see what I was writing. I told her I would tell her later. She pretended to look away. I started writing again, only to glance up and find her reading my message: "I will not be returning Victoria to the Centre today…" She might have had an idea we wouldn't be going back: it was Saturday – the day we were due back at the Mediation Centre, and she hadn't even met her Daddy yet. We both looked at each other. I had wanted to take the time to explain things to her gently, but it hadn't worked out that way. She went very quiet for a while, taking it in. I explained as best I could, and she soon came round. Considering that it was the only upset she had had during the whole journey, our rescue operation had been remarkably gentle on her – something I had set my heart on. When we stopped for a meal, Graham had her giggling away again, even though he didn't speak a word of French…

Once the phone call to the Mediation Centre was done, our last challenge would be the short ferry trip from Scotland to Northern Ireland. It had been quite a journey. Once again, we didn't get the boat we had intended to take, but at least this one was going the right way… Victoria felt like watching a film, so I went with her, while Graham and Irene hopefully got what little rest they could on the seats in the lounge.

Arriving in Larne late that night was Graham's worry. If the Mediation Centre had contacted the police, we could have problems… But Northern Ireland welcomed us without a police officer in sight, and we arrived at our friend Samantha's home, where Axel and Elvira were waiting for us, in the early hours of Sunday morning.

As Victoria got out of the car, a little uncertainly, her Daddy came out of the house and immediately held his arms out wide, a big grin all over his face as he came to welcome her home. Victoria couldn't mistake him – that was her Daddy all right, though she hadn't had any contact with him at all since that day more than seven years ago when he had sat her down on my knees in the police station and kissed her goodbye. As she said to me later, the strange thing was that she didn't feel there was anything strange about it at all ! She and Elvira were to share a double bed at Samantha's that night, and of course Elvira had to be woken up to give her big sister a welcome home hug. Then they both snuggled down next to each other, looking like two peas in a pod. We prayed together (for the first time) and thanked God for our safe journey home – then I had to lie down between them to calm their excited giggles and get them off to sleep.

Victoria was home. As we stood looking down at our two daughters asleep in the same bed – in the same country – for the first time in their young lives, we were deeply thankful. We refused for the moment to ask the question "For how long?" that was hovering over us. God had brought us this far. Surely He would not let us down now. But then God's ways are not our ways. We always think the easiest way is best, but God knows better. We had not quite reached the end of our journey down Heartache Road.

18

The backlash
July 28, 2000

Just being family

Our first couple of days at Samantha's and the next week that we spent on holiday near the North Antrim Coast were a very special time. Victoria was delighted to be with her Daddy, and he was the one she wanted to sit beside, sit on his knee, play volleyball with. She even drew a side-view sketch of him as he sat on the sofa next to her – a good likeness, too. We took in the Giant's Causeway, the Carrick-a-Rede ropebridge and Dunluce Castle. Victoria ran everywhere in a sort of wild exhilaration and Axel spent a lot of his time running after her !

She enjoyed Portrush, running and shouting boisterously on the beach, asking her Daddy for piggy-backs, lifting me up at least a foot off the ground – we made sure we got a photo of that – or paddling in the cold sea with Elvira. The trampolines in Portrush were a great favourite with them both, as was Water World. Samantha had kindly thought to give us money especially to buy Victoria some new clothes, and she enjoyed choosing her own in the July sales in

Coleraine. I had brought her an English book for young learners to look through and she applied herself well to it now and then… but couldn't be persuaded to even try bacon and eggs for breakfast – uggh !

At nighttime Victoria wanted me with her to get her to sleep. In her great this-is-my-family adventure, I sensed that I was the one she came back to because of the time we had spent together in France. It was Axel that she asked to explain about her grandparents, though – why they had been against us, why we had stayed at a distance from them… it was painful for both of them, but Victoria needed to know it to be able to make sense of things for herself, and Axel was careful to show her that his parents had been misled by the outright lies of people with malicious intentions.

Victoria was at last getting to know her Daddy again – and Axel was adapting to the reality of having an often unpredictable ten-year-old daughter instead of the three-year-old he had been so close to. What's more, both Victoria and Elvira had to accept the unavoidable fact that they could no longer get "only child" treatment, and it did make a lot of difference to their everyday life.

The naturalness of our family reunion sometimes made us forget these facts, but we had everyday reminders of the work that was still to be done – Victoria and Elvira both had fairly strong characters and friction was inevitable, and (we had to remind ourselves) healthy. The girls had to learn that being a "big / little sister" didn't necessarily mean what they automatically thought it did. So we laid down clear rules for family peace – each member was to be respected and given their rightful place. It was something that would take time, and we would have to make allowances at times, but little by little we were fitting together.

Our faith was absolutely vital in this process. Elvira had prayed many times for Victoria to come home and now she had seen the answer to that prayer – but she hadn't bargained on all the side effects it would bring with it ! What she did understand (after a little reminding) was that Victoria had suffered from not being with her Mum and Dad – and because she understood that, she was able to let things go that otherwise could well have festered. Elvira had loved her big sister from the first day she saw her in France, and she soon settled down in a very determined way to make Victoria love her back.

Victoria, we must remember, had been plunged from a Roman Catholic view of Christianity into our Biblical faith. It soon transpired that she had found Roman Catholic church services in France to be "frankly boring – always the same" and that this impression had made her almost cynical about 'religion'. But she was sensitive and sincere, with a very logical mind. She soaked up our explanations about God and man and sin, and was forever asking questions – often logically critical but also surprisingly deep.

That very first Sunday night she had been to church with Axel, and this had started the questions. Then, after our week's holiday and another day at Samantha's, we all went together to church in the evening – Axel was translating for her at that stage, as her English wasn't yet strong enough.

"Daddy, what does it mean to be 'ready' ?" she suddenly asked him in a whisper.

"It just means you need to be saved," Axel answered. She had tears in her eyes.

That evening, as she was about to get into bed, she needed to talk (that was to become Victoria's "talking time" – and was to keep her and me awake for hours during the months to come). That night, though, she really had something on her heart.

"I think God was speaking to me tonight, Mummy," she said, a little hesitantly.

"That's great, Victoria," I told her.

"But what should I do ?" she asked. I explained to her very simply that all God wanted her to do was trust the Lord Jesus to forgive her sin and come into her heart and life forever.

Victoria was saved that night. For her it seemed a most logical thing to do and she went to sleep in peace while we rejoiced with our friends, as did the preacher and the members of the Free Presbyterian church we had attended that night. We had not expected this so soon, and for us it was as though God had sealed with His approval our decision to bring Victoria home. Our family was now truly united – we could pray together.

But after our week's holiday, we had decisions to make…

Home at last

Victoria and Elvira were happy to be home, and Victoria loved her room – we had painted it the colour she had chosen: sky-blue. It was the first time we had been home since bringing Victoria out of France. Except for Jacqui and Cecil, Stephen and Samantha and of course Graham and Irene who already knew, we had told nobody else about the escape from France – the consequences of our decision were our responsibility and we didn't want to implicate anybody else.

After discussing the situation with Stephen and Samantha that day, we had decided we should go home and live as 'normally' as possible. Of course, the French authorities had our address, but at the same time, their case against us was strong in slander but weak every other way. Would they really come after an innocent mother who, after more than seven years of proceedings, had brought her own daughter home with her in desperation?

We could have left Northern Ireland for New Zealand if we had really wanted to, but for several reasons we felt it better to stay. To start with, most of our help and support had until now come from Ulster. It had been thanks to the very faithful and constant prayers and help of the Christian people of Ulster – mainly from the Free Presbyterian churches – that we had come this far, and it seemed right to stay close to them. After Victoria's homecoming, and the joy of being reunited at last as a family, all we wanted was to continue on the way we were going, in the midst of the people who had helped us get there.

Then there was Axel's family to consider. Once Victoria was out of France he had rung his parents to reassure them that she was all right and to invite them to come and see us in Northern Ireland. He wanted to resolve the "family conflict", he told them, and asked them not to lodge a complaint against me. They agreed with both those suggestions, but weren't sure about when they would be coming to Northern Ireland. Axel still longed to be able to speak with his parents freely at last, after so many years of misunderstanding and outside interference in family relations. And now that Victoria was back with us in her rightful place within the family – plus the fact that the grandparents had not lodged a complaint against us, which was proof of their good will – we all felt the time had well and truly come to be reunited with them too. With that possibility in mind, Ulster was definitely the place to be.

So we decided to settle down to as normal a life as possible and if the French authorities initiated proceedings, we would simply defend ourselves. They hadn't made a move against my bringing Victoria home yet – and the longer they waited, the better for us. We lived in hope.

The French Judiciary takes revenge

At 7:45 the next morning there was a knock on the door. Several knocks. Louder. The letter box was being rapped. I rushed downstairs with my heart in my mouth – through the net curtain I could see several men standing outside, cars all round the house as far as I could see, and one man standing at the door with an official card in his hand, pressed up against the glass pane. Now my heart really began to thump, as I signalled to them to wait and went to get the key – starting up the stairs first to hiss to Axel:

"It's the police – I'm going to have to open up !"

Axel was looking out through the net curtains upstairs.

"They've got the house surrounded, I'd say," he said.

"What'll you do ?" I asked him. He shrugged his shoulders. He didn't care what the French authorities did against him, as long as Victoria was with me – but if they were threatening to split the family again, he would be better staying quiet and making sure we were together for good before he came out into the open.

"Just don't say anything about me for the moment if you don't have to," he said. I returned downstairs.

"Are you Delwyn May Jones ?" asked the officer with the card, as soon as I'd opened the door.

"Yes, I am," I answered. "You'd better come in."

I could feel the shock washing over me, and my legs had gone weak. Trust the French authorities to do things this way, I thought.

There were so many people out there – officers from Scotland Yard's Extradition Squad, RUC (Ulster Police) officers, social workers (I later learned that the RUC officers were from the Child Abuse Unit – I hate to think what they expected to find). I had been half-expecting a summons to the police station, but I certainly hadn't been expecting this. Thankfully only two of them came in straight away, introducing themselves as DS Bell and DC Robinson, from the Scotland Yard Extradition Squad.

"Is your daughter Victoria with you ?" asked the Detective Sergeant.

"Yes, of course, she's upstairs asleep," I answered. This was getting awfully like February 1993. But my answer seemed to reassure them. DC Robinson went quietly upstairs to check and came back downstairs looking surprised. "They're lovely children," she said. "what's the younger one's name ?"

"That's Elvira," I answered, suddenly feeling very defensive. "She has nothing to do with this," I added quickly. They apparently hadn't expected to see Elvira there. In fact, the whole situation was starting to make very little sense to them: the French authorities were "concerned" for Victoria but had made no mention of Elvira. But if I was not a "fit and proper" mother, why take one child and leave the other ? My head was spinning at the time, anyway. I could only hope that Axel had somehow disappeared somewhere.

They must have realized I was shocked. They sat me down on the sofa in the living room and the Detective Sergeant started explaining that the French authorities had initiated extradition proceedings against me for removing my daughter from France without the authorities' permission. I nodded.

At that stage another plain clothes officer entered, along with two women (social workers) and introduced himself as DC Weber. As they looked round the living room – Axel had only finished redecorating it a couple of months ago – they seemed slightly uneasy. Our home didn't really look like a 'cult' "hang-out", I suppose. I was ill at ease too – I still had just my nightdress on with a fleece jacket flung over the top. DC Weber kind of excused himself and continued the explanations. It was all done very quietly and sensitively. I was impressed by their attitude – a big change from the French police gung-ho attitude I had experienced in France. They would have to take me to London that day, he said. And Victoria would have to go into care…

"Why ?" I asked them, suddenly panicked.

"Just while you're not there to care for her," one of the social workers reassured me.

"No, no, you can't do that to Victoria," I said, my voice rising. "it's going to be 1993 all over again for her. You don't realise everything she's already been through…"

"It'll only be for a few days, until you return from London," – it was one of the social workers reassuring me again, logical and reasonable. She was a nice-looking person, but I instinctively didn't trust them – not after my experience of French Social Services.

"Can I ring a friend ?" I asked suddenly. I needed someone else's opinion on this, since I couldn't talk to Axel. Jacqui was the only person I could call on at this hour. She would come as fast as she could, she told me when I rang. She sounded shocked as well. This was of course what she had been afraid of.

A repeat of 1993 ?

We had to wake the children of course – more memories of 1993. Elvira was her usual bubbly self, but Victoria was more aware and very quiet. I explained to her – in French – that I had to go to London for the day because the French authorities were complaining about me taking her out of France, and that somebody else would look after her until I got back. She was almost crying. I could see in her eyes her fear of losing us all over again and being sent back to France.

"Why can't Papa look after me ?" she asked.

"We can't mention Papa," I told her. "You know he's in a difficult situation." Thank goodness we were able to speak in French. I realised she needed to see me strong.

"It won't be for long," I promised her. "Let's trust God, Victoria – He knows what He's doing, all right ?" She nodded, still tearful.

The girls quickly got dressed and while I was packing things for them the other social worker – Rosemary Morris, the senior social worker, I was to find out later – said she needed to ask a few questions and fill in some forms for Victoria. Then she started asking questions about Elvira.

"Hold on," I said. "Elvira's not going into care – she can stay with friends."

"Oh, I thought she would be wanting to stay with her sister," said the social worker, as reasonable as ever. Five minutes before she had not even known Elvira existed, but now she saw no reason why a perfectly happy and healthy child shouldn't go into care!

"She's only been with her sister for a few days !" I exclaimed. They had no idea what they were dealing with. "She has nothing to do with all this, and… and I can't do that to her, she would be absolutely lost in care. Elvira can stay with friends," I repeated. "Actually, why can't they both stay with friends ? You can ask for whatever guarantees you want. I'm Victoria's mother, and I want her with friends."

But they refused to budge from their view that Victoria had to go into care because of the French authorities' "concerns".

I went into our bedroom to get a few things for myself and found Axel behind the door. I couldn't really talk because DC Robinson and Rosemary Morris were just outside in the hall. I whispered to him that I had to go to London, that they were putting Victoria into care and that Jacqui was coming for Elvira. He just nodded. Now it was clearer than ever that he should stay hidden for the moment – he had to make sure that Victoria was going to stay with me. By the time Jacqui arrived I had finished getting our things together. Now the police were hurrying us: if I wanted to get to court in the afternoon and return home in the evening, I would have to get a move on.

Jacqui was shocked, worried, and upset. Not surprisingly. The situation couldn't have looked worse.

"Can Elvira stay with you ?" I asked her, while the girls were still upstairs. "They were talking about putting her into care with Victoria, but I said no."

"Oh, of course, love," she said, tears in her eyes at the mere thought of Elvira in care. Then she had the same thought as me. "But can't Victoria come with me as well ?"

I turned to Social Services again, but their answer was still no. It was so unfair, and that was the worst part of it: Victoria was the one who would suffer the most from all this, and yet the French authorities were claiming to act in her best interests !

Going quickly upstairs for something at the last minute, I had a moment to give Victoria a hug and say a few words and found Elvira sitting on our bed, staring at the wardrobe opposite with a mysterious smile on her little face.

"Daddy's in there," she whispered to me, pointing to the wardrobe. "I'm making sure no-one finds him !" It was all an adventure for her – and it was better that way.

I couldn't help smiling. All the police were downstairs now anyway – and had been repeating to me that it was time to leave.

"I think he'll be all right now," I told her. "You can come back up with Jacqui when Mummy's gone."

"Will you be back tonight, Mummy ?" she asked.

"Tonight or tomorrow, my love," I told her. "Now you be good with Jacqui and look after our secret Daddy, all right ?"

She nodded and we went downstairs with Victoria, who was waiting for us in the hall, uneasy, protesting that she wanted to stay with me. Jacqui was wiping tears from her cheeks as she took Elvira's hand, and Victoria was clinging to me with a look of desperation on her face.

"Just a minute," I told the Extradition Squad officers, and with Victoria, Jacqui and Elvira we had a little pray. It was heartbreaking to have to leave Victoria, who was almost in tears herself. Only just reunited with her family, in a new country, where she didn't understand the language, and here she was being plunged into State care – again. And I was helpless to do anything about it, once again. I had to leave her behind

Out into the open

The officers tried to keep me talking in the car on the way to the airport, but the moment came when it was all just too much. I had to turn away from DC Robinson as the sobs just overcame me, shaking me uncontrollably as I put my hand over my face. Victoria on her own, amongst strangers whom she could barely understand...

The rest of our journey to London was mostly spent in conversation. DC Robinson sat a row in front of the other two, beside me, and asked me for the whole story – were the others listening, I wondered ? It didn't matter. I tried to give her the general gist without going into too many details, and I think she got the picture – she asked me when I was going to write the book ! She had children of her own and could sympathize. It was almost as though she regretted doing her job that day.

"I know today is difficult for you," she said, "but I really think all this could actually help your situation… you know, bring it all out into the open." She was giving me something to hold on to, and I appreciated it.

If these officers had been more than correct at home, there was now a respectful friendliness about them that was an unexpected help to me through those difficult moments when I was trying not to think of Victoria "in care". Perhaps I appreciated them because I had been accustomed to the brutality of the French police. There was certainly none of the shallow bravado, callousness and mockery that the police officer who had questioned me on 10 February 1993 and his colleagues had been a perfect example of… These were people who could be moved by the plight of a desperate mother.

The three of them kept everything low-key and relaxed – no-one would ever have guessed that they were cops and I was a prisoner. You would have thought we were taking a day out to London. The Detective Sergeant left us on our arrival at Heathrow, while DC Robinson, DC Weber and I were escorted to a police van waiting discreetly outside a side door. There were only two seats, but DC Weber said he would "sit behind", which I discovered meant sitting on the floor behind bars – obviously where I was supposed to be. At one stage I could hear DC Weber on his mobile, desperately asking for more precise information from the French authorities, which I can only suppose he never received.

We spent ages, it must have been an hour or more, waiting to get into the police station at Heathrow – all three of us standing in a queue outside, silent most of the time. By now they had informed me that it wouldn't be possible to get me into court today, so I was going to have to spend the night in the police station there and appear before Bow Street Magistrates' Court the following day. They even got me laughing about spending a night at the station "with the TV and the electric blanket". I knew it would be far from it, if conditions in French police stations were anything to go by. I told them I was getting used to spending time in police station lock-ups anyway...

They had also contacted a solicitor for me. I had wanted to do things thoroughly – go through the whole list to see who was available and then choose – but they kind of looked at me and said tactfully: "Well, let's start at the bottom of the list for a change, shall we – do you want a man or a woman ?" After all our run-ins with women judges, women prosecutors, women social workers and women lawyers in France, I had no hesitation in asking for a male lawyer. So we got a Mr Zullrich, who said he would be there to represent me in court the next day and would come to see me shortly beforehand, if he didn't make it to see me at the police station that evening. Thankfully, money was not a problem – because I was on Income Support I shouldn't have a problem obtaining legal aid.

When we got into the station and I saw all those cells with just a little square barred window in the iron door, reality finally started to sink in. What's more, almost everything I had brought with me had to be left behind in one of those big plastic bags for personal belongings. DC Robinson came close to overlooking a small razor-sharp metal paper-cutter that I was about to take in with me in a plastic case with a few pens – I thought they were being picky, to be honest, but once I got into the cell I was glad she had taken it out: it meant I couldn't even think about it, or the possible uses it could have been put to...

A police station is not a hotel

All alone in a cold concrete underground cell with nothing to do, my mind started whirling. At least there was a plastic foam mattress and a blanket in here, and the cell was quite big: about three metres square. I kept asking to phone, asking to see a solicitor ("you're in the queue, Madam", I was told) – anything to get out of that loneliness or get talking to someone. I spent some time writing down what I would say to the judge the next day – I knew nothing of the way British courts functioned, and that only my solicitor would be saying anything; but at least it took up time.

At one stage I was almost sure I was going to be sent to France – after all, I had confessed to my crime, I was indeed guilty of not having returned Victoria to the Mediation Centre. I was sure the French authorities would argue that that settled the case – "so send her back here" would be their line. I paced my cell to keep warm, keep moving and try to think clearly.

I did have my Bible. Tucked in amongst its pages I found notes I had taken down on the back of an envelope from a sermon preached on Psalm 3. It spoke of the word "Selah", commonly found in the Psalms, meaning a "pause for rest" – and went on to show how we needed to learn the "selahs of life": when it was time to rest, pause and wait patiently upon the Lord. There was the rest of salvation, of supplication, of submission and of Sunday. I knew the first, and was getting to know the second and fourth better, but it was the third – the rest of submission to the will of God – that struck me that night. Sometimes when we can't see where we're going, and our path can be painful, the preacher had said – we need to discover the secret of that "selah", peacefully resting in and submitting to the will of God. Those thoughts from Psalm 3 were to remain wonderfully with me through that cold, gloomy night and through the court hearing the next morning too. God had once again unfailingly given me strength when I needed it.

I did see the "on duty" solicitor – one who came round when your own solicitor couldn't come in, to talk and give advice. He was very reassuring, saying that in his opinion I would be freed tomorrow on bail, under a few conditions, and that I had nothing to worry about. Unfortunately, after our experiences in France I was unsure as to whether British solicitors were to be trusted !

I got a glimpse of the shower facilities in the police station that evening – there was only a swing door that was open at the top and bottom, to allow supervision, I suppose.

"I think I'll give it a miss," I said to the policewoman with a wry smile.

"As you like, Madam," she answered, rather tight-lipped. "This is a police station, not a hotel." The next morning, though, I was dying for a shower and when I saw that the policewoman would be the only one there, and standing just outside with her back to me, I decided to risk it after all – and it was worth it too, even though there were only paper towels for getting dry… I had no fond farewells to say to that cell. As I left the police station though, I was amused and cheered to hear the policeman at the door mutter, in such a thick Cockney accent that I didn't understand straight away:

"Picking on poor, innocent immigrants – I dunno !"

Next up was the trip to court in a police fourgon, locked up in a tiny compartment with a small, dark glass window. The wall was only a foot from my face and covered with graffiti. I couldn't help wondering whether the people outside could see anything of me.

At the court Mr Zullrich, the solicitor, appeared at the hole in the door. He apologised for having to speak through it.

"So what's your story, then ?" he asked. "From what I've heard it sounds like something out of a spy thriller."

I had to smile. He was quite a character, and I liked characters. He couldn't believe the story, of course, shaking his head in disbelief and throwing questions at me all the time. My concern was that I needed to get home to Victoria and Elvira. Mr Zullrich hoped to get me out on bail without any complicated conditions, possibly just a curfew and an interdiction to travel outside of Northern Ireland… he would see me in court.

When I got in there, through the defendants' entrance, of course, the court seemed huge, solemn and quite dimly lit. From where I was told to sit, on the defendants' bench, I couldn't seem to hear extremely well either, so I had to strain my ears and leave the rest to Mr Zullrich.

The high point of the hearing, as far as I was concerned, was when DC Weber spoke on behalf of the Extradition Squad.

"If I had known yesterday what I know today," he said, "I would never have signed the warrant for Mrs Jones' arrest." He couldn't have been any clearer. The slander from the French authorities had not stood up to British scrutiny.

I was only asked to confirm my identity at the beginning and agree to the bail conditions at the end, and that was it. As Mr Zullrich had hoped, there were no complicated conditions. I was to live and sleep at home between 11:00 p.m. and 7:00 a.m. and not allowed to apply for travel documents. There would be a full hearing sometime in October. I thanked Mr Zullrich (who thoughtfully gave me twenty English pounds to get myself something to eat – Northern Ireland bank-notes aren't always accepted in England), and went to wait for my belongings in the big plastic bag. It felt as though I was coming out of prison.

As I finally stepped out into the London sunshine, I felt a wave of relief sweep over me: I was free. The sky looked bluer and the air felt fresher – and that was in inner London. One night locked up in a cell had been quite enough for me. The first thing I did was to find a phone box to tell Axel and Jacqui that I was out... The worst had happened but I was still there – and I was hopeful we were nearing the end of the road. Axel was there with Stephen to meet me at the airport and they got me sitting down for something to eat and drink and even got me laughing over the whole episode. As the saying goes in Ulster, if you didn't laugh you'd cry...

"I want to be with my Mum"

If I had thought it was all going to be plain sailing from then on, I should have thought again. To start with, Social Services refused to return Victoria to my care as soon as I was back in Northern Ireland, because they were still concerned about the French Government's "concerns" for her: there were rumours – rumours from France about the alleged 'cult', rumours about the accusations against Axel, and especially rumours that the French authorities were going to be using the Hague Convention to get Victoria returned to France.

After meeting with them, I was relieved to hear that I was going to be able to see Victoria the following day (under supervision), but I was horrified that in spite of all the explanations I gave them about how Victoria had been separated from me in France, they were still going to keep her separated from me now ! I protested by withdrawing my consent for her to be in care, which I had given them on July 28 before leaving for London. Social Services then said they would simply apply for an extension of their Emergency Protection Order. We seemed to be back into conflict yet again.

Victoria was tearful when I saw her and wanted only one thing – to be back home as soon as possible. All I could say was that she should keep telling everybody that, because I was telling everybody that too, and together we would get there in the end. At least here nobody could influence her against me, but in her isolation and desperation, with everything else she was going through because of this repeat of our 1993 separation, she could easily have given up and turned back to an easy life in France with her grandparents. But Victoria knew what she wanted. When her grandparents rang her at her foster home the day after I saw her (I wasn't even allowed that number myself!), she told them in no uncertain terms that she wanted to stay with her *Maman*. She had made her choice, and it was a brave one.

Social Services nevertheless obtained their extended Emergency Protection Order at an initial Family Court hearing on August 2. Thanks to Mr Wright, I had been able to contact a reliable solicitor, explain the case to him briefly over the phone and provide him with the file of evidence in our favour – the doctor's health certificates, a copy of Victoria's health book, family photos of her when she was small, as well as more recent proof showing there had been no reason for the French Judiciary to keep Victoria separated from her mother and little sister.

Then there was a hearing on August 4, and although I hadn't actually been summoned to it, I thought I should at least be present. Jacqui went with me and the official at the door kindly let us in.

"I have learned that the mother of the child Victoria Schmidt is present in the courtroom though uninvited," stated the judge, a few minutes later, to my surprise. "However, we shall continue with the hearing, please."

Axel was also being represented by then, by a young solicitor that Mr Hart, my own solicitor, had recommended.

The solicitor appointed by the French Government stated that Victoria had initially been withdrawn from my care to protect her

from the vicious 'cult' her parents belonged to, etc. The judge turned
to my solicitor to ask him what he had to say to that. There was a
hush in the courtroom.

"Mrs Jones belonged to a small evangelical church, your
Honour," stated Mr Hart, my solicitor, simply and clearly. I felt like
cheering. The judge asked to see the family photos – not just to skim
over and discard them, like the judges who had been dealing with
the case in France, but to really examine them.

"Certainly looks like a happy, healthy child," he remarked. I
started breathing again. This judge was actually taking our evidence
into account ! I know it shouldn't have seemed such an event, but
after having seen it set aside for so long in France I was over the
moon.

But the hearing was not over yet. Outside the courtroom Social
Services had been talking of putting Elvira into care as well… The
judge didn't mention it, though, to my greatest relief.

"I believe we have an illustrious personality in our midst,"
announced the judge, "and we would be honoured to hear what she
has to say to us."

So the M.E.P., designated by the President of the European
Parliament to look into Victoria's case, had the opportunity to say a
few words – which she had never had before the judges dealing with
Victoria's case in France.

Most importantly, the Family Court judge ruled that day that I
should be allowed to see Victoria every day until the next hearing,
which the judge was referring to the High Court because of the "high
profile" of the case. It would be fast-laned, he said, looking at me.
Although it was a relief to know I would be seeing Victoria more
often, I knew it was also going to be a very painful time.

True enough, every time I saw Victoria she couldn't bear the
thought of leaving me – and I hated separating from her. For our
first couple of supervised visits we had to be observed by an
interpreter – to make sure I wasn't telling Victoria anything in French
that I wasn't supposed to ! Victoria's distress at being separated from
me was very evident, and I was tormented once again by my own
helplessness – all I could tell her each time was that I was doing
everything I could to bring her home. The interpreter, a retired French

teacher, looked ill at ease himself at being asked to do such a dirty job: reporting to Social Services what was obviously so personal and painful to us. I was touched when he let me encourage Victoria spiritually and glossed over it in his comments to the Social worker. Victoria desperately needed encouragement. Spiritually she was just a babe, and her faith in God was already being put sorely to the test.

At the next visit I learned that the interpreter had refused to continue with the work, as he didn't agree with what Social Services were doing to us. His help and his stand were an encouragement to me, and even Denis Hamilton, the social worker, who I would say was relatively sincere and unbiased, could see how wrong it all was. Victoria was now refusing to get into the car at the end of visits, she wasn't getting on with the elderly lady she had been placed with – she could hardly communicate with her, to start with – and visits with me, which she looked forward to, only caused her more distress when she had to leave. The situation was intolerable, and painful for everyone – even the social worker couldn't suggest any way of alleviating Victoria's distress. Social Services depended on the court and were only carrying out orders, they said, but we knew their recommendations could influence the court a great deal.

Several politicians who had been informed of our difficulties made representations to Social Services, which undoubtedly helped. But help was also on the way from a different and unexpected source.

Pressure on the grandparents

Back in France, the judiciary had been furious, of course.

First of all, the grandparents received a visit from the police while they were still away on holiday. They were questioned at some length about the whole case and were finally asked the burning question.

"Are you going to lodge a complaint ?"

Axel's Dad had been expecting it and had his answer ready – a firm "no".

Then Madame Barnier had cried over the phone to Axel's Mum. "Are you not worried about Victoria ?" she was asking. Are you not going to be lodging a complaint was again the question between the lines.

"Why should we be ?" asked Axel's Mum. "Victoria is with her mother." The Judiciary had always done their best to make them distrust me and vice versa, but with Axel in contact with his parents now, their little game was up.

After the grandparents spoke with Victoria on the phone on August 2, they also wrote to the judge for children. They had spoken to Victoria in her foster home, they wrote, where it was impossible for her mother to influence her, and she had clearly told them that she wanted to stay in Northern Ireland with her *Maman*. They therefore renounced their custody of Victoria "with relief in [their] hearts".

That phone call had a story of pressure behind it, too. Incredibly, my daughter's number in foster care in Northern Ireland, which I had been forbidden to know, had been communicated to UNADFI ! That organisation was always in the know whenever there were any legal proceedings concerning any people they had imperiously labelled a 'cult'. They attempted to drag the grandparents back into collaboration with them by holding Victoria's phone number out to them like the proverbial carrot. However, the grandparents had long been disillusioned with UNADFI and were not about to let themselves be enticed back into associating with them: they rang the Ministry of Justice to find out the number for themselves.

So UNADFI was obliged to do their dirty work by themselves. On August 8 there was a French radio report telling of my dastardly deed (imagine – an innocent mother had dared to take her own daughter home to live with her !) and this was followed by articles in French newspapers and a shocking one in the New Zealand Herald. Of course, UNADFI knew how to slant everything so that it sounded horrific, and all the worst old accusations were dug up and slung around. I had a horrified letter from the family in New Zealand along with a copy of the article, and poor Derek and Lilian, who hadn't been able to reach us on the phone, thought we were all in prison and had almost jumped on a plane to come and see us ! We had agreed with Axel's Mum and Dad that we would say nothing to the press, though, and the family in New Zealand followed suit – let the press ramble on, we weren't going to enter the fray.

But the worst of the French Judiciary's push for a complaint from the grandparents was through the examining judge in Versailles – a certain Monsieur Charpier, known for his crackdowns on big-time criminals – who summoned the grandparents to the local police station. There they were asked, or rather subtly ordered, to sign some forms, which turned out to be an application for Hague Convention proceedings so that Victoria be returned to France. It seemed that the French Judiciary simply could not bear to think of us being a united and reconciled family once again.

Thankfully Axel was there to talk to his parents about the agonizing situation Victoria and I were in because of our continued separation and the short, supervised visits. When he informed his Mum and Dad that it was mainly because of the Hague Convention proceedings that this painful separation was being prolonged, they immediately wrote to the French Minister of Justice to retract the application they had been forced to sign, and we gave the translation of their letter to my solicitor in Belfast, who forwarded it to the Belfast High Court and to Social Services. They also wrote to the French examining judge and to the French police, to make quite sure that everyone knew that they were entirely supportive of their granddaughter's wish to remain in Northern Ireland with her parents. It was an isolated and courageous stand to take, but some-how our newly-found family union seemed to have inspired them with courage.

With the Hague Convention proceedings dealt with, and nothing concrete having come through from the French authorities about the 'cult' accusations, the only other thing that could possibly prevent Victoria's return home were the accusations against Axel. He decided it was time to take things into his own hands.

Axel's bid for justice

Axel's only reason for keeping a low profile until then had been to help me regain and keep custody of Victoria. The French authorities had known he was in Northern Ireland since March 1995, but hadn't done anything against him as long as they had a hold on Victoria in France. With a hearing about Victoria's case coming up in Belfast on August 16, Axel decided to go and see Social Services and put everything plainly before them: Victoria's abduction by police without any kind of prior investigation, the false accusations against him, and the way he had been convicted two years later to justify and cover up Victoria's disparition. Stephen accompanied him, but of course had to remain outside.

"Victoria desperately needs to come home now, as I believe you are aware," Axel told the Social Services team. "If you see me as an obstacle to Victoria's return home, I am fully prepared to move out – immediately."

Social Services must have been a little taken aback by his forthrightness.

"Well, at the moment we are still seeking further information from the French authorities about this whole case," said the senior social worker, Emma Lambert (Rosemary Morris happened to be away on holiday that week).

"Yes, sure, I understand that," replied Axel, "but you will get a lot of garbage from the French !" He asked to be given a say about any documents they received from France, gave them Elvira's school report, as proof that she was well brought up, happy and normal, and said that his home was open to them if they wished to investigate further.

"And here's my CV, so you know who I am," he added.

"Mr Schmidt, could I ask whether you would agree to taking part in a family assessment ?" asked Mrs Lambert. Axel saw no reason why not – and so the meeting ended. All the cards were on the table and Axel had made his position clear. As long as Victoria was safely with me, he didn't care what it cost him. If the French authorities wanted to come after him now, he would be standing his ground.

Axel returned home, and ten minutes later the phone rang. It was Denis Hamilton, who told me that the Social Services team had decided that at the hearing due the next day (August 11) they would be asking for Victoria to be returned home and they themselves would be withdrawing from the case. I was delighted, and so relieved – but he had more to say.

"We actually don't see any reason why she can't come home tonight, since we've already made our decision," he said, "so you'll probably be seeing her in about an hour."

"Brilliant !" I almost yelled down the phone at him. I thanked him and hung up. Axel was waiting to see what that had all been about.

"You must have made some impression on them," I told him. "They're bringing Victoria home tonight !" We were all ecstatic. Elvira was dancing around in glee and then bouncing up and down on Stephen's knee.

In fact it must have been only about half an hour later that we had a knock on the door. I was upstairs and came down to see Victoria flying in through the front door and literally jumping into her Daddy's arms. Denis Hamilton was on the doorstep, smiling at her enthusiasm. We could only thank him again – at least he went home that evening knowing he'd made one family happy. Stephen was still with us and I could see the tears in his eyes – the old softie.

So Victoria was home, legally and lawfully home, after so many years, so many people's prayers and so much tension and stress. She had spent two weeks in care in Northern Ireland, compared with the two years in care in France plus the five and a half years with her grandparents under the judge's orders. It was true that proceedings were still on-going, but we felt they were off to a good start. Things were being brought into order at last.

The French authorities had only one last hold on our family – but we knew they weren't the kind to let go easily. Now was going to be perhaps the most trying time of this whole long ordeal for me. They had often attempted to pressure us as a couple into separating of our own accord but now they were going to use force – to separate me from Axel.

19

Oh to be united for good at last
July 2000 – November 2002

Just a check-up

Now we were not only together, but we were legally together. We at last settled down to normal family life. I confirmed to Elvira's school that Victoria would be attending from September 1st, and she was officially enrolled. Both girls had taken to attending gymnastics twice a week and both of them had also made friends in the small Free Presbyterian congregation where we had attended the night Victoria was saved. That was going to be essential for Victoria as she adapted to life in Ulster.

For the first time since February 1993 I felt myself actually beginning to relax and just enjoy the satisfaction of being a mother and wife at home. Being able to care for Victoria and Elvira with Axel's support and without anything else weighing on my mind, was unexpectedly a luxury. There was only one hitch: I couldn't stop myself from waking early every morning with my stomach in knots. I knew it wasn't logical – the situation was out in the open now and there should be no further reason for a police intervention like the one on July 28 – but there it was, and it was worse every time there was a hearing: August 2, August 4, August 11, August 16...

Axel was out cutting the grass just the day after Victoria got back when we had a call from Social Services. What they now wanted was Axel's consent for them to check his convictions in France and the United Kingdom with Interpol – just to check the facts he had given them. Axel agreed, of course, and they came round a little later to get his signature for it.

Now Victoria needed more explanations – her separation from us had inevitably brought back memories of 1993, and she wanted to know the whys and wherefores of it all, once and for all. Axel sat down with her and they had a good talk. It seemed that she needed to get things sorted out in her mind so as to be able to put it all behind her and get on with life.

We also got on with decorating her room a little more – she chose a border and Axel designed a desk-and-bookshelf unit for her. Then we had news that Axel's Mum and Dad were thinking of coming to visit from August 24 to September 1st. For Victoria that was extremely important – she needed to know that the people she loved most, her parents and her grandparents, were reconciled and united around her; for Axel and I it was to be a special moment, especially for him, as we welcomed his parents to Ulster without the contentiousness that had disastrously stymied family relations in France; and for Elvira it was the wonderful discovery of a "granny and granda" who had been unknown entities for her until then.

Then, three days after their request for information, on 15 August 2000, Social Services informed Axel that they had received answers to their inquiries through Interpol and were now asking him to leave the family home while they carried out further investigations. What seemed to trouble them most was that back in 1995 Axel had been given an eighteen-month prison sentence, which for them naturally indicated that a "serious level of harm against children" was involved. The French Judiciary had known exactly what they were doing and what the consequences would be for Axel when they had meted out that unjust and unsubstantiated sentence.

Axel immediately agreed to their request – he had said he was prepared to do this and he fully intended to keep his word. This was going to mean not seeing the girls except during supervised visits and not coming to the house at any time, even when the girls were at school. It was inevitable that the family 'balance' we were just getting used to was going to suffer.

Over the years I had become used to being considered as 'separated' to all outside intents and purposes. Now though, I was going to learn what it was really like to be a single Mum. To start with, there were simple little round-the-house jobs that Axel would have done, from cutting the grass to organising the roof-space or locking up at night. Not only did I now have to take on these kind of extra practical responsibilities, but I also had all the 'family management' problems to cope with on my own – being fair between the two girls, making allowances when necessary and drawing the line where I had to, and trying to give them the good family times they needed as well.

Where I especially felt the strain was when the two girls had conflicting interests. Normally this wouldn't have been a problem with Axel at home, but now, for example, I had to try to get Elvira to sleep in the car while we waited for Victoria to come out of gymnastics. Elvira's constant colds and eventual asthma problems date from this difficult time. Because of the five-year difference between the two girls, they were interested in very different activities, and catering for these as a single parent was exhausting. I lost more weight. The actions of the French authorities were still affecting us in our everyday life. Would we ever be free of them ?

Axel's parents' visit at the end of August was to prove a very welcome respite: Social Services had decided that we could be together as a family as long as we were with the grandparents, though we were still limited in that my bail conditions required me to be back home every night, so the girls and I couldn't be away for more than a day at a time.. Humiliating, but we didn't care – being together was good for everybody, and if this was what we had to do to keep Victoria with us, so be it.

Axel's parents discover Ulster

It was extraordinary for Axel to be able to welcome his parents in a relaxed, affectionate way, literally with open arms. To see him walking and talking with his Mum and Dad, both together and separately, did my heart good. To see Victoria and Elvira happy with their grandparents *and* their parents was a treat as well: everything was at last coming together and it was vital for both the girls. It was also a novelty for me to have Axel's parents' support and confidence at last, something the accusations in France had deprived us of for too long. For the grandparents I felt their visit was a help in adapting to their new life without Victoria – they undoubtedly missed her sorely. They had done more for Victoria than they had ever done for any of their children, as Axel could see. They had brought over some of her things with them… Meeting Elvira was also a novelty for them. In the letter they wrote to Madame Barnier on their return to France, their first conclusion read: "Elvira is a very joyful and spontaneous child, at ease and sure of herself." She had been a discovery for them as well.

This didn't mean we were agreed on everything. Axel's parents still believed that our church had been a "cult" etc. They had believed it for so long and acted so often in consequence, that it was extremely difficult for them to take in even the possibility that the reality was altogether different from what others – especially Axel's brother René and his wife – had told them time and again. We knew it had been impossible to persuade them otherwise (impossible to even talk about it calmly) because of the context in France, but even we were amazed at how a pack of malicious lies had become an entirely accepted and acted-on truth for them. Now they were seeing and experiencing the reality for themselves and starting to reconsider, but it was still very difficult for them to come to terms with it.

They could see that our faith was genuine and authentically personal; that our decisions and actions were based on Biblical principles and our faith in them; that we were responsible parents who loved our children and wanted to give them the best we could.

All this was totally contrary to their perception of us up until then – they had been given the image of an irresponsible, naïve couple who had let themselves be taken in by people with sinister intentions. Now they could see what we had been trying to tell them: we *knew* the truth about our life in the church, we *knew* the value of what we had received there, and at last we were able to show them this in a simple, everyday way.

Axel himself felt he also needed to put things right, and asked their forgiveness for his attitude – not for the position we had taken in keeping quiet about Victoria's birth, or in defending the church, both of which we were still entirely convinced had been the only honest and appropriate options given the circumstances – but for the lack of consideration he felt he had shown towards them all those years ago. He was dismayed to see that they had been coerced into this fight against the "cult", and it had got them into a position which they could now see simply didn't make sense.

My parents-in-law also discovered that Northern Ireland was not the 'pit' they had been brought to believe: they found their stay at Jacqui's B&B delightful (what Axel had dreamt of when he was working in the house in 1995-96 had come true), they immensely enjoyed visiting the tourist attractions round the North Antrim coast – all the sights we had been to with the girls in July, plus a visit to the Auld Lammas Fair in Ballycastle and a few sights around Belfast. They especially seemed to find the people they met unexpectedly likeable: open, out-going, caring, generous – and of course there was always that wicked Ulster sense of humour ! "*Sympa*," was invariably the word they used. Axel's Mum told him at one stage that if she had known what our situation in Ulster truly was, she would have been more favourable towards Victoria's return home. Sadly, it was only our removal of Victoria from France that had allowed them to realise this.

Axel's parents made good use of their time in Ulster. After arriving on August 24 and spending the first five days being with the family and meeting friends, their last three days were spent meeting with the Guardian ad litem (appointed by the Court to represent Victoria's interests), being interviewed separately by Social Services, meeting the girls' school principal and being shown round the school, meeting solicitors and barristers dealing with the case to tell them personally what their position was; as well as going to see the girls at gymnastics and purchasing a piano so that Victoria could continue to play.

Most importantly, they were able to be present at a Social Services Case Conference about the girls, where they clearly stated their position and the very favourable impression they had been given of Victoria's life with her family in Northern Ireland. It was quite intimidating having to speak in front of about twenty people, including medical representatives from our family GP's surgery, police representatives and other "concerned professionals" (our case was obviously still considered to be 'high profile'). Many of the concerns expressed were however much allayed by the clear position taken by Axel's parents: Victoria had not suffered any emotional trauma by being brought to Northern Ireland, and the grandparents made it very clear that they believed Victoria's place was with her parents – so what was the problem ?

I was personally extremely glad for the presence and support of the girls' school principal at that case conference. Axel and I and the two girls had been to see him that morning with Axel's parents, and had been able to explain the situation to him. Having known Elvira fairly well, he was the only one at the Case Conference who confidently voted against putting the girls on the "potentially at risk" register. It was a courageous stand against Social Services' interference into our family life, and the kindness and understanding he showed that day were exemplary. He was undoubtedly aware of the heartache and difficulties we were going to face as a family, and evidently concerned that interference was unnecessary and would be destabilizing – and he was going to be proven right.

That afternoon a meeting had been arranged with Dr Ian Paisley. All four of us went, leaving Victoria and Elvira at Jacqui's, but it was the grandparents that Dr Paisley was there to speak to – Axel and I just translated. Once they were in his office, Dr Paisley didn't stay behind his desk - he pulled a chair up beside them.

"I'm a father and a grandfather, too, you know," he said to them. The scene was set, the conversation was warm and interesting, and

Axel's Mum and Dad were soon smiling, even laughing. It was like a celebration of our family reunion more than anything else.

"Time for you all to turn the page and not look back," said Dr Paisley. He really had a way of speaking to them personally. Axel's Mum and Dad were at ease, yet respectful.

At the end Dr Paisley prayed, and gave them one of his books, personally signed especially for them.

On their last evening with us Jacqui threw a goodbye party at her house, and we had a last meal with them the next day after Axel's Mum and I had picked the children up from their first day at school – the first day ever for Victoria in an English-medium school. Axel saw his parents off at the airport with a lump in his throat. Their time in Northern Ireland had passed only too quickly and once again he had to separate from us...

The last snatch

We had four hearings in August, first at the Family Court in Belfast and then at the High Court. At the last one on 16 August, care and control of Victoria had been entrusted to me. The next hearing was due on 5 September 2000 – because Hague Convention proceedings were involved, we had to attend a hearing every three weeks. We were hopeful that they would soon be dropped, since Axel's parents had withdrawn the application that the examining judge had 'requested' them to make.

Court hearings always seem to be long, drawn-out affairs. In Northern Ireland, at least the judge truly kept to a judge's role – he kept his distance from the different parties and encouraged them to consult and discuss with each other as much as possible, so that when the court convened, everybody's position was clear and the judge didn't waste time listening to the parties arguing between themselves – as had been the case in France. This meant that our solicitors and barristers represented our interests not only before the judge but also in discussions with the other barristers involved. This kind of 'negotiating-before-going-into-court' was a relief to us – far better than getting into court and then being put on the spot. We simply made our position clear to our Counsel (barristers) so that they could put that across to the other barristers and eventually to the judge. The barristers here were no "auxiliaries of the judiciary" as we had so often seen in France !

So on 5 September 2000 Axel was due to meet with his solicitor and barrister at 11:00 a.m. and I was due to meet with mine at 11:30 a.m., although the hearing was only due to take place at 2 o'clock in the afternoon. We were expecting to spend a long day in court. Axel was staying with Professor McLeod and I would be leaving the girls off at school to meet Axel at the Royal Courts of Justice.

The Courts are an impressive place, especially when entered for the first time: once through the security check, the big pillared entrance rose dauntingly before me, then it was through the double doors past the reception and announcement area to the main hall, a long high room with benches at intervals along the sides and round notice boards down the centre of it, where people were discussing their business in quiet tones. It seemed there were forever people waiting for hearings or looking for their legal representatives, and as soon as we came through the big double doors at the entrance end and down the steps, everybody's eyes seemed to be following us to see if we were the people they were waiting for – or just out of curiosity. We found somewhere to sit and joined the waiting, watching eyes.

Looking up as someone came down the entrance steps, I suddenly realised I recognised that face – it was DC Weber, of the Scotland Yard Extradition Squad. He even nodded at me. I could only assume he was here on other business – his nod had reassured me it wasn't my case he was looking into, anyway. I did mention it to Axel though.

"What do you think's going on ?" I asked him. "It's strange him coming all the way from London to here, don't you think ?"

I could see Axel did think it strange. We watched people going past. Our solicitors came to see us and went away again. DC Weber had been in and out of the hall, too, speaking to people. I was feel the tension building.

More time passed. Stephen had come to be there with us, and we talked things over a little. Axel's solicitor was there too.

"I think they're here to arrest me," Axel said to me, but I didn't want to believe it. He had just finished speaking when we heard a voice ring out.

"Mr Schmidt !" He turned to see who was calling him – it was DC Weber, hailing him from the other side of the hall, signalling to him to meet him outside. Axel and his solicitor headed out. After a while we went to see, and learnt that DC Weber had to take *Axel* to London this time, on an extradition warrant from the French authorities once again…

Axel confirmed his identity to them and seized the opportunity to make a written statement in which he declared that his arrest was part of a "pattern of religious persecution by the French Government".

Apparently nabbing people when they appeared for a court hearing was uncommon… I was more angry than upset at first. Axel had only come into court to support me and help settle things down for the family – would they never leave us alone ? After all these years, too, when they had known he was in the UK and had done nothing about it. This was pure spiteful revenge, once again. They had no real concerns about the danger Axel might pose to society, or they would and should have done something sooner. In our case they were obviously determined to try every dirty trick in the book.

Social Services were there outside as well, and the senior social worker's attitude seemed to be that this was the beginning of the end for Mr Schmidt. That was him out of the way! Denis Hamilton, the social worker who had been in charge of Victoria's case, was a little uneasy, though.

"What should I tell the girls this afternoon ?" he asked Axel. He was the one who had to deal with the situation on the ground.

"Don't worry," Axel answered. "Delwyn will see to it." It was going to be difficult telling the girls though – they had been due to see their Daddy at the Social Services venue that afternoon and they were going to be disappointed.

I was able to talk to Axel briefly. With the police watching a couple of yards away, I could only kiss him goodbye and see if I could do anything for him. He was calm – in a way it was a relief for us both that things had come to a head now for him too. We were both also determined to resist extradition proceedings and I hoped that like me, Axel would be back in Northern Ireland in a couple of days.

He left with the Extradition Squad officers and Stephen and I returned to wait for the hearing to take place. How many times I had appreciated Stephen's constant support. He seemed to be able to look at the situation from such a reasonable point of view and say: Axel will be back soon, don't worry, as though he had it all worked out – and it usually did turn out to be right too. There never seemed to be a reason for tears when Stephen was around. Yet as my indignation turned to upset, it became harder to hold them back. The French authorities had succeeded in separating us again. I knew what awaited Axel, the anguish of the cell and the worry for us and the moments of doubt when it seemed as though the French authorities were bound to crush us in the end. But would God fail Axel? I didn't believe so.

HMP Brixton

Axel was headed for worse than the police station at Heathrow: after appearing before a judge in Bow Street Magistrates' Court, he was immediately imprisoned in Brixton HMP. He had a week to arrange sufficient bail conditions to satisy the court that he was not going to disappear again.

Axel took to praying and fasting – and speaking to those around him. He had promised himself long ago that if ever he landed in prison, he would use the opportunity to speak to others of Christ, to help those around him if he could. While waiting at the court he started talking to his Jewish fellow prisoner, and they spoke together at some length. This man was very open to hearing about Christ, and providence was to bring them back together again a week later, when they both appeared before the same court for the second time. By then Axel was spiritually even stronger, and his Jewish acquaintance got the full benefit of the Gospel message loud and clear. Before they parted he wanted to know what Bible he should buy !

My sister Jeanette was working in London at that time, and when she heard that Axel was in Brixton she immediately offered to go and see him – he was the mysterious French brother-in-law she had never met, after all. I think the visit did them both good.

Not long after Jeanette's first visit, Axel got talking to another fellow prisoner, this time a French-speaking Muslim ("Ah, you are a Frenchman !" he said to Axel) who was delighted to find someone else who spoke French. When Axel shared with him the change Christ had made in his life, he was attentive too, but he knew only too well the stark reality of the law of Islam: if he converted to Christ and returned to his home country, he would most certainly be killed. He prayed devoutly three times a day, facing east – towards the wardrobe, as Axel remembered it. The wardrobe was towards the east, he was reminded of it three times a day. Axel, on the contrary, seemed privileged to be able to pray in any available corner without worrying which way was east. When his Muslim friend fasted, which he did, he simply saved up his meals during the day and then ate them all at night-time, according to his custom. When Axel fasted, he gave his uneaten meals to his appreciative cell-mate.

This Muslim also spoke three languages, English, French and his native tongue, but he couldn't write in any of them. So Axel sat down beside him two or three times to show him how – it wasn't too difficult, since he could already read without a problem. Axel also wrote some letters to his friend's solicitor to try and help him get out of prison. Axel's efforts to help this man did not go unnoticed: he was surprised to see that the prison inmates who served the meals, most of whom were black people like his cell-mate, gave Axel double helpings and were very respectful towards him… After his release, when this man wrote his first letter, it was one to Axel.

He was encouraged to receive a visit from a Free Presbyterian minister working in London, and he kept himself busy in his spare time by writing letters and doing a lot of reading – as ever, he had taken his Bible with him into prison, in fact it was the only thing he had taken in with him – reading Psalms, Proverbs and especially the book of Esther… His next hearing was on a Wednesday, and he decided to set apart Monday to Wednesday as three special days of fasting and prayer, just as Esther had done. On he read, into the book of Job, then Ecclesiastes and Proverbs again. He was praying to be released that Wednesday. If he wasn't, he would have to wait another whole month to have his appeal heard – and he knew we needed him back in Ulster.

Back home I spent two increasingly difficult weeks with the girls. Determined not to mention the word "prison" to them, I had had to explain that their Daddy had been kept in London for a little longer than we had thought, because his case was a little more complicated than mine. I had spoken to our London solicitors several times and only knew that they would be making a request for release on bail on the Wednesday. They were asking me for the names of anyone who might possibly be able to stand surety for Axel.

Here again, Stephen came to our rescue, personally contacting the different people who were to stand surety for Axel, on top of the security paid to the Court by Axel's parents. Of course, all the old accusations were brought out in court by the British prosecutor, speaking on behalf of the French Government. The four people who had accepted to stand surety had made a special effort to come to London from Northern Ireland for the bail application hearing, and they were all questioned one after another. Councillor Wright was the first to come under the prosecutor's fire, which flamed on for about half an hour in a desperate attempt to dissuade him and the other sureties from supporting Axel. These loyal people were superb in their stand that day. One by one, they unflinchingly maintained that the behaviour the defendant was accused of was totally out of character with the person they knew – Axel Schmidt. The French Government, it appeared, would have infinitely preferred that Axel stay in prison ! At last I could give the girls some positive news – it had been decided that their Daddy would be coming home just as soon as the solicitors could make the necessary arrangements.

Now it was a race to get the security money in so as to get Axel out, and unfortunately the money from Axel's parents in France was a little complicated in coming. They had made sure that enough money be sent to cover commission charges so that the whole sum was paid into the Court's account, but somehow somebody human blundered, and the amount that eventually came through was seven pounds short. Worse still, Axel's solicitors could do absolutely nothing to help him – they were strictly not allowed to pay any part of the security money. For the sake of seven pounds Axel was stuck there in prison… could nobody help him ? Then my sister Jeanette unexpectedly returned to see Axel again – and yes, she knew Bloomsbury Place, she might just be able to take those few pounds round to our solicitors and get Axel out of jail – if he really wanted to !

Axel stood in front of the huge iron prison door, waiting. Slowly, ever so slowly, it opened, revealing little by little the colours and variety and opportunities of the outside world – opening onto free-dom. As he walked down the quiet street leading out of the prison he thought back – a fortnight before it had seemed that everything was over for him, and now by the goodness of God he was walking out free. The emotion of it was in his eyes that evening when Stephen and a friend met him at Belfast International Airport and he saw it reflected in their faces; reflected in Professor McLeod's words too when Axel got back – "I was moved to tears when I heard you'd been arrested, Axel". Thanks to true and upright Ulster people who were prepared to take a stand for a friend and literally put their money where their mouth was, he was back home – a free man at last.

So in spite of the French authorities *coup* on 5 September, Axel was present once again at the next hearing on 25 September. His reappearance must have seemed like someone rising from the dead. Social Services could say nothing except well, we were still in a precarious situation – we might both still be extradited to France… they were still waiting for something concrete against Axel to come through from the French authorities, but all they had received was a vague one-page rag of a document that was more like a "tabloid-newspaper article" than a serious legal *chef d'accusation*, as my solicitor put it. The judge allowed Social Services to withdraw from the case that day, so they were no longer a party to the proceedings.

"Nice to have you back," was my solicitor's only comment to Axel – with a smile. Axel's return could only make our solicitors more confident. The judge stated that "the court would be very interested to know what there really is against Mr Schmidt", looking fixedly at Axel himself. Axel nodded – the judge had

understood that Axel had nothing to fear on that account: there were
accusations against him, but nothing to back them up.

A family under assessment

However, Social Services had not finished with us – now that the
investigation stage had seemed to go as far as it could, it was time to
get into the second stage of their dealings with us: the family assessment. Of course, now that Axel was back from London and free on
bail, we were pressing for his return home – they had asked him to
move out of the family home for "the investigation period at least",
which gave us some hope that he might now be allowed home. They
had had plenty of time to observe us during contact and the girls had
already clearly expressed their wish to have their Daddy back home
again.

Social Services' decision to keep him away during the
assessment period was going to have a lasting impact on our family.
At that vital time of "tying the family knot", as it were, one
important strand was missing – Axel. It was going to make it harder
for Victoria to adapt to her new environment and it deprived both
our daughters of their Daddy's support at a time when they vitally
needed it. In such adverse circumstances, it was amazing that their
school studies and behaviour did not visibly suffer. Axel and I took
to fasting every Sunday once again.

The family assessment began on November 1st and weekly
one-and-a-half hour sessions continued on for twelve weeks. It was
harrowing at times – especially when we went over Victoria's
abduction by the police in 1993. It made me loathe to go back
for the next session. It wasn't the same as talking about it with
friends or sympathetic listeners. The Family Care Unit people who
carried it out were pleasant, and always questioned us sensitively,
but they could only listen as professionals, from an objective,
almost clinical point of view, and for some reason this made it much
harder for me. The stark reality of what we had been through was as
though laid out on the table, and it hit me harder than I had expected.

The main objective of the family assessment was to give Social
Services not only an insight into the events our family had lived

through, but an understanding of our intentions and reasons for taking certain action, such as refusing visiting rights when Victoria was little, Axel's flight from France and Victoria's removal. What we didn't want was for it to turn into an inquisition bringing up all the old and unfounded accusations against the church in France – we had to keep to the subject, so we had to remain on our guard to a certain extent, but such lines of questioning were not indulged in.

While the family assessment was on-going Axel was to continue to live at Professor McLeod's house, not far from Belfast, and come in three times a week for visits with the girls, leaving us in a terrible void at the weekend. The girls' assessment of the family situation was given to Social Services loudly and clearly: they wanted their Daddy home. Elvira wrote it on a big piece of paper and stuck it on her bedroom window so that everyone going past could see it. Victoria discovered the usefulness of fax machines and both of them wrote Axel endless faxes telling him in their own personal way that they wanted him back: Victoria tended to order him back "immediately", while Elvira told him she loved him and missed him. Victoria even wrote one of these messages on a large piece of paper during a contact visit one day and held it up to the one-way mirror (a mirror for us, but a window for the social worker on the other side) for them to see. What could we say ? We could hardly discourage her, given the circumstances. We protested mildly.

After seeing Axel inside, the girls loved to play at running in turn into his arms outside before leaving, to which the social workers turned a blind eye (they could see us from inside the building anyway). The problem then was getting them away from him and into the car. I often had to start driving off to get them in. Then came the day when Axel had just carried Elvira into the car and I turned round to find her in tears.

"I want Daddy to be with us at home, too" she said to me. "Why can't he ?" She had had her Daddy at home almost all her life, and she couldn't understand this restriction. I felt angry that things had come to this, but I was once again helpless to do anything. I could only tell her that we hoped Daddy would be able to come home soon

– and I made sure Social Services were aware of the pain they were putting our little daughter through.

When Axel's younger sister Marianne came to see us for a few days towards the end of the year 2000, we all enjoyed having her. Axel took her round the sights of Ulster, the three of us met for a meal and she spent an evening at home with the girls and I.

She especially appreciated being able to make sense at last of everything which until then she had known from much the same point of view as Axel's parents. None of all the rumours she had heard corresponded with the plain reality. Back home it took her three weeks to get the reality into place in her head – a "horrible" thing to go through, she said. A pack of lies can make people act in a way they never normally would towards others, and she was having to come to terms with it. She told us that her predicament was only a fraction of the one her parents, Axel's Mum and Dad, found themselves in – she told us they had been extremely depressed for weeks after they had returned from their trip to see us in August, just trying to take it all on board…

She seemed to enjoy her evening with the girls and I, and was surprised to hear that Victoria had got into the habit of talking my ears off at night-time.

"That's great to hear !" she said to me. "She never used to really talk in France." She appreciated Elvira's character, but understood my problem with the girls' age difference – there were five years between her eldest boy and young daughter, and she knew the difficulties there could be when their Daddy wasn't around to help.

Axel's brother René came to see us as well. Axel told him simply that he needed to repent for what he had done, and reassured him that he would not be taking reprisals against him, which he could so easily have done.

My sister Jeanette came and stayed with us at home for a week or so, too, which I enjoyed. She could see the two girls kept me busy. She was on her way home to New Zealand, and we would have loved to be able to go with her for a visit, but it wasn't time for that yet. Perhaps that time would come, but for the moment the extradition proceedings against Axel and I meant that we could not travel anywhere…

326 All To Bring Victoria Home

Still wanted in France

Extradition proceedings initiated by the French Government against me were to lead the British authorities on a wild goose chase over the next two years.

On 28 November, when we were roughly a third of the way through the family assessment, I was once again summoned to London. There had been much debate inside the court because the "authority to proceed", which the French authorities needed to continue the proceedings, had been sent to the court unsigned. Contrary to the prosecutor's arguments that the authority to proceed had still been sent, even if the signature had been overlooked, the judge had concluded that without a signature the document was not valid and therefore the case was dismissed. It was said on such a low tone that it sounded as though it had been merely postponed. When I finally got outside and our London barrister told me clearly that "dismissed" meant it was all over for me, I had to ask him to repeat please – it was so unexpected.

Then six months later I received a phone call from my solicitor in Belfast telling me that he had been contacted by the Scotland Yard Extradition Squad: the French Government were relaunching extradition proceedings against me ! It seemed they would just never give up... This time though, DC Robinson arranged to meet me at a police station not far from home – not a full-scale police intervention this time. The officers there had a good laugh when I asked DC Robinson what I was supposed to fill in at one place on the form – all right, so a police officer isn't allowed to 'influence' an arrested person, but could she not simply tell me what on earth I was supposed to put in that blank ?

I was eventually committed (i.e. the proceedings were given the go-ahead by the Home Secretary), and almost a year later, in April 2002, both Axel and myself were due for the hearing before the High Court in London, the next stage in extradition. The day before, however, I received a phone call from our London solicitors – not a surprise, there were often last-minute arrangements to make and we had been fairly regularly in contact over the last few days. To my astonishment, he was pleased to inform me that the French Government had now dropped their request for my extradition !

"Do you mean it's really completely over ?" I asked, a little incredulous.

"Well, we're half-way there," he said. That was what I expected – strings attached.

"Half-way there," he repeated, "because we've still got Axel's case to go."

So it really was all over for me…

The extradition request against Axel was more sustained. In fact, Axel wondered whether by dropping the case against me that day before the High Court hearing wasn't just to give the French Government an excuse to be sure to nail him. At any rate, he lost his appeal and his case went before the House of Lords. After that there would only be the Home Secretary to appeal to.

By now, however, his case was looking fairly strong. Rebecca and Philippe, the parents of the two boys Axel had been accused of "mistreating" had written a witness statement to say that such a thing had never happened. Abbé Hamelin also helped by writing a witness statement describing what had happened at the trial in February 1995 and stating that a close advisor to the Minister of Justice had told him back in 1994 that there was "practically nothing" in the file against Axel. Evidence had also now been produced that the French Government had known that Axel was in the UK since 1995, yet had done nothing for five years. Finally, Axel's extradition would plunge us, his family, into the difficulties and trauma we had already known, and would seriously disturb the girls. This was also a factor that must be taken into account in extradition cases.

Although Axel could ask to be tried again on his return to France, he knew that because of the French Government's policy against "cults", which had been revealed as persecution against us, he would never be given a fair trial in France and the French Judiciary would seize the opportunity to convict him by any means available.

This case remains a matter of concern and prayer for us.

United at last

After twelve weeks of questioning us about "all aspects of our life", the Social Services Family Care team were finally able to ascertain that we were a loving, caring, strong family unit; that Axel and I were sensitive to our children's needs and that we had always acted with their best interests first and foremost at heart. They expressed their opinion that our "fears" of persecution in France were "genuinely felt" and in conclusion recommended that Axel could "return home and live normally with his wife and children". The false image of an "unfit" mother and a "dangerous" father was a thing of the past: all the problems that had been invented in France had been shown to be non-existent.

Social Services still said that the Court might not follow that recommendation – just to keep us in suspense – but the social worker had said to Victoria that he hoped her Dad would be back with her the following week. When she smiled, he remarked that that was the first time she had ever smiled at him ! On 2 March 2001 the Court did follow the Family Assessment recommendations, even granting Axel care and control of Victoria on an equal footing with myself. That afternoon he was home.

Social Services of course continued to make weekly then (once the girls' names had been removed from the child protection register) monthly visits, and Axel's final move home didn't actually happen until a couple of weeks later, because he had to ask permission from the Court in London in order to change his address – and the French Government *naturally* objected to it, making a formal hearing necessary. So for two weeks he only left home after the children were asleep and returned the following morning before they were awake. It was a bit of a strain, but Victoria and Elvira couldn't get normality fast enough, and if that was all it took… We weren't going to let these things make the slightest difference – our family was together at last.

Around this time we received a letter from Madame Fontaine, President of the European Parliament. She was writing in response to a letter that I had written to inform her of the excellent progress Victoria was making in adapting to life in Northern Ireland and to thank her for her much-appreciated efforts in helping me in the past. She simply acknowledged my letter and wished Victoria all the best in the future.

Victoria was doing so well in her last year at primary school that the following year she was accepted without a problem into the grammar school of her choice. She continued to excel in her musical studies too, passing her Grade 5 piano examination with distinction and racing through the first three grades of violin in her first year. She also enjoyed gymnastics and other sports. Events from her past emerge from time to time – she remembers being pulled into the police-car that day and calling *"Maman* !", and crying on her arrival in State care. But that's another story… From the interiorised tom-boy she was when she came, she has turned into a sensitive young girl who is far wiser than her years in some respects, yet sometimes wishes she could stay a child – she missed out on so much of a normal childhood.

Elvira has shown much maturity in coming to terms with her sister's arrival, though of course the odd sparks still fly at times. Her sister's brilliant results at school have inspired her with a little of that "I-can-do-this" spirit that is characteristic of Victoria, and she is doing better than she ever has done at school and in her other activities. Only now, when I see the result of our family being back together again, do I realise how much she was affected by her sister's forced absence and the strain that had placed on us.

Both girls are looking forward to going to New Zealand some-time in the near future and seeing my Mum again (who hasn't yet seen them together though she has talked to them on the phone) and the rest of the family there. For the moment they are both very fond of their paternal grandparents, who have been over to see us five times already. We all have excellent memories of their second visit at Christmas 2000 when they came with Axel's two younger sisters and family. Over these visits we have come to understand each other and enjoy each other as family. People have often remarked on what a "normal" family we appear to be – and it is true that in some mysterious way our difficult family past seems to have bound us all closer together. For us that can only be explained by the grace of God.

People have also said "You have been so strong !" Have we ? In the quiet of our study at home, sitting in front of my computer, with Axel at his working-from-home business beside me and the girls out at school, I don't feel we have been very strong – not with our own strength anyway. We were in a hopeless situation, but we had a very strong, desperate motive – our love for our child – and so we turned to God in our helplessness and He faithfully answered prayer, giving us wisdom and strength when we needed them, and the love, understanding and help of people close to us, both near and far, whose faithfulness, dedication and courage have deeply impressed us.

He answered our prayers, and the prayers of every dear Christian whose heart was burdened for a little three-year-old French girl who had been unjustly separated from her parents.

"Blessed be the Lord, who hath not
given us as a prey to their teeth."
Psalm 124:6

UHRW MISSION
To protect our Freedoms
Freedom of Speech - Freedom of Religion - Freedom from Want - Freedom from Fear
Through True Democracy for All the People of Northern Ireland

ANNEXE

1. Introduction

1.1 The Ulster Human Rights Watch Organisation

The Ulster Human Rights Watch (UHRW) is a major Human Rights organisation in Northern Ireland whose mission is primarily to protect the human rights and fundamental freedoms of all the people of Northern Ireland, whatever their class, creed, or political opinion, within the framework of genuine democracy. It specialises in in-depth analysis of legislations and their practical implementation, particularly in Northern Ireland but also in the whole of the United Kingdom as well as in other countries. It also engages in a thorough examination of cases where human rights abuses are alleged to have been committed.

1.2 Paving the way to widespread religious persecution in Europe

The UHRW investigation into the case of the Schmidt family has revealed grave violations of the most basic human rights and has prompted the Ulster Human Rights Watch to analyse the system that has been devised and implemented by the French Government against religious minorities labeled as "cults". We will first of all in (2) give an overview of the process for devising and implementing a system against cults. Then in (3) we will expose the reinforcement of the system within the Civil Service, the Judiciary, and Parliament.

2. Overview

2.1 The Process

The French system designed to target cults is based on a sustained collaboration between the Legislative, the Executive and the Judicial Powers. The Legislative Power (*Assemblée Nationale* and *Sénat* – National Assembly and Senate), has issued several parliamentary reports on "*sectes*" (cults in English) which have made recommendations to the Government and the Judiciary, and has also voted new laws to facilitate the fight against cults. In applying the recommendations made in the parliamentary report, the French Government has created a vast network at every level of its Civil Service, from the *Ministères* (Government Departments) to local district authorities, whose duties are to gather information and co-ordinate actions against cults. In line with the parliamentary report, the Judiciary has organised close co-operation between prosecutors and judges[1], at the request and under the supervision of the *Chancellerie* (Ministry of Justice). The fact that the three major powers have united to fight against what they call cults, has totally undermined the possibility of any mechanisms of balance and checks, or of accountability, which are essential in a democracy.

2.2 The system originally implemented

The first parliamentary report was prepared by a Member of Parliament at the request of the French Prime Minister and published in 1983 under the title: "Cults in France: Expression of Moral Freedom or Factors of Manipulation". Following this report, the French Government developed a policy against cults. In answer to a question asked by a member of the French National Assembly in June 1987, the Minister of the Interior revealed that concerted action between the different State Civil Service Departments in order to deal with the cult issue was already being taken. The main Government Departments who initially implemented this policy were the Ministry of the Interior, the Ministry of Justice, the Ministry of Finance and the Ministry of Education. Any religious group arbitrarily labelled a cult, regardless of the doctrinal basis of its beliefs, could be submitted to endless investigations (preliminary police inquiries, criminal investigations by the Judiciary, tax control etc.), all conducted with the purpose of bringing about its closure.

3. The reinforcement of the system within the Civil Service, the Judiciary, and Parliament

3.1 The Civil Service

In 1995, in order to give new impetus to the fight against cults, the National Assembly established a Parliamentary Commission to Inquire into Cults. A new report[2] was prepared and published on 10 January 1996.

3.1.1 The absence of a legal definition for the word "*secte*"

Soon after beginning its work, the Commission realised that there was no legal definition of the word "cult". Neither the French Parliament nor the Government or even the Judiciary have ever been able to give any definition of this term. The Commission eventually declared that it should have stopped its work since it was confronted with the impossibility of defining a "cult". However, in order to be able to continue with their work, the Commission hastily decided to "retain the common direction that the public opinion allots to the concept"[3] as the definition of the word "cult". This so-called definition only confirms the absence of any proper definition for a word whose meaning has been totally distorted through years of propaganda carried out in the French media, mainly by anti-cult lobbies[4] supported by the French Government. Today the word *secte* has an extremely perjorative and even defamatory sense in France. It has therefore become an arbitrary criterion which has been applied in the report to all kinds of religious minorities, ranging from Evangelical churches to Satanist organisations[5].

[1]   In France judges and prosecutors belong to the same body of civil servants. They are called *magistrats*. A judge during his career can become a prosecutor and vice versa.
[2]   Report made in the name of the Board of Inquiry into Cults (*Rapport fait au nom de la Commission d'enquête sur les Sectes*), unanimously adopted by the Commission on 20 December 1995 and published on 10 January 1996, No 2468.
[3]   Page 14 of the Parliamentary Commission report.
[4]   *Centre de documentation, déducation et d'action contre les manipulations mentales* (CCMM) and *Union Nationale des Associations pour la Défense des Familles et de l'Individu* (UNADFI). The latter is a dangerous extremist organisation which has infiltrated the democratic institutions of the French Republic.
[5]   Page 51 and 52 of the Parliamentary Commission report.

3.1.2 The creation of a specialised Government body and network to fight against cults

As a result of the Parliamentary Report's recommendations in January 1996, the French Government enforced a more radical policy and set up a more efficient system to fight against cults. All Government Departments and all civil services at every level were obliged to take part.

3.1.2.1 A specialised Government body in charge of the fight against cults

On 9 May 1996 the French Government created an *Observatoire Interministérielle sur les sectes* (Interministerial "Observatory" on Cults), presided by the Prime Minister, in order to gather information and make proposals in view of improving the means available to fight against cults. This new body was soon replaced on 7 October 1998 by the more extreme *Mission Interministérielle de Lutte contre les Sectes* (Interministerial Mission to Fight Against Cults[6]), working in close association with the Prime Minister. The Mission is made up of six permanent civil servants. The President of the Mission is appointed for five years by presidential decree[7]. The Prime Minister appoints a General Secretary, whose duty is to co-ordinate the work of the Mission's members.

The Mission itself consists of two groups: the *conseil d'orientation* (orientation council) made up of nineteen members of which five are Members of Parliament, and who give their views on the cult issue; and the *groupe opérationnel* (operations group), comprising fifteen high-ranking civil servants appointed by the Ministers of eight Ministries: Employment and Solidarity, Justice, National Education, National Police, Foreign Affairs, Economy and Finances, Defense, Youth and Sport[8]. Periodically, the President of the Commission organises 'operations group' meetings in order to exchange information and co-ordinate actions in the fight against cults[9]. The rest of the time, these high-ranking civil servants work as the Mission's permanent correspondents within the different Ministries.

The duties and powers of this Mission are as follows. It receives information on cults from the different civil services, who are obliged to report this; it incites public services to take the appropriate measures in order to fight cult actions which impinge on the dignity of the human being or are a threat to Public Order; it informs and trains civil servants in methods to be used to fight cults; it informs the public of the dangers of cults and takes part in work concerning cults within international bodies such as the European Union, the Organisation for Security and Co-operation in Europe and the United Nations. The Mission therefore has sufficient power to promote and co-ordinate actions against any group labelled as a cult, or against any individual accused of being a member of a cult, without any hindrance or safeguard.

3.1.2.2 A specialised network within the French Civil Service

Several Ministries have undertaken to co-ordinate the fight against cults within their own department and have subordinate civil servants operating at regional and local levels.

The Minister of the Interior issued two circular letters to all the *Préfets de Département* (Heads of District) on 31 October 1997 and 20 December 1999, instructing the Heads of District to create a *cellule* (cell) within each District. Each special cell is made up of civil servants from the regional and district employment department, from the academic inspection department,

---

[6] *Décret* No 98-890 signed by the President of the Republic and the Prime Minister.
[7] Mr Alain Vivien was appointed by a *Décret* of the President of the Republic dated 23 November 1998.
[8] *Arrétés* from the Prime Minister of 23 November 1998 and of 21 December 1999.
[9] Article 5 of the *Décret* of 7 October 1998.

from social services (*DDASS* and *DRASS*), from the customs administration and from the tax administration. The Interministerial Mission to Fight Against Cults is automatically invited to take part in each 'cell' meeting, which is presided over by the Head of the District. The purpose of the cell is to assist the exchange of information between the different State services and to mobilise all the services of the State against the "cult phenomenon". The Interministerial Mission is closely associated with the work of each 'cell', which must be set out in a report.

The Ministry of Youth and Sports has constituted a network of correspondents in all its regional departments. Following the recommendations contained in the Parliamentary Commission's report in 1996, the Ministry organised a nation-wide media campaign targeting all religious minorities labelled as cults, without distinction.

The Ministry of Employment and Solidarity also issued a circular letter on 3 October 2000, instructing all central civil services to appoint correspondents. These correspondents operate under the control of the *direction de l'action sociale* who liaise with the Interministerial Mission to Fight Against Cults and meet once a month. The Ministry instructs its regional departments to appoint a regional correspondent on cults, who participates in the specialised cell set up by the local Chief Prosecutor at the request of the Minister of Justice. All correspondents must take part in training sessions on cults. Central and local civil services must at the same time carry out any investigation relating to an alleged cult.

The French State has therefore set up an extensive network within the Civil Service of every Government Department as well as at regional and local levels, with the aim of gathering information on cults and coordinating the struggle against them.

3.2 The Judiciary

On 29 February 1996, the Minister of Justice sent a circular letter to all Chief Prosecutors and Public Prosecutors, instructing them as to the means they should employ against cults. Exchanges of information between prosecutors and the different regional and local civil services were to be intensified in order to reinforce the means of fighting against cult excesses. The Minister insisted that any denunciations received by prosecutors must be systematically followed by an investigation. Prosecutors must therefore choose between ordering a preliminary inquiry to be carried out by the police, or a criminal investigation to be carried out by an examining judge. Prosecutors were pointed to specific provisions of the Civil Code and were advised to use these provisions to deal with children whose parents belong to a cult. Advice was also given for applying special measures (originally designed for the mentally handicapped) to young adult members of cults. The Minister instructed prosecutors to cooperate increasingly closely with judges, and in particular with judges for children, thereby making null and void the principle of the independence of the Judiciary.

In the second circular letter to Chief and Public Prosecutors, issued on 1st December 1998, the Minister of Justice stated that the Ministry (*Chancellerie*) follows all proceedings involving cults and takes an active part in the elaboration and implementation of the Government policy in this domain. The Minister indicated that a "specialised cell" was being constituted within the Ministry of Justice's *Direction des Affaires Criminelles et des Graces* (Direction of Criminal affairs and Pardon), led by a *magistrat* (either a judge or a prosecutor). The Minister confirmed that anti-cult organisations such as UNADFI (despite the fact that the actions of this extremist organisation against individuals or groups are not submitted to any proper form of accountability) must be closely associated with the Judiciary's work at every level, from the Ministry down to the Public Prosecutors. Every Chief Prosecutor was instructed to designate a member of the prosecuting department as "*correspondant-sectes*" (cult correspondent) in order to coordinate actions against cults and to organise meetings with other civil services.

Public Prosecutors must in particular define a concerted policy with all the other civil services specified by the Minister in order to deal with minor-aged children whose parents are members of a cult. The Judiciary is therefore closely associated with the system set up within the French Civil Service to fight against cults. In such conditions, the independence and impartiality of judges, particularly examining judges and judges for children, are no longer guaranteed.

3.3 Parliament

On 18 December 1998 the French Parliament voted a law which aimed at allowing State authorities to control the teaching of children, whether in private schools allegedly run by cults, or at home when schooled by parents accused of being cult adepts.

More recently, the French Parliament voted a law on 12 June 2001 creating the new criminal offence of "brainwashing". According to this law, the new offence is committed when a person "fraudulently abuses the ignorance or weakness" of a person "who is in a state of psychological or physical subjection" in order to make this person do something "which is gravely prejudicial to him/her". The definition of this offence is extremely vague and its interpretation is aleatory, and could easily result in trumped-up convictions. It is intended to be used against religious minorities.

By the same law a new provision (Article 2.17) was introduced into the Code of Criminal Procedure by which certain organisations, such as the extreme anti-cult lobby UNADFI, were given the power to initiate criminal proceedings against alleged cults without the approval or even the intervention of the Public Prosecutor.

Finally the law gave the Judiciary the possibility of ordering the closure of any religious group as soon as the group itself or its leaders have been convicted of two offences, however minor. The application for closure of a religious group can be lodged by the Public Prosecutor at his own initiative or at the request of "any interested person" such as an anti-cult lobby. The reinstatement of a religious group previously closed by the Judiciary is an offense punishable by a fine or a prison sentence.

The recent powers granted to anti-cult organisations now make them able to initiate criminal proceedings against any religious group that they have labelled a cult; obtain two or more convictions from a compliant judiciary; and finally, request that the Public Prosecutor lodge an application to have the targeted religious group legally closed, never to be reinstated.

4. Conclusion

The French State system to fight against what it calls "cults" (although no reliable legal definition of this word has ever been given) has gravely undermined the basic principles which underpin any democratic system, particularly the principle of the separation of powers and the principle of independence and impartiality of the Judiciary. This can only result in extremely serious violations of human rights and fundamental freedoms, especially for Bible-believing Christians, as demonstrated in the case of the Schmidt family. In doing so the French State has paved the way to widespread religious persecution in Europe, since it encourages other States to engage in the same fight against "cults".

PO Box 163, Lisburn, Northern Ireland, United Kingdom, BT28 3UN
Tel: 07759212861 Fax: + 44 (0) 28 3834 7221
e-mail:info@ulsterhumanrightswatch.co.uk
web: www.humanrights.uk.net